HOUSE SIGNS AND COLLEGIATE FUN

HOUSE SIGNS AND COLLEGIATE FUN

Sex, Race, and Faith in a College Town

Chaise LaDousa

INDIANA UNIVERSITY PRESS
BLOOMINGTON & INDIANAPOLIS

This book is a publication of

Indiana University Press
601 North Morton Street
Bloomington, Indiana 47404-3797 USA

iupress.indiana.edu

Telephone orders 800-842-6796
Fax orders 812-855-7931
Orders by e-mail iuporder@indiana.edu

♾ The paper used in this publication meets the minimum requirements of the American National Standard for Information Sciences—Permanence of Paper for Printed Library Materials,
ANSI Z39.48—1992.

Manufactured in the United States of America

Library of Congress Cataloging-in-Publication Data

LaDousa, Chaise.
House signs and collegiate fun : sex, race, and faith in a college town / Chaise LaDousa.
p. cm.
Includes bibliographical references and index.
ISBN 978-0-253-35642-0 (cloth : alk. paper) — ISBN 978-0-253-22326-5 (pbk. : alk. paper) 1. Universities and colleges—United States. 2. Universities and colleges—Social aspects—United States. 3. Signs and signboards—United States. 4. College campuses—United States. I. Title.
LA227.4.L34 2011
306.43′2—dc22

2010050903

1 2 3 4 5 16 15 14 13 12 11

For Michael from Ohio

Determining what popular culture means
is not a matter of semantics.

—JOHANNES FABIAN,
Moments of Freedom

CONTENTS

PREFACE

Although responsibility for the ideas presented in this book is ultimately mine alone, students engaged in much of the fieldwork on which this book is based. While I cannot re-create the energy that fueled the seminars in anthropology that brought us together, I hope that my students' unanimous enthusiasm for the investigation of the world of their peers will be obvious throughout. I can only guess that the reader of this book is or has been a student of some kind in some sort of institution, probably several. Just as my own students—especially the ones who participated in the activity that we studied—learned much about the cultural category they supposedly occupied by becoming increasingly displaced from it, I hope that this book will afford new insights by virtue of displacements I cannot anticipate.

It is true that I hope this book will grab the reader with its theme of collegiate fun. But this book also provides a framework for understanding culture in a particular way. The notion of culture that inspires this book—embodied in the ethnography of speaking and its developments—finds attention to context to be a necessity in the study of meaning. In turn, an interest in context entails an interest in the uneven deployment of meaning-making resources. Some of the theoretical foundations of such work can strike students of cultural analysis as difficult. One of my goals in writing this book is to make some of those theoretical foundations clear. I hope that the cultural manifestations of collegiate fun that are the focus of this ethnography will make learning about those theoretical foundations enjoyable. And for cognoscenti, I hope that this book will give you as much cultural vertigo as the project gave me. I was an undergraduate student myself at the college "where fun comes to die." It's funny how things come full circle.

ACKNOWLEDGMENTS

I am most indebted to the students at Miami University who were involved with this project. Research subjects invited us into their named houses and indulged our concerns with wit and verve. Students in my course asked questions, listened patiently, and discussed the recorded interviews in class. Given the promise of anonymity made to the research subjects, I cannot name them. Because I have used pseudonyms throughout the book, I can name the student researchers. They are Mark Amos, Melissa Asbrock, Robert Bell, Sabrina Bourgeois, Christine Chynoweth, Sean Clark, Jonathan Devore, Christopher Fox, Alison Goebel, Jonathan Green, Curtis Howard, Sarah Kittleson, Jennifer Kline, Jonathan Littig, Jessica Lodwick, Heather Luker, Gia Mandala, Ellen McGovern, Justin Miller, Christopher Reese, Brittany Siler, Aggy Stevens-Gleason, Joseph Teed, Nicholas Tymitz, and Lauren Walsh. None of the student researchers is responsible for the arguments made in the book.

I will never forget the lessons of my first teacher in anthropology, McKim Marriott, or those of my first teacher in folklore, James Fernandez. My mentor, Susan Wadley, continues to offer criticism, advice, and friendship. No amount of thanks would be enough. Ann Gold's laughter and incredible encouragement helped me to see the worth of this project early on. Christopher DeCourse, William Mangin, and Deborah Pellow offered hearty laughter at a talk I gave on the project at Syracuse, and I thank them for it. Robert Rubenstein continues to offer support and advice. Other dear friends from Syracuse have, at various points, commented on aspects of this project and offered much-needed support. They include Eric Estes, Joanna Giansanti, Mailan Gustafsson, Anthony Kwame Harrison, Mark Hauser, and Kalyani Menon.

In each of my academic jobs, I have had an incredible colleague who showed me the ropes and offered seemingly unlimited generosity. Susan Paulson at Miami University, Kathleen Skoczen at Southern Connecticut State University, and Bonnie Urciuoli at Hamilton College have made the last ten years richer by far. Others at these institutions have contributed much to this project. They include Bob Applebaum, Erol Balkan, Joyce Barry, John Bartle, Mary Jane Berman, Lisa Bier, James Bradfield, Donald Carter, Steve Ellingson, Tomomi Emoto, Stacey Giroux, Haeng-ja Chung, Jim Hamill, Gordon Hewitt, Jenny Irons, Alfred Kelly, Jennifer Kinney, Anne Lacsamana, Madeleine Lopez, Joe Manzella, Heather Merrill, Nona Moskowitz, Ann Owen, Jeff Pliskin, Deborah Pokinsky, Patrick Reynolds, Mike Rogers, Elena Schmitt, Charlie Stevens, Lisa Trivedi, Robin Vanderwall, Chris Vasantkumar, Chris Wellin, James Wells, Chad Williams, and Dawn Woodward. I must thank Jim Hamill in particular for suggesting that I teach the class that led to the project and for many midday discussions of house signs over "rabbit food." Mailan Gustafsson, Nona Moskowitz, Bonnie Urciuoli, and James Wells read all or sections of the manuscript and offered excellent suggestions for revision. Indeed, Bonnie Urciuoli read the manuscript twice and has offered the warmest friendship one could dream of. Students at Hamilton College who read the manuscript and offered criticism include Jane Fieldhouse, Eleanor Goldman, Elizabeth Gordon, Fiona Kirkpatrick, Callie Krumholz, Helen Rogers, Alicia Wright, and Emily Zeidler.

Other colleagues have provided encouragement and advice. They include Barney Bate, Harris Berger, Laura Brueck, James Collins, Sonia Das, Giovanna Del Negro, Virginia Domínguez, Paul Garrett, Rudi Gaudio, Kira Hall, Jane Hill, Matthew Hull, Misty Jaffe, Krishna Kumar, Nita Kumar, Sarah Lamb, Gabriella Modan, Rakesh Ranjan, and Jim Wilce. Thanks also to two anonymous reviewers for the *Journal of American Folklore* and three anonymous reviewers for Indiana University Press. Although we met only briefly in a K&B in New Orleans, my intellectual debt to Richard Bauman will be obvious throughout.

Joseph Urgo and Patrick Reynolds, Deans of Faculty at Hamilton College, provided generous support enabling the publication of some of the book's images. They must also be thanked for their encouragement and sage advice.

Staff members at Indiana University Press have been a joy to work with and have made this a better book. Rebecca Tolen guided me through the stages of publication with firm direction and gave excellent editorial advice and suggestion as did her assistant, Peter Froehlich. Elaine Durham Otto further polished the text to make the book a smoother read. Brian Herrmann provided final production guidance. It has been a pleasure to work with these people.

My mother, Dickie Wagner, and her parents, Charlie and Eva Nettles, are responsible for the education I received—and most everything else—in my younger life. My mother is one of those people who make friends wherever they go, and I have enjoyed living in a world filled with them. Thanks for everything, Mom. Thanks also to Mary Attwood, Marie Desjardins, Jo Faulk, Renee Lapeyrolerie, Laura Sanders, Jenny Sandlin, Tom Secrest, Jennie Stearns and Tim Veenstra for warm memories. Kimberly Williams, her husband, Travis, and her children, Porter and Ella, and Edie Doss and her husband, Grayson, have filled my life with love. Charlie Nettles and Marilin Sailor deserve special thanks for being there. Tom Ladousa and Bob Wagner are two of the funniest people I know, and I cannot help but think that they have something to do with this book. Jay, Kelli, Aiden, Frank, Terri, Christian, Maryann, Bill, Ken, and Sabrina make Parkway East a special place. Speedy is my own little Sisyphus. And then there is Michael, as well as Ann, Michael, Maggie, Cory, and Stephen. Michael's love has made so much possible daily.

An earlier version of Chapter 2 was published as "'Witty House Name': Visual Expression, Interpretive Practice, and Uneven Agency in a Midwestern College Town," *Journal of American Folklore*, 2007, 120(478):445–81.

TRANSCRIPTION CONVENTIONS

,	short pause (less than one second)
.	long pause (approximately one second)
(2)	pause of indicated number of seconds
::	preceding sound lengthened
- - - - - -	said quickly
~~	said laughingly
bold	said loudly
. . .	speech trailing off / fading
⌈	beginning of overlap with speech positioned below
|	beginning of overlap with speech positioned above and below
⌊	beginning of overlap with speech positioned above
#	laughter
" "	quoted speech
[ ]	transcriber's comments

HOUSE SIGNS AND COLLEGIATE FUN

INTRODUCTION

House Signs and Their Display

Even the fun of college life was a learning experience.

—MICHAEL MOFFATT,
Coming of Age in New Jersey

On being hired by the Department of Anthropology at Miami University in a visiting teaching position, I drove to Oxford, a town in southwestern Ohio, to meet a realtor and secure a place to live. As I drove into town, I saw a huge sign attached to a house with the words "Pee-wee's Playhouse" painted on it. I saw yet more signs attached to houses, more than I could remember after six blocks or so. I had never seen anything like them. At the same time, they seemed right at home in a college town. I asked the realtor about the signs, and he replied that they were the reason I should not live in the Mile Square. This was all student housing. He said he would be willing to rent me a house in the Mile Square, but the rent for an entire semester would be due upon signing the lease, the typical practice when students are involved. He also said that the noise would be too distracting for a professor. As the realtor drove me to what he described as a more suitable environment, a new set of apartments not far outside the Mile Square, he noted the absence of house signs during the last half-mile of our journey. "There are students here," he said, "but they don't party as hard as those in the Mile Square."

Over two hundred house signs dot Oxford's residential landscape. Students attach large signs made out of wood, metal, or plastic to their houses, exhibiting to passersby countless messages, linguistic and pictorial. House signs cannot be missed given that they are the most visible features in Oxford's public signage apart from the advertising erected by businesses, traffic signs erected by the city, and the signs erected by the university announcing the names of buildings and other campus features. House signs are distinguished from commercial, civic, and university placards in two ways. They tend to look less carefully or uniformly constructed. Writing styles are not typographically standardized, and the homemade images are attention-grabbing. On the other hand, they invoke—through words sometimes complemented with illustrations—practices (e.g., studying), objects (e.g., beer cans), and/or physical conditions (e.g., a hangover) that are linked by their salience to "student life." In a college town, one is not surprised to find labels such as "Boot 'N Rally" (vomiting and regrouping to drink more) and "Beer Goggles" (finding others more attractive than one would were one sober) attached to houses in which students "party."

Colleges, occasionally even real ones, have provided the characters and scenes for films and novels. Some films such as *Who's Afraid of Virginia Woolf* (1966), *Mona Lisa Smile* (2003), and *A Serious Man* (2009) depict various aspects of college life, but do not revolve around college fun. Much more common, however, are films that include fraternity brothers, sorority sisters, pledges, nerds, band members, football players, cheerleaders, Reserve Officers' Training Corps cadets, graduate students, professors and administrators, their spouses and children, and many others engaging in or trying to thwart all manner of collective drinking, sexual experimentation, and rule-breaking antics.

Campus Squeeze is a website that includes, among other things, a list of "The Sixteen Best College Themed Movies." The website praises the attributes of its winner by referring to partying and its accoutrements:

> *Animal House* is the college movie to which all other college movies are compared. It has everything: sex, drugs, alcohol, the fat friend who parties harder in one night than you will in your entire life, and of course, douchy rich kids trying to narc on the cool kids' good times. If you were indifferent about going to college after high school, *Animal House* got your mouth watering at the prospect of partying higher education style. Even if college life isn't exactly the same as it was in this movie, you may have found that it's not that different, either.

The website uses words like "douchy" and "narc" that come from the world represented by the movie at the same time that the website equivocates on the

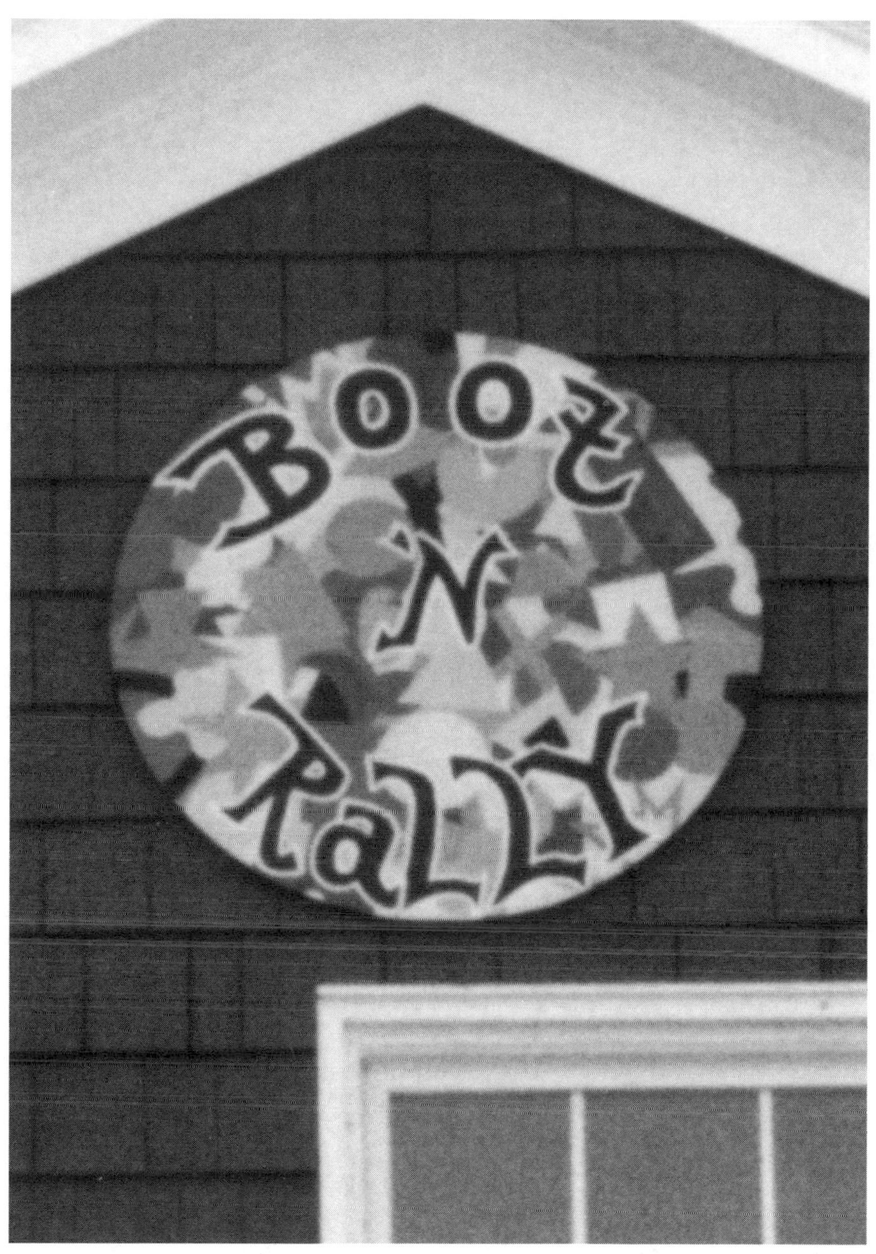

FIGURE 0.1. Boot 'N Rally

movie's representativeness of the life of the current viewer. Whether or not art imitates life, *Animal House* "got your mouth watering at the prospect of partying higher education style."

Rather flirtatious with the possibilities of the means of representation, if not with the specific people and places being represented, is Tom Wolfe's novel *I Am Charlotte Simmons.* Wolfe claims, "This novel is not based on any real college, not even partly," yet he thanks his "two collegians" who "rescued me when I got in over my head trying to use current slang." He explains to them, "Your father had only to reassemble the material he had accumulated visiting campuses across the country" to write the novel (2004, ix). Having thus blurred the boundary between the fictive and the real, Wolfe opens the novel with a conversation between two drunk male students talking while using the toilet. The first line is between them, and it involves sex (and sexism): "Whattaya mean, a slut? She told me she's been re-virginated!" Reminiscent of the scenario suggested by the house sign Boot 'N Rally, Wolfe continues to build the restroom scene: "Urinals kept flushing, boys kept disintegrating over one another's wit, and somewhere in the long row of toilet cubicles somebody was vomiting" (2004, 3). College provides a stage on which intoxicated, sexual, and playful banter is to be expected.

Of course, one does not have to travel to a cinema or rent a DVD to see *Animal House,* nor does one have to purchase a paper copy of *I Am Charlotte Simmons* to own it. They are readily available for purchase on the Internet in electronic form. Yet the consequences of these developments for the representation of college fun pale in comparison to other possibilities provided by the Internet. Countless websites have emerged. From PubClub.com's "Top 10 College Party Schools: 'Win or Lose, We Booze!'" to CollegeTips.com's "College Party Themes & Ideas," the Internet has served as a platform for a massive proliferation of representations and suggestions that combine alcohol and sexual experimentation in college. The first website, for example, specifies where the most fun can be had, while the second suggests party ideas, many based on dominant males and sexually subservient and promiscuous females, as in "CEOs and Corporate Hos," "GI Joes and Army Hos," "Golf Pros and Tennis Hos," and "Pimps and Hos."

Joining the fray of representations of college fun are those not meant to be fictional or promotional, but rather descriptive—often critical. Barrett Seaman's *Binge: Campus Life in an Age of Disconnection and Excess* is based on visits to prestigious colleges and universities across the United States. Although Seaman includes themes like studying and diversity, the lion's share of the book is devoted to partying. Seaman even offers advice:

> Students and professors getting to know each other better isn't going to stop dangerous drinking, drug use, and date rape. Nor will it reverse the rise in depression and general anxiety that reflect larger cultural traits. But it can serve to curtail abuses by keeping the focus of campus life on the fundamental purpose of college, which is to learn and grow while learning. (2005, 272)

Murray Sperber's *Beer and Circus: How Big-Time College Sports Is Crippling Undergraduate Education* focuses on large universities and shows the ways in which NCAA membership, entertainment that revolves around alcohol, and increasing classroom size and decreasing contact between students and professors have come to change a number of schools. Finally, numerous websites (StopHazing.org), documentaries (*Haze*), and books (*Wrongs of Passage* and *The Hazing Reader*) foreground the harmful effects of alcohol abuse in college, especially in the pursuit of joining a fraternity, sorority, or sports team.

There is no doubt that drinking, drug use, and sexual activity are key aspects of college fun. But it is important to consider the ways in which college fun is represented as well as how such representations are used, often by different people for different ends. A website picks out a particular representation, a movie, and addresses the reader in order to urge her to compare the movie with her own experience. Tom Wolfe's novel depicts fictional places by using language that is meant to resemble that used by real people, but leaves it to the reader to make comparisons. Investigative reports provide a way to put these representations together with the activities they represent, urging the reader to see excess and the possibility of curtailing the activities. These films, books, and websites thus represent a core set of activities quite differently and provide different clues about the people they represent and those for whose consumption they are created.

What they do not provide, however, is an account of how students produce, reproduce, and engage with such resources for representation. What college students produce, how they reflect on their productions, and the relationship between the two may teach us something about the possibilities and limitations of fun in their lives. House signs provide a medium that represents college fun. Alcohol, sex, and—less often—drugs take their place on the signs, but signs accomplish many effects beyond representing these three realms.

We can acknowledge the pervasiveness of alcohol, drugs, and sex in representations of collegiate fun while maintaining a focus on what students are producing by treating fun as something like a keyword in the parlance of Raymond Williams. He explains that keywords "are significant, binding words in certain activities and their interpretation" such that they provide clues to the social and cultural worlds in which they are important (1983, 15).[1] A keyword like fun is relevant to a great range and variety of college students' activities because, as Williams explains, "the most active problems of meaning are always primarily embedded in actual relationships, and that both the meaning and the relationships are typically diverse and variable, within the structures of particular social orders and the processes of social and historical change" (22).

Someone completely ignorant of collegiate fun would learn quickly about "the structures of particular social orders" that shape it by discovering that it is rarely had—or depicted as being had—in academic pursuits or alone. It would also be clear that the idea of college without any fun is preposterous. Such an experience would be incomplete, even though what constitutes college experience varies greatly from person to person, college to college. Overt descriptions of what college is might foreground academic studies, but for college to be complete, there must be fun. Note that neither of these insights has anything to do with alcohol or sex per se. Indeed, a space might open wherein the necessity of consuming alcohol and experimenting with sex might be questioned. There are many websites, for example, like eHow.com's "How To Have Fun in College without Drinking," which suggests that college students engage in activities such as pranks, movie nights, and sleep!—all without the use of alcohol. Such websites show that having fun is crucial and goes beyond being involved in specific activities.

By understanding fun as a keyword in collegiate life, we begin to understand that this notion can include particular activities, but also includes a general disposition to the world. This is precisely what three scholars found in their ethnographic research at institutions of higher education in the United States. Michael Moffatt (1989), Rebekah Nathan (2005), and Mary Grigsby (2009) have published ethnographies of collegiate life based on interviews, participant observation, and long-term residence in dormitories. These studies show that collegiate fun rests on a disposition—an understanding of the self and its relationship to others—as well as on particular activities. The three ethnographers demonstrate that fun plays an integral part in undergraduate life and that it relies on and reproduces allied dispositions such as being "cool" and being an "individual." All three studies show that fun is born in partying, whether at parties or in carefree behavior elsewhere, and that the successful realization of partying depends on a laid-back disposition that is not overly concerned with the attitudes and opinions of others.

Studies such as these take us beyond an understanding of fun that depends on specific and easily demonized activities to one that rests on ideas of a self that is amenable to participation in those activities. They bring together the activities and interpretations that Raymond Williams considers necessary for an account of the production of meaning—that is to say, the production of culture. Ethnographies of this kind provide an important corrective to the common view that activities are equated with groups because the individuals in those groups possess some shared substance, some essence. At different times, that substance has been understood to be race, nationality, ethnicity, or culture. For example, while conducting research for this book, I heard about "Oxford culture," "Miami culture," "student culture," "faculty culture," "college culture," and "house sign culture." Like other works of ethnography, this book will show that the links between groups and substance are not natural but rather are human endeavors that are malleable over time.

Forms of culture emerge in particular contexts, make possible particular results, and entail particular constraints. Language, which is a part of culture, enables us to view culture as changing, contingent, and not specific to any group. Judith Irvine offers a particularly elegant explanation:

> Communities—whether they be "speech communities" or other kinds—are not givens, objects existing prior to the conduct of social life. Instead, they must be constructed, and continually reconstructed, in and by discursive and other interactional practice; and as they are constructed, they can be imagined. (1996, 124)[2]

Referring to house signs as the product of Miami culture or student culture, for example, is itself an act of cultural production and one that involves imagining a community as the site of a cultural activity. Who produces the culture? To what ends? Are there other ways of seeing house signs as significant? Who produces them? To what ends? And, most important, how do we bring the different answers to bear on one another? We will see that there is no one-to-one relationship between people and house signs—or any other cultural phenomenon, for that matter—and that an exploration of signs' creation, interpretation, and use can show us that culture is a process, not a substance or essence.

The analytical framework for understanding cultural production as a process will unfold over the next two chapters. Chapter 1 shows that the creation and display of house signs mark certain temporal and social transformations in the way college students engage in fun. While displaying house signs on rented off-campus houses may be an activity specific to students in Oxford, Ohio, from the 1970s to the present, the use of puns and double entendres involving alcohol and sex invokes much older images of American college students. Fun and the independence and freedom that fuel it have been a feature of college life since the beginning of higher education in the United States, but the residential situations and leisure activities that underpin house signs reflect some of the transitions in ways of having fun and interacting with others more broadly, characteristic of late twentieth-century college life. Thus, even if college students were to be considered a single community, their disposition to fun has changed quite radically over time. Chapter 1 ends by demonstrating why it is also crucial to understand that the people who produce (perhaps better put, reproduce) identities, places, and activities have ideas about how they go about doing it. Reflections on culture from person to person may differ radically in how they represent culture. Understanding this is a first step toward an analytical stance.

Chapter 2 addresses complexities entailed in the notion of community. It demonstrates that understandings of house signs are related to location in larger social groups. What these signs represent depends on one's social location because one's social location is partly established by what one makes of house signs. For example, students living in houses with signs, students conducting an ethnographic project as part of an anthropology class, my colleagues, an author of another book on house signs, and I may all give different answers to questions about what house signs represent. To develop a framework for analysis in which cultural production and reflection can be viewed in social context, house signs as well as the discourses about them are treated here as texts situated in chains of production. The chapter introduces a conceptual apparatus, semiotics, for tracing text production and uses it to demonstrate how people's position in relation to the production and interpretation of house signs can be analyzed.

I then offer three extended considerations of the complexities involved in the creation, display, and interpretation of house signs. Chapter 3 deals with people who envision special uses for the signs. A small group of residents of named houses believe that house signs reflect their Christian faith. They differ markedly from other residents in believing this, and residents of other houses may be unaware that there are Christian signs in Oxford. Those students interpret the Christian signs in ways that make sense to them and the salience of Christianity disappears. Chapter 3 shows that group formation itself is mediated by interpretation that is socially located.

Chapter 4 describes people who believe that their residence in a specific part of town enables them to benefit from the qualities embodied by house signs generally. This group's signs refer to the fact that they live in a part of Oxford called the Ghetto. Indeed, they explain that the Ghetto is a special place because this is where the disposition to the world that all house signs are supposed to offer can be realized to its fullest. The students are able to engage in these reflections on the Ghetto because they imagine the real ghetto to be located at a great distance from Oxford. Oxford's world of house signs constitutes a community, in part, because of its imagined difference from elsewhere. Race is relevant to the difference between the Ghetto and the real ghetto, but the maintenance of Oxford's house sign world depends on this fact remaining unspoken and thus hidden.

Some students living in named houses critique some of the ways in which house signs portray social difference, specifically via images of gender and sex, and this is discussed in chapter 5. Women sometimes point out that women and men create and use signs differently, and yet they claim that they can't be offended by house signs—as do many who see their signs as a reflection of their Christian faith. Residents have different ideas about what the effects of a sign on onlookers might be, but the stance toward signs that characterizes the house sign community at large prevents critiques from being more salient.

Anatomy of the Project

This book emerges from an ethnographic research project conducted by different people at different times. As a visiting assistant professor at Miami University, my main duties were teaching introduction to cultural anthropology and a seminar in linguistic anthropology. The syllabus for the seminar included recent work in anthropology focusing broadly on questions of identity, and I asked the students on the first day of class whether they might like to apply the concepts from the course in some sort of ethnographic investigation. A student asked, "What about house signs?" and everyone agreed that a concerted focus on a single phenomenon would provide a common ground of discussion.

We decided we would devote at least the first hour of each three-hour class meeting to discussion of the reading assignments and the rest to an exploration of the relevance of the course topics to our unfolding project. We concurred that our first step should be to make some sort of record of the signs. The first time I taught the course, the students and I met on a Saturday morning in order to walk around the Mile Square. I photographed the signs as we walked, noting the street addresses. I used seven rolls of film with thirty-six exposures each. The second time I taught the course, I distributed disposable cameras to the students and had each choose an area to photograph. Once they had photographed the house signs in their sections of town, the students brought their cameras to class, and I had the film developed. The photographs, spread out on the large seminar table, became the subject of discussion in class.

It might have been wise to record the class discussions to get some idea of the ways in which we produced our reflections on the pictures in front of us, but we did not. Our first inclination was to work with what we had, the photographs, and to begin to sort the house names into categories. Next, we decided to find out if and how people living in houses with signs reflect on their own signs and those of other houses. We attended a training session of the university's institutional review board for research involving human subjects. The session stressed the necessity of minimizing any risk of harming the physical safety and psychological well-being of the people involved in our research project. Back in class, students created lists of houses whose residents they wanted to interview based on what they took to be common themes, such as signs involving alcohol or street location. Less commonly, students picked their favorite signs based on noteworthy artwork or vibrant colors.

The students visited the houses, explained the project to the residents, ascertained interest, made appointments for interviews, and left copies of the consent form approved by the institutional review board for all residents of the house should anyone not present want to participate. If residents in one house were uninterested or inaccessible, the student moved on to the next house on the list until the student had interviewed residents from two houses. Each student interviewed residents of a third house whose name was drawn from a pool of the houses not selected earlier. None of the student researchers had trouble completing the assignment because residents of named houses were generally eager to be interviewed. Interviews were scheduled beforehand to ensure that most residents would be home, and all interviews were done while at least half of the residents (varying from four to twelve per house) were present. The first time I taught the course, nine students interviewed twenty-seven houses' residents, and the next time, seventeen students interviewed fifty-one houses' residents.

The class created a list of ten questions, but students were encouraged to deviate from the list and conduct open-ended interviews.[3] Because our goal was to discover how residents of named houses talk about house signs, even if in an interview that might seem artificial relative to other contexts, we pitched the questions with which we started interviews broadly. Why is it important to live in a named house? Did you pick the name and how? What do you think people think when they see your house sign or hear your house name? How does your house name reflect who you are? These questions turned out to be extremely productive, and interviewers turned out to be adept at asking questions based on the answers to our stock questions. In many interviews, residents interacted with each other as well as with the interviewers, something we took as evidence that the interview context did not entirely distort how residents might talk about house signs.[4] Interviews ranged in length from twenty minutes to two and a half hours. Students could accompany each other on interviews or conduct them alone. Students requested my presence in nine interviews.

The students taped their interviews and used three- to five-minute segments to write a final paper engaging with the overarching theme of the course: the reproduction of culture in context. Upon completion, as stipulated in the course syllabus and in the proposal approved by the university's institutional review board, students gave me all of their photographs and tapes and agreed to allow me to use them for future publication. In the consent form, we promised to keep the identities of the residents confidential. I have given house residents and student interviewers pseudonyms in the transcript excerpts and have omitted the dates from descriptions of fieldwork and presentations, which all took place in the last fifteen years. The people who lived in the houses depicted herein are not necessarily the same people who participated in the interviews. Thus the residents who displayed house signs depicted in the figures cannot be matched with the residents whose interviews are presented.

Transcripts of recorded conversations in this book are not presented in the literary style typical of the rest of the text. Elinor Ochs (1979) explains that transcriptions are hardly natural representations of what happens in moments of verbal interaction. Elizabeth Fine notes that "speech and writing employ two different kinds of symbolic systems, the former using not only acoustic signals but gestural signals as well, and the latter using only a sequence of visual signals arranged on paper" (1984, 96). Mary Bucholtz (2000b) explains that transcriptions mark choices about what is transcribed and how it is transcribed, revealing that scholars selectively represent aspects of their fieldwork and engage with socially and politically significant aesthetic possibilities of graphic representations of speech. I have tried to avoid rendering speech in such a way that it might be perceived as nonstandard. For example, I have avoided allegro forms, speech represented as casual or authentic (e.g., wanna, betcha, how ya doin'?); dialect respellings, speech represented as local or regional (aw kay, how awr yoo dooin'?); and eye-dialect, or speech represented as rustic or simple (I alreddy sed swell) (Jaffe 2000, 2007, and Preston 1982, 1985, and 2000).[5] I have indulged in respellings when it seemed to me that the speaker was diverging from her or his way of speaking just prior to the speech in question—in order to mimic someone else, for example. I have also done so when the respelling does not seem to me to unduly stigmatize the represented speaker. Indeed, no house resident that I met during interviews or heard while listening to interview tapes was a speaker of what might be considered in the United States to be a nonstandard variety of English.

Even with such precautions, some of the house residents, upon seeing our transcriptions in a public presentation, told us they were surprised that the transcriptions made students look stupid. When I asked them to elaborate, they said that the transcriptions showed students hesitating, starting the utterance and suddenly changing the topic, and frequently uttering things like "um" and "like." My guess is that rendering transcriptions of interviews in the literary prose characteristic of the rest of the book would change their reception, but I have made the choice to render them as I have for a number of reasons. As I listened to the audio recordings, I came to appreciate the complexities involved in rendering the speech I heard in a graphic form because the speech I heard was so complex. Interview subjects talked about house signs in an orchestrated way that I think is worth trying to represent. Indeed, everyone does certain things to emphasize points, indicate that something is funny, or express solidarity with or distance from peers. I have tried to present extended examples of talk so that readers might find contradictions and inconsistencies in my arguments about what speakers are doing in the transcripts or might find significance where I have not seen it.

The world of parties that occur in named houses will remain relatively unexplored in this book, save one held in a part of town called the Ghetto, described in chapter 4, where the public nature of parties becomes a part of reflecting on the neighborhood. Juxtaposing students' typification of parties while they reflect on house signs with what really happens at parties is not my aim. I was unwilling to attend parties in the houses because I did not want to change the dynamics of parties with my presence. At the same time, this should not be taken to imply that my students found instant rapport with residents of named houses. My students were as unfamiliar with the significance of a house's name for its residents as I was. Indeed, only one of my students lived in a named house, and the house is one that residents of other houses describe as "dumb." This student explained to the class that he didn't feel that his house was one of the better known ones and that he would hesitate to speak for the residents of other houses. Nor did I feel comfortable asking my students to attend parties as part of the research. Discussions of house signs do not focus a great deal on what happens at parties. Occasionally, one of my students signaled recognition of a house's name by virtue of the fact that she had been to a party there, but reflections on house signs did not involve recounting what happened at a party or characterizing parties more generally. Just how house signs are connected to parties and partying will be discussed below.

A Brief History of House Signs and Habits of Their Display

While nothing about Oxford or Miami University accounts for the existence of house signs, the students who display them inhabit a quintessential college town (Gumprecht 2008, 4). In late August, 16,000 Miami University students join Oxford's 15,000 permanent residents. The presence of students has shaped Oxford's economy in ways typical of college towns. Bars and a large dance club occupy prime real estate downtown, a short walk from campus. Many of the youths who attend private high schools outside of town are children of professors, and so salient is the term "townie" that I heard townspeople themselves use it with one another in barber shops, the supermarket, and Oxford's central park.

It is impossible to fully explain why house signs became such an important part of public space in Oxford. Students tell me that these signs have been around since the early 1970s and that The Ivy League was the first. It seems that they were correct in the matter of age.

Initially I had no good reason to doubt that The Ivy League was the first house sign. In fact, students and townspeople alike commented on the sign's simplicity of design and lack of salacious metaphorical play (unlike Octopussy, Morning Wood, and At Church and Almost High), suggesting that it represents a less corrupt time. I was so convinced by these explanations that I published an article in 2007 repeating this information.

Imagine my surprise, then, when I read in a book (discussed more fully in chapter 2) self-published by Reginald Olson, former Director of Miami

University Campus Ministries, that The Pit was the first. Olson learned this from the Miami University yearbook. He writes:

> According to the 1983 *Recensio,* the naming of off-campus houses began in 1973 with some men naming 112 Tallawanda "The Pit." Shortly afterwards, neighboring houses were named Hut Hut (a football quarterback's signal) and Fox Den. Originally an annex to a fraternity, and later used to house football players, the Hut Hut house was named by a group of girls who later moved in and purportedly named it after one of their boyfriends' "peculiar laughs." (2000, 13)

Only after reading Olson's account did I begin to wonder why people might believe that The Ivy League was the first house sign. This idea seems to correspond to a venerable quality similar to that invoked by the identification of Miami University as a "Public Ivy" (Moll 1985).

Oxford's population rose significantly between 1960 and 1970, resulting in the construction of new housing beyond Oxford's Mile Square, the town's original boundary measuring one square mile (Blount 2000). Many residents moved from the Mile Square to the new neighborhoods, renting their former houses to students. Increases in the number of students living off campus provided renters for the new housing being built outside the Mile Square. According to Ellison, in 1955–56, 72 percent of the 5,219 students lived on campus, whereas only 60 percent of 12,442 students did in 1974–75. By 2001–2002, 42 percent of 16,757 students lived on campus. He summarizes:

> These trends [in the changing situation of student residence] appeared because Miami enrollment continued to expand throughout the Public Ivy era [1970–96] without a corresponding expansion in housing. . . . Off-campus options became more attractive for students—new apartment complexes designed with appealing amenities, as well as more rental properties available near Uptown [the commercial district abutting the campus on the west] as faculty and staff moved out of the Mile Square. (2009, 331–32)

Students who live in the large apartment buildings outside the Mile Square do not display signs. The one exception is an area north of the Mile Square on the east side of town where many students live. This area is called the Ghetto, which refers to the shoddy construction of the houses, comparatively cheap rents, and a lax atmosphere conducive to partying. Some house signs use the label in their messages: Ghetto Fabulous, Ghetto Super Stars, and Too Poplar for the Ghetto. Very few students who were interviewed were aware that

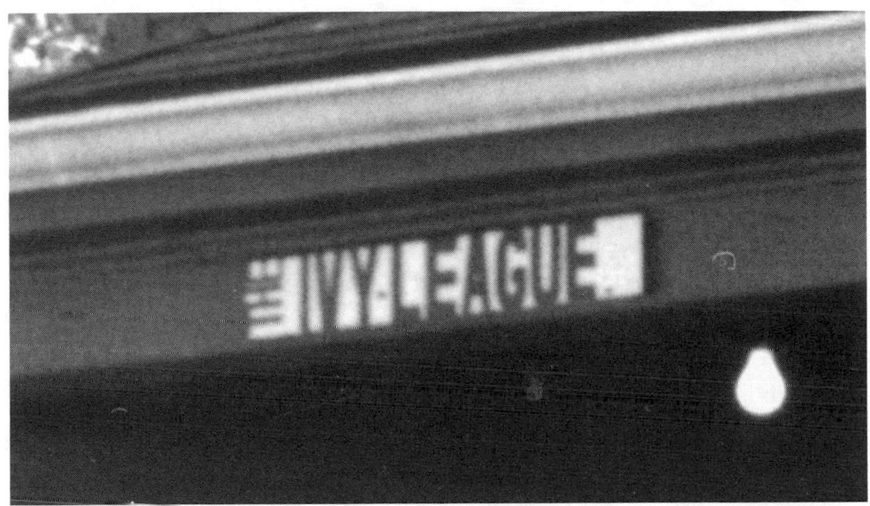

FIGURE 0.2. The Ivy League

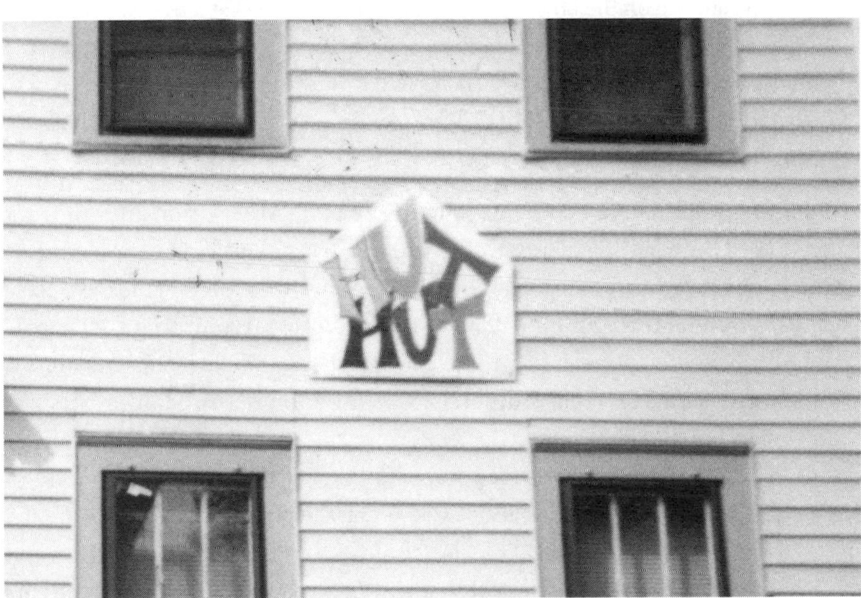

FIGURE 0.3. Hut Hut

the Ghetto is nearly as old as the Mile Square and that the Ghetto used to be the black section of town. Indeed, most residents of named houses are white. Miami University's 2007 *Diversity Update* shows that 85.3 percent of undergraduate students were white, while 3.2 percent were black, and 1.9 percent were Hispanic (Stevenson 2007).[6] Very few students of color live in named houses. One student told me that he was tempted to bring his Jewish upbringing to bear in a house sign that would lampoon recruitment advertising by the university that he believed exaggerated the minority presence on campus. But, he explained, house signs are not the platform for such serious statements, an opinion voiced by other students we interviewed.

In an interview with eighth-graders at a middle school in Oxford, a local man described the loosening of restrictions on African American residence and was asked what had stayed the same. He replied:

> Nothing. The street layout is the same for the mile square, but other than that, nothing has stayed the same. When I was living in Oxford in those days, all of those houses that are rented to students today were single family homes, peaceful, no signs up on the house, Tappa Keg a Day and all that stuff. Families were wholesome. The students lived on campus, and of course earlier, before some of the liberalization took place, blacks had to stay in the private homes, had to rent rooms from private families. They couldn't stay on campus. That changed. But basically there's really nothing the same in Oxford. (Pettitt 2007, 37)

For many students, living in a house is an attractive option after the first two years of required residence in the university's dormitories. Residence in named houses presupposes the ability to pay rent in Oxford. Typical of a college town, rent is rather high when compared with surrounding rural areas or nearby cities. Such spatially inflected differences are characteristic of how students envision social class differences as dividing them from others. As Ortner has noted, "Americans do recognize class in some form. Or rather I should say, *some* Americans recognize it, from a particular point of view" (2003, 41). Students rarely talk about social class differences among students, but much more often talk about locals, "townies," or residents of nearby rural or urban areas as occupying a lower social class than themselves. Students refer to Hamilton and Middletown, nearby cities in which Miami University branch campuses are located, as "Hamiltucky" and "Middletucky." The nicknames suggest a lower social class standing than that of Oxford by intimating that people and poverty associated with Kentucky have crossed the Ohio River. House signs provide a way to talk about stigmatized others—such as

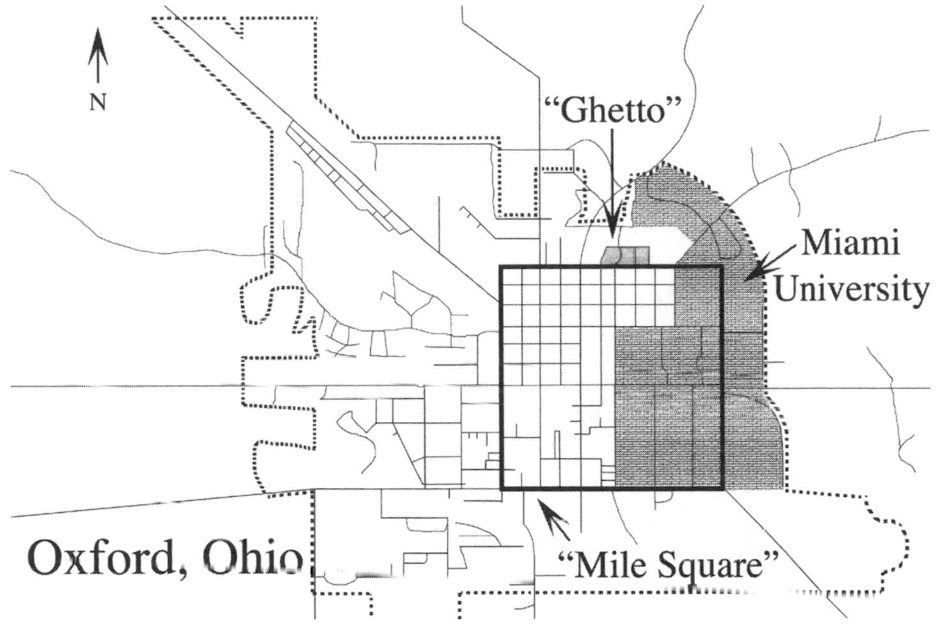

MAP 0.1. Map of Oxford

FIGURE 0.4. Ghetto Superstars

"townies," "hillbillies," or residents of ghettos—by focusing on such things as hairstyles and accents, but rarely refer to social class.

An interview conducted with four sophomores shows that houses offer special qualities not found in dormitories or apartments:

> VICKY: now are you guys interested in living in a house, and if so, why or why not(4)
>
> LIZ: um, I really wanted to live in a house this year . . . next year, but my friends and I couldn't find one, so::, and because you have to get houses so early in Oxford, we ended up just getting an apartment because it was just a whole lot easier in the end(2)
>
> ROBBIE: um, I'm really interested in living in a house(2) I like the freedom, and, uh, you can be in a house all year. you don't have to leave for special breaks or anything like that. you can do whatever you want(3)
>
> STACEY: um, I definitely wanted to live in a house. I wanted that over an apartment because I wanted to have more living space and I thought a lot of the apartments in Oxford didn't really offer that, and the house that we found was really coo::l and had everything that we wanted like our own washer and dryer and all that stuff, so yeah, I definitely wanted to live there
>
> REBECCA: I'm really excited about living in a house only because of my friends(3) I really just wanted to live close to them and that's . . . I mean if everyone had wanted to live in the dorm, I probably would have done that too

When asked whether they would want to have a house sign, even the girl who will live in an apartment replied affirmatively:

> VICKY: OK, would you guys want to have a house sign. why or why not(2)
>
> LIZ: Uh, yeah, because I think it just makes living in the house a whole lot more fun, even though that sounds really stupid. I think it just shows the personality of the people that live there(2)
>
> ROBBIE: Um, I agree with that too. it, uh, shows a little bit of our personality, it kind of shows who we are. people can sort of see . . . you know, get an idea of who we are from looking at our house name. it's neat

STACEY: yeah, it's . . . seeing the house names around, it like kind of just gives a little bit of spice to the off-campus life, so it looks really cool and I think it'll be cool

REBECCA: well, the house I'm moving into is already named, it's called Animal House, but I think it's a really crappy name, so I'm sure we'll change it as soon as we move in

These remarks give a sense of how little residence in a named house determines the social habits and bonds of the residents. Although our class project involved but a single researcher living in a named house, we came to know some things about the social relations among residents. At the most encompassing level, we found that this included many practical requests and obligations like borrowing a car, repaying a very small loan, or settling a cigarette debt. Remarks and requests emerged as asides in interview conversations. We also discovered that most houses were made up of residents of a single sex. We encountered no couples living together in a named house. Residents poked a good deal of fun at the very few who had a steady partner, someone always living elsewhere. We encountered no house in which residents revealed that a housemate engaged in anything other than heterosexual activity. We asked why living in a named house was important, and answers generally focused on how well the house name was known and not on social activities among housemates. In spring, members of the class might note that residents were cooking on a grill in the front yard, but this was true of both named and unnamed houses. Indeed, it seemed to us that "friends," the category of people said to live together in named houses, required little in the way of explicit explanation, as long as such people were not hostile or romantically involved.

Not only was the category of "friends" quite flexible and its requirements undefined but residents made explicit that some cared too much about their house sign and name. In an interview with the residents of Hot Box, the women poke fun at the ways in which the residents of End Zone put their house name on items in the house. My student Jenny and I ask the residents whether they have anything that has the house name on it, and the residents point to End Zone as an example:

JENNY: do you have anything in here that like says Hot Box or . . .

GIRLS: no

ALI: T-shirts

LILY: no

MEG: yeah we're not that obsessed with our sign

CHAISE: do you know if other people have like T-shirts for their houses or . . .
LILY: the people next door actually are quite into their name. End Zone, they have, did you go there, oh my god they have like a table, like posters like everywhere like I'm sure they have, they have to have a shirt
MEG: yeah they have a, yeah they have a ⌈table, outside
LILY: ⌊cups that are like Hot Box like, uh not Hot Box but End Zone like, everywhere is⌈End Zone, everywhere
MEG: ⌊yeah, picture frames with End Zone underneath and like all the roommates in it

Their commentary shows that some house names provide a way for the residents to frame and display their friendship. By and large, however, such display is rare and often decried as going too far.

While some houses retain their names through many sets of residents, on the whole, names change very unevenly. For example, Rebecca plans to change the name of the house into which she is about to move. Philosophers of language such as Kripke (1972) and Putnam (1975) have demonstrated that proper names rest on a baptismal event when a group bestows a name on a person, place, idea, etc. Since the baptismal event by which the first and oldest house with a sign (The Pit or The Ivy League) was named, a house's tradition has come to depend on its name's inheritance or maintenance by successive inhabitants. Many signs include the year in which the house was named. Sometimes students painted the date on their sign in order to substantiate the house's tradition or "pedigree."

Sean, a resident of Gutter Balls, for example, uses the verb "to be born" to specify the year in which the house was named.

BEV: tell me about your house and about the name(2)
SEAN: well, our house was born in 1997, and the wrestlers used to have it and when they left, they passed it down to one of the guys' little **brother. he** named this house Gutter Ba::lls and the sign is a picture of **two large bowling balls** and a pin, a **large** pin in the middle. there's bowling balls. and that represents us, we're called Gutter Balls. but we hate bowling, none of us

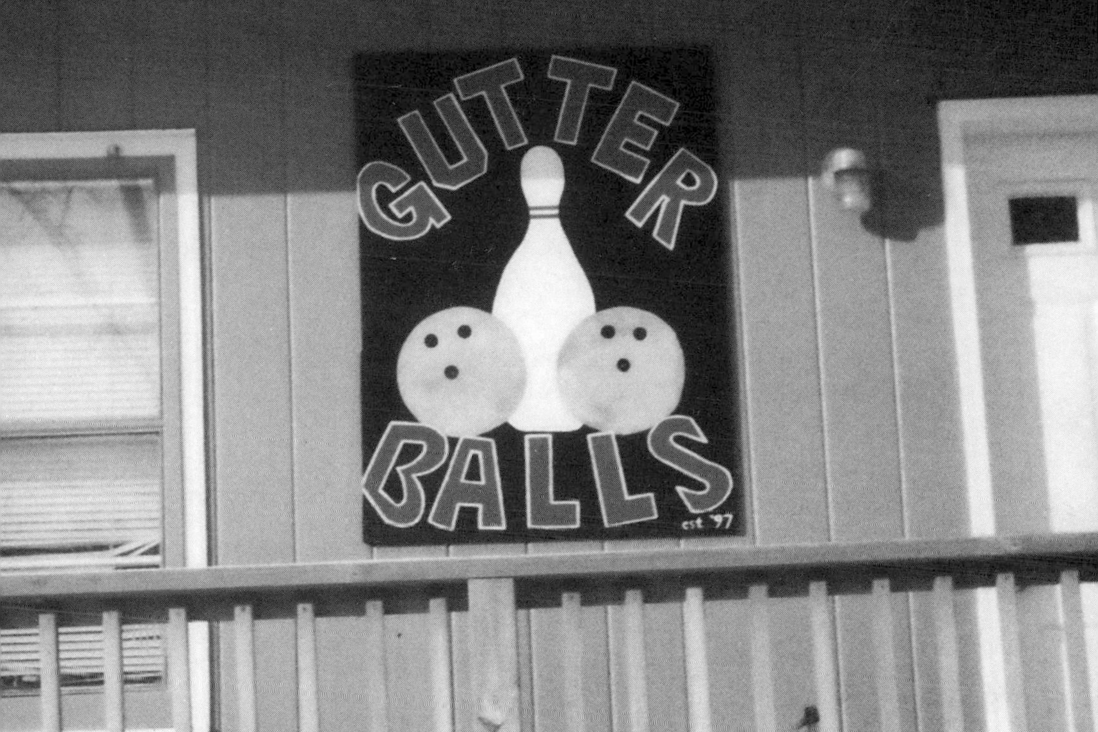

FIGURE 0.5. Gutter Balls

bowl . . . and the only reason worth going to the bowling alley#
is to see the mullets, the hairdos

ALL: #

SEAN: that's it for Gutter Balls(2) this house will go on forever because anyone who lives here will be too lazy to make a new si::gn. so it will just be known as Gutter Balls

Sean never makes explicit how the name should be understood, but there is giggling and loud talking as he describes the sign.

The residents of Unplanned Parenthood explain that their house went without a name the year before they moved in:

JAY: so, you said this . . . this one had a different name
NICK: ⌈**yeah**
SKIP: ⌊Bed No Breakfast
TODD: Bed No Breakfast
SKIP: it used to be called ⌈Bed No Breakfast
NICK: ⌊**last** year it wasn't called anything though
SKIP: there was no ⌈house sign
JAY: ⌊no house sign

TODD: **we** didn't really like that so(2)
SKIP: yeah, we didn't like that that much
JAY: so, do you think you'll pass this one down when you lea::ve
SKIP: ⌈I hope so
NICK: ⌊**yeah,** yeah
TODD: I hope . . . I hope whoever gets it next year keeps the na::me
JAY: yeah
EMMA: will you leave the sign, then, for them
SKIP: u::m, yeah
NICK: I think so, ⌈yeah
TODD: ⌊yeah. we'll probably talk to them first(1)
EMMA: will you be living here next year
TODD: no
NICK: we're all ⌈graduating
SKIP: ⌊yeah

In many interviews, residents gave evidence that the baptismal event of naming a house was a complex mediating factor long after those who named the house moved out (Rymes 1996, 2001a, 2001b). Some said they promised previous residents to keep the house's name; others reported having to decide whether to keep the name or change it; and others described holding competitions and voting on the cleverest name. The residents of Come-N-Go kept the name because it was already well known.

LOU: did you guys name your house or was it named before you guys moved in here
SUE: it was named **before** ⌈we got here
WENDY: ⌊before we got here(2)
VAL: we actually thought about changing the name(2)
SUE: a little bit
VAL: a lot
WENDY: we couldn't come up . . .
VAL: we were gonna call it Your Mom's House
ALL: #
WENDY: but there was already a house named Your Mom
SUE: we didn't know about it then, we didn't change it because it was named the year before and so we just figured that people had already known it and people were asking us where we were living. it was just easier to say . . . well this is what it is, it was like

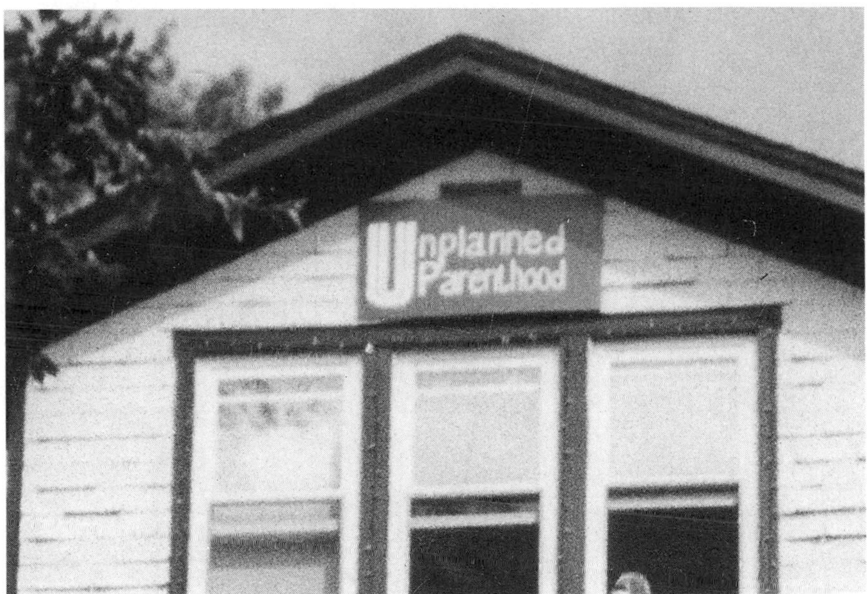

FIGURE 0.6. Unplanned Parenthood

> harder to say . . . what we're changing it . . . we don't know what we're changing it to. so it was just a convenience thing, and we just kept it.

The comments by the women of Come-N-Go might be understood to affirm Sean's claim that sometimes new residents are too lazy to create a new name for the house. Or the same comments might indicate that the residents of Come-N-Go appreciate the social recognition the name offers.

Only two house signs seemed to be too salacious for prolonged public display. While walking to the university, I would see 3 Chicks and a Cock (three chicks and a rooster or three young women and a penis) spray-painted on a dilapidated piece of plywood that was positioned in different areas of the front yard of a house for a two-week period before it finally disappeared. Residents explained that the only sign that had to be removed because of complaints was Nothing Butt Sex. I never found out who had asked for it to be removed or to which house it was attached.

In Oxford, house names can be used apart from their depiction on house signs. For example, interviewers arrived at one house to find residents dressed in matching green T-shirts with their house name written across the front.

FIGURE 0.7. 3 Chicks and a Cock

They explained that they wear the T-shirts when they host or attend parties together. However, only two other houses were identified where residents did this. When the residents of Hot Box chide the residents of End Zone for doing this, they are reflecting the rarity of such activity.

The *Miami Student Amusement* conducted a poll in 2002 about the ten most infamous house signs. The list included Morning Wood and Octopussy. It also published a list of "House Sign Superlatives" and bestowed its "Amusement Awards." The categories are not entirely representative of the way residents reflect on signs. Entirely alien to the ways students talk about house signs, for example, was the notion that a sign might be pretentious. Even so, some of the commentary does hint at the importance of elements that did figure prominently in students' reflections, such as a distinction between "dumb" and "clever" signs, the prevalence of signs that involve alcohol and the partying that goes along with it, the prevalence of names taken from popular media venues, and the great importance of sexually charged signs.

Finally, a sandwich shop near campus used house names for several of its menu items. No particular domain of meaning dominated, as the manager explained to me that anyone could suggest names and sandwich ingredients and that suggestions were hardly confined to house names.

Table 0.1. Joke Awards for House Signs Announced by the *Miami Student Amusement,* January 24, 2002

House Name	Award	Commentary
Pop-N-Wood and Morning Wood	Most Immature	Come on now, do you really need to advertise this? It might have been cool in junior high, but you're in college now.
Ivy League	Most Pretentious	If you belonged there, you wouldn't be here.
Betty Ford Clinic	Most Addictive	Was it even a contest?
Dollhouse	Barbie	Somewhat basic, but we do go to Pretty Girl U.
Endzone	Ken	It's an All-American name, much like Ken, and an excusable one for your house.
Shanty	Most Boring	What is the point in hanging this sign up? We thought "shanty" could describe all of Oxford's housing.
AA	Most Honest	At least these housemates can admit their vices and enjoy them.
Ho-Tel 6 and No-Tell Motel	Hide the Sign when Mom Comes	Not sure these signs are anything to be proud of, similar to the traditional Miami uptown attire.
Catch-22	Most Educated	Very nice name, but exactly how many housemates have read the book or know what the phrase means?
Dude, Where's My House? and Menace to Sobriety	Best Take-off of a Movie Title	Dude, we just liked them.
As Good as You'll Get	Worst Take-off of a Movie Title	The movie might have left us with a warm, fuzzy feeling inside, but this sign just leaves us feeling nauseated.
Cruel Intentions	Most Ambitious	Scandalous. This name was well chosen and the most realistic of Miami night life.
Good 'N Plenty	Midnight Snack	We appreciate this sign for its ambiguity. Read into it what you will.
Gutterballs	Mind in the Gutter	The sign says it all. Guys will be guys, but at least they're good sports about it.

Continued on the next page

Table 0.1. *Continued*

House Name	Award	Commentary
Tom Collins and Red Stripe	What the Hell, Who Cares	What is really the purpose of these names? First impressions are everything, and yours leave us less than satisfied.
Deez Nutz	Most Likely to Get Pissed Off If They Don't Get an Award	The name of the house has been around for at least five years, so get no real credit for the sign or choice to leave it up.
Witty House Name	Witty House Name	Very nice name from some sarcastic and "witty" people. Thanks for the entertainment.
Alpha Sigma Sigma	Most Supportive of Greek Life	This sign makes us laugh every time we see it. Are they saying something about Greek Life?
Four Play	Most Honorable Intentions	We think this is always an enjoyable sign. Enough said.
Wendy's Backyard	Most Unoriginal Sign	This sign is the epitome of Richard T. Farmer [the name of the business school] creativity.
Bring 'Em Young University	Most Original Sign	As if we wanted them old.
Pissonia	Most Offensive	We kind of wonder if King Library's most recent book-peeing celebrity ever lived here.
Syc-A-College	Most Creative Sign	This sign is particularly relevant to those of us who have been here five years.
Octopussy	Worst Sign Overall	Is anyone really a fan of the p-word?
Tappa Kegga Day	Best Sign Overall	It's always good to have a personal mission statement. And we think this is a good one for everybody.

Source: Adapted from Melissa Paniagua, "Hey Baby, What's Your Sign?" *Miami Student Amusement*, January 24, 2002.

FIGURE 0.8. Crammed Inn's Welcome Banner

Residents of named houses often used their house names in messages displayed on cloth banners. These messages marked a specific occasion, such as parents' weekend, and always in a transparent, albeit humorous, manner. The residents of Crammed Inn, for example, added a checklist to the message "Welcome to Crammed Inn Mom & Dad" that included the name of a credit card, food, and clothes. The welcome banner reinforces the connection between house signs and students because it makes explicit the students' dependence on parents. The residents of Cosmopolitan similarly welcomed their parents using their house's name, but integrate a design element from their sign, a martini glass, into the message on the cloth banner. They sign their welcome, "your girls," preceded by a red heart.

Other occasions marked by cloth banners were specific to individual houses. The residents of Sex on the Beech advertised a party on a cloth banner, mentioning the name of the party, Beech Fest, the date, Sat. Sept. 14, and the command to "Come Thirsty!" Banners, however, were rare. Students explained that parties rarely needed advertising, because word of mouth was more than sufficient. I can only guess that the residents of Sex on the Beech used the banner to advertise Beech Fest because it was early in the academic year, when students might be relatively unaware of who lived in what house.

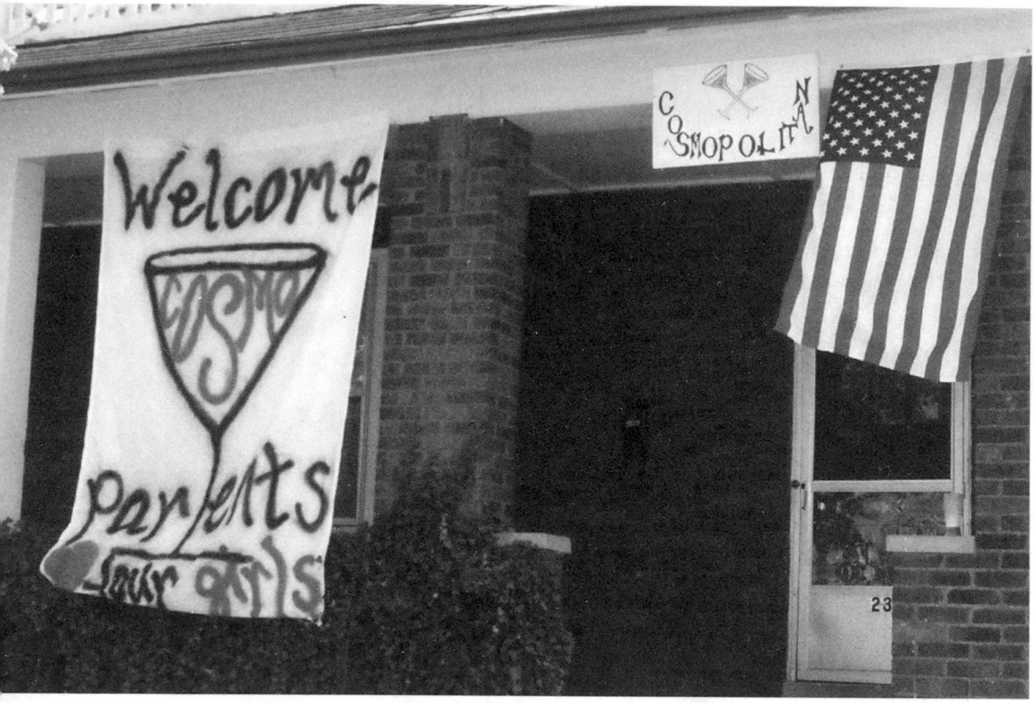

FIGURE 0.9. *Above.* Cosmopolitan's Welcome Banner

FIGURE 0.10. *Below.* Sex on the Beech/Beech Fest Announcement

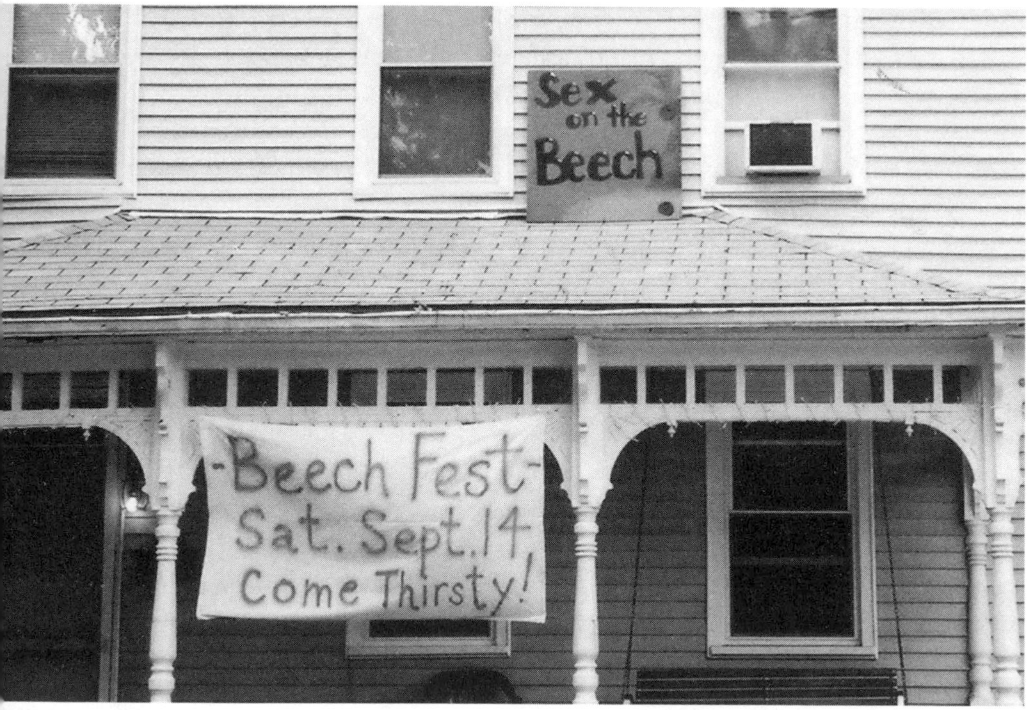

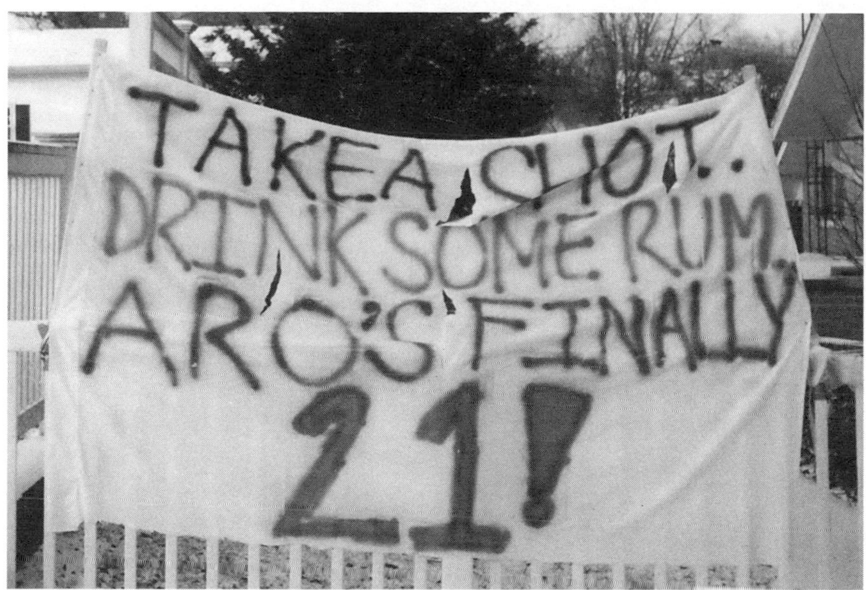

FIGURE 0.11. TAKE A SHOT . . .

Most commonly, banners commemorated a resident's twenty-first birthday. In Figure 0.11, residents have couched their birthday wishes in a rhyme: "TAKE A SHOT . . . DRINK SOME RUM . . . ARO'S FINALLY 21!" This banner makes explicit why the twenty-first birthday is important: the ability to consume alcohol legally. Whether they welcome parents as part of a university event, advertise a party, or celebrate a friend's ability to drink alcohol, the banners involve activities significant to college students.

The only place I found house signs detached from their houses was in one of Oxford's bars, across the street from the sandwich shop. A number of examples of house names—Morning Wood and Octopussy among them—were attached to the walls. A bartender told me that when a number of house residents graduate together, they "retire" their sign to the bar so that other students will see it. New residents sometimes use new pictorial and design elements but maintain the name. Most names in the bar still exist around town, and the bartender said that during homecoming, visiting alumni often check to see whether the house where they lived still bears the same name.

There is no question that house signs invoke alcohol, sexuality, and—less often—drugs, the accoutrements of partying and collegiate fun so well represented in the mass media and of such concern to critics of student life.

But house signs also invoke social boundaries and contexts that mass media representations and the exposés written about college fun cannot explain. A sign sometimes plays with the fact that the house sits beside a specific institution. Residents sometimes care a great deal about whether the next group of residents will maintain their house name, while others seem not to care at all. And, perhaps most obviously, it is students who name their houses. While they often borrow elements of names from the world of the mass media, they do not simply reproduce those names. Indeed, Rebecca, the sophomore who will be moving into a named house, finds the name Animal House to be "crappy." House signs have a complicated relationship with partying and college fun more generally.

CHAPTER ONE

Bed Booze & Beyond: History and Ethnography of Collegiate Fun

Words, expressions, and forms of discourse sometimes die quickly as institutional projects are abandoned or radically reconstituted, sometimes slowly weather away, gradually or unintentionally altered in the course of prolonged daily use in relatively stable projects. Old meanings are likewise disrupted or altered, defeated or disfigured. New words and usages are adopted as significantly different institutionally embedded projects are introduced.

—ALLEN PRED,
Lost Words and Lost Worlds

Even a brief glance at the list of names of houses in Oxford (Table 1.1) confirms something noted by anthropologists, folklorists, historians, and sociologists who have studied life in U.S. colleges and universities: having fun is of paramount importance in the lives of students. The first three house names, for example, invoke something like the familiar trio, "sex, drugs, and rock 'n roll." The sign 3 Chicks and a Cock suggests the transgressions of group sex while playing with a word for a young woman and a more vulgar word for a penis. 4 Non-Blondes is the name of a band, and like 3 Chicks and a Cock, hints at the number and sex of the house's residents. The name 6 Pack suggests the number of the house's residents, and perhaps the sex, too, since "six pack" can refer to the pattern of muscles on an abdomen. The name also invokes beer because whether in bottles or cans, the beverage is commonly sold in sets of six. Further down the list one finds Alco Hall, Alcoholics Unanimous, and Ale Road Crossing.

Table 1.1. Selected House Names in Oxford

3 Chicks and a Cock
4 Non-Blondes
6 Pack
:10 Spot
12 Feet Inn
AA
ΑΣΣ
Absolut Angels
Absolut Chaos
Alamo
Alco Hall
Alcoholics Unanimous
Ale Road Crossing
Animal House Knowledge Is Good
Arsenal
Asspen
At Church and Almost High
Bamm Bamm: Come See the Bedrock
Band of Brothers
Bed Booze & Beyond
Beech Bunnies
Beer Goggles
Betty Boops
Betty Ford Clinic
The Big Kahuna
Blonde Moments
Blue Lagoon
Blue Moon
Boardwalk
The Boobie Trap
Boogie Nights
The Boom Boom Room
Boot 'N Rally
Booze Inn
Bored of Education
Bottoms Up
Boutique Hall
Box Office
Boxed Inn
Brew-Ski
Brick House
Casa Blanca
Casual Six
Catch 22
Century Club
Champagne Room "Rules Were Meant to Be Broken"
Che
Cheers
The Chick-Inn
Church Key
City on Down
Clothing Optional
Cocktail
Cocktales
Collgirls
Come-N-Go
Copa-Cabana
Corner Pocket
Cornered Inn
Cosmopolitan
Crammed Inn
Crib of the Rib
Cruel Intentions
David Hasselhoffbrauhaus
Deez Nutz
Deuces Wild
Dillywhop
Dirty Dozen
Dirty Martini
Dirty South
Dis-Graceland
Di-Vine
Dogg Pound
The Dollhouse
Dude, Where's My House?
Dysfunction Junction
End Zone
Fill'er Up
For Sale
Four Play
Fourever XXI
Fox Den
Freshmen O Rientation
FUBAR
Fully Loaded
Gallery
Game On We Shoot. We Score
Gary Coleman Fan Club
Genital Hospital
Gettin' Lucky
Ghetto Booty
Ghetto Super Stars
Gimme Shelter
Girls Gone Ghetto
Girls Gone Wild
Girls on Top
Glory Days
Good + Plenty
Goodfellas
Green House
Green Machine
Gutter Balls
Hacienda
Hangover Here
Happy as a Clam
Happy Hour 60 Wasted Minutes
The Heisman
Hell's Belles
Hit & Run
Hoe Down
Home Alone
Home Plate
Hootersville
Hot Box
Hotel California
Ho-Tel 6 "We'll Leave the Light On for You"
Hut Hut
Immaculate Consumption
Immoral Support
Inncoherent
Inn Pursuit

Table 1.1. *Continued*

The Ivy League
Jäger Städium
Jaundice
Keg Stand
Kinkytown
Kokomo
The Land of Oddz
Last Call
Lazy Dayz
Leave It to Beaver
Lemon Spritzer
Lily Pad
Limelight
Liquor Juggs
Liquor Up Front, Poker in the Rear
Little Women
Live Bait
The Living WC
Looks Te-quil-ya
Main Event
Main Squeeze
Melee
Miami U Short Bus
Miami Vice
Miss B. Haven
Moist
Moon Inn
Monkey Business
Morning Wood
The No-Tell Motel—Pay by the Hour—
The "O" Face
The Oar House
Octoballs
Octopussy
Paid Vacation
The Panty Shanty
Parliament Oxford, Ohio
Party Foul
Pebble Beech
Peeps
Pee-wee's Playhouse
The Petting Zoo
Pheromones
Pitcher Perfect
The Playm~~ate~~eight Mansion
Poisoned Ivy
Poplar Cherry
Poplar with the Ladies
Pop-N-Wood
Pour House
Precinct 109 "Spread 'Em"
Project Mahem
Pucker Up
Raisin' Hell
Red Stripe
Reunion
Risky Business
Rolling Stoned
The Rusty Trombone
Sanctuary
Scooby
Scrappy
Señor Ayitas
Serendipity
Set Sail
Sex on the Beech
Shanty
Simply Irresistible
Six Appeal
Six Geese a Layin'
Slow Idaho
Slump Busters
South Beech
South of the Border
Spoiled Beeches
Spring Chicks
Spring Fever
Stagger Inn
Startin' Early
Stop Inn
Stop Making Sense
Strangers with Candy
Subject to Blackout . . .
Sugar Shack
Syc-A-College
Tailgate (Miami)
TKΔ Tappa Kegga Day
Team Ram-Rod
Tequila Mockingbird
Three's Company
Tipsy Chicks
Tom Collins
Tony Danza
Too Poplar for the Ghetto
Top or Bottom?
Treehouse
Trouble in Paradise
Tuna Sandwich
Unbuckled
Unisix
Unplanned Parenthood
Up Your Alley
Uptown Girls
The Usual Suspects
Waffle House
Waste of Space
Well Hung Over
Wendy's Backyard
West High Life The Champagne of Houses
Where Is Our Sign?
Where the Sidewalk Ends
Where the Wild Things Are
Whine Cellar
White Castle
White House
White Trash
Wigwam
Witty House Name (Preferably with a Drug, Sex, and/or Alcohol Reference)
Wrong House
Yabba Grabba Brew
Yellow Submarine
Young and Restless

When considered together, the six examples show that house signs themselves are fun, as they take advantage of sound patterns, play with the ways sound is represented visually, and borrow and manipulate words and phrases wholesale, all toward the creation of puns, double entendres, and humor more generally.

A number of ethnographic studies have explored what makes the college years so charged with the production of fun. These studies have shown that the connections between this period of life and the expression of fun have shifted over time with economic, institutional, sociocultural, and political aspects of life in the United States. Less attention has been paid to how students reflect on fun as they are (or are not) having it.

Beer Goggles: Introducing Collegiate Fun

One of the major reasons the folklore produced by college students in the United States is so charged with images of booze and sex is that the age most associated with the college experience falls between the dependence of childhood and the independence of adulthood.[1] Adolescence is a period of life full of ambiguity structured by such new realities as the age of consent, labor laws, registration for military service, and the drinking age. Each of these involves transformation—from constraint to liberty or vice versa. The period is marked by transition from the dominion of parents to the support of the self, with a time in between partially devoted to study. Studying itself is fraught with contradiction when viewed through the lens of productive economic activity, since it provides no immediate sustenance. Ultimately, education guarantees nothing, not even a job, which today is the most widely cited reason for attending school (Levine and Cureton 1998).

The uncertainty of college studies only becomes more complex when academic success depends on the authority of professors as well as the diligence of the self. Barre Toelken captures the transitional and ambiguous qualities of the category of the college student:

> Old enough to drink, work, fight in wars on the one hand, dependent on money from state or parent, dependent on the tests of overbearing professors, dependent on the vagaries of a changing job market on the other. Independent adults they may be, but their arrested youth allows them, in the words of one cynical professor, to have their parents and eat them, too. (1986, 524)

New responsibilities and freedoms make for a complex period of life, increasingly so given that state funding for education has been rolled back in recent decades and more burden has been shifted to students and supportive families. College student life blends the partial and multiple involvements and responsibilities of a period left behind with those of a period not yet reached.

Only adding to the anxiety of the period, the medical professions and media alike have depicted adolescence as a time ripe with the possibilities of delinquency, the emergence of yet unseen mental illness, and the mistake that carries catastrophic consequences in later life (Cohen 2002 and Lesko 2001). Daniel Suslak (2009, 203) nicely characterizes the sense of exaggeration emergent from the life period, including the energies devoted to a response:

> Following swiftly in the wake of modern adolescence's arrival on the scene are the inevitable moral panics about the role of the adolescents in the local social order. They get viewed as irresponsible, wild-oats-sowing, not-yet-fully-formed adults. Enormous resources get spent on socializing them to uphold local values and reproduce the local social order. Yet the very institutions created to accommodate them—particularly schools—serve to further set them apart from both their elders and their younger siblings and cousins.[2]

Given that the energies devoted to adolescence as a problematic period have been brought to bear in colleges and universities, among other institutions, it is not surprising that the institution has provided a context for the emergence of as well as a theme for a great deal of folklore and expressive culture.

Trangressive fun thus emerges from but also speaks to the ambivalent position of the college student, most often rendered as psychological:

> College students, often away from parents for the first extended period, perched on the edge of adulthood, anxiously anticipating their entry into a real world of competition, failure, and success, engage in a number of exaggerated traditions which speak to the pressures and stresses of their psychological position. (Toelken 1986, 523)

It would seem that the psychological insecurity of college emerges from a time and space "betwixt and between," in the words of Victor Turner, more defined times and spaces. Indeed, college might be described as a time and space for enacting what Turner called a "ritual of status elevation" wherein the "subject or novice is being conveyed irreversibly from a lower to a higher position in an institutionalized system of such positions" (1969, 167).

College folklore attests to the idea that these transformations are riddled with ambivalence. A good deal of student folklore concerns the institutional roles and relationships in which students find themselves newly entangled.

In his extensive review of the folklore of college students, *Piled Higher and Deeper* (PhD), published in 1995, Simon Bronner notes that a good deal of anxiety surrounds the authority of professors and the fairness of academic evaluation procedures. Bronner presents lore, for example, that describes students whose extensive preparations lead them to fail, impossibly eccentric or capricious professors, tests that contain tricks that guard against cheating, or recycled term papers that receive comments revealing the professor's humorous acknowledgment of plagiarism.

Bronner presents an example of a mock exam circulating at a university in Oklahoma in 1988. It implicitly criticizes an overly demanding set of questions that cannot possibly be answered in the time allowed. The mock exam begins routinely enough: "Instructions: Read each question carefully. Answer all questions. Time limit—4 hours. Begin immediately." The exam is divided into common subjects of study such as "History: Describe the history of the papacy from its origin to the present day, concentrating especially but not exclusively on its social, political, economic, religious, and philosophical impact on Europe, Asia, America, and Africa. Be brief, concise, and specific," or "Medicine: You have been provided with a razor blade, a piece of gauze, and a bottle of Scotch. Remove your appendix. Do not suture until your work has been inspected. You have fifteen minutes." The exam proceeds in like manner through Public Speaking, Biology, Music, Psychology, Sociology, Management Science, Engineering, Economics, Political Science, Epistemology, Physics, Philosophy, and General Knowledge. The exam ends with "Extra Credit: Define the universe. Give three examples" (Bronner 1995, 63–65). The mock exam is particularly clever because it uses the instruction and question format of the very thing it seeks to criticize.

House signs find their closest expressive cousin in the most studied aspect of college lore, which has been collected and published under the label "slang." In her *Slang U: The Official Dictionary of College Slang,* Pamela Munro explains, "Most authorities conclude that slang is language whose use serves to mark the user as part of a distinct social group, and we have used this criterion in deciding which expressions qualify as college slang" (1989, 3–4). Like all slang, college slang is hard to define because it changes rapidly. Connie Eble explains that less than 10 percent of the slang terms she collected in 1972 at University of North Carolina at Chapel Hill were still in circulation in 1987 (1996, 15). Whether an expression will survive for very long or venture beyond the confines of the people who first use it is impossible to predict. Eble notes that "the slang of a group proliferates around topics of importance to that group" (1996, 51). Like other scholars of youth, Eble notes that college slang emerges in a period of insecurity and liminality:

> College students are always living up to the expectations of others—family, home community, and teachers, for example. Although slang may provide college students with a means of subtle rebellion against all these pressures, the opposition to authority appears to be rather playful and occurs in predictable areas, obligatory and automatic rather than heartfelt. Slang mainly provides college students with a means of feeling connected to other people subject to the same insecurities. (1996, 129)

Many of the words that make up college slang bespeak the unevenness of academic life, such as courses that require vastly different amounts of work, or students who are overeager and too close to the faculty:

> Students identify easy courses as guts, cakes, puds, puddings, cinches, snaps, skates, and breezes; hard courses are bitches, screamers, grinds, and ball breakers. During the nineteenth century, zealous students were called digs, fags, grubs, polers, or blues. Today, they are grinds, grunts, gunners, geeks, gweeps, dweebs, and throats. Students who gained teachers' approval were bootlicks, fishers, piscatorians, toadies, and coaxers. Now they're brownnoses and ass lickers. (Bronner 1995, 41)

Eble notes that students can downplay their own academic prowess with the term "geek," in phrases such as "I'm geeking tonight, so I can't go out"; "I'll probably geek over to Davis library around 7"; and "Let me geek down these last few notes, and then I'll go out" (Eble 1996, 111). A mere association with school can render negative connotations: "*Booked* means 'ugly,' and *published* means 'very ugly': 'You might think that guy is booked. Well, his roommate is published'" (Eble 1996, 60). Few words of genuinely positive value have emerged to describe classes or students in the folk argot of academic life. One is "ace," which Eble defines as "perform well, make A," but it is a rarity (1996, 145). Most terms refer to perceived inconsistencies in the face of a standardized grading system, or allegiances to authority figures who dole out those grades.

House signs in Oxford rarely speak to such academic concerns. A handful of signs do use elements in their names that pertain in some way to the university. Names that mimic conventions for naming university buildings include Alco Hall and Boutique Hall. Jäger Städium plays with the visual representation of the stadium's name, Yager Stadium, to remind one of the

German spirits, Jägermeister. Tailgate (Miami) invokes a popular activity at sports events and includes the name of the school. TKΔ Tappa Kegga Day and AΣΣ play with the practice of using Greek letters to name fraternities and sororities. Freshmen O Rientation invokes a rookie student level and a university-related activity. Animal House Knowledge Is Good is the name and mocking mantra of a movie, even if dated, about college life.

The Ivy League includes reference to the halls of ivy, an expression for institutions of higher education. Miami U Short Bus includes the name of the school and a derogatory name for a vehicle.[3] Manipulated names of spring break destinations include Asspen and South Beech. College sports serve as the basis for Hut Hut, The Heisman, and The Oar House. Books that might be assigned in class include Catch 22, Little Women, and the altered Tequila Mockingbird. One might argue that these signs simply invoke aspects of college life, however, and do not assert the same kind of anxiety mixed with disaffection that Bronner's and Eble's examples do so well.

Three house signs do resemble the examples Bronner and Eble discuss in that they are oriented explicitly to aspects of academic life. Poisoned Ivy includes an august reference to the institution but couches it in the name of a plant that causes discomfort and a rash. Syc-A-College playfully integrates part of the street names, Sycamore and College, on which the house is located to create the phrase "sick of college," which expresses malaise. Finally, Bored of Education manipulates the spelling of the word "board" to transform a common name for a public school committee into a statement of malaise. Given the total number of house signs presented in Figure 1.1, however, three signs form a tiny minority. Even if the house signs that involve any sort of academic or university-related concerns were included, they would make up only a small proportion of the total.

Much more common than house signs that include some academic or university-related theme are the signs that involve drinking, sex, and the music, films, and advertisements of popular culture. Many of those signs that do involve college life in some way or another also reference drinking and sex. Asspen, for example, is a house sign that has made sexual the name of a destination for spring break, and Tequila Mockingbird is a house name that has manipulated the name of a book such that it invokes alcohol. Barre Toelken notes the prominence of such themes in the folklore of college students:

> Student customs extend far beyond the issues of academic anxiety. . . . Collectors of student folklore have noted extensive drinking games ("Cardinal

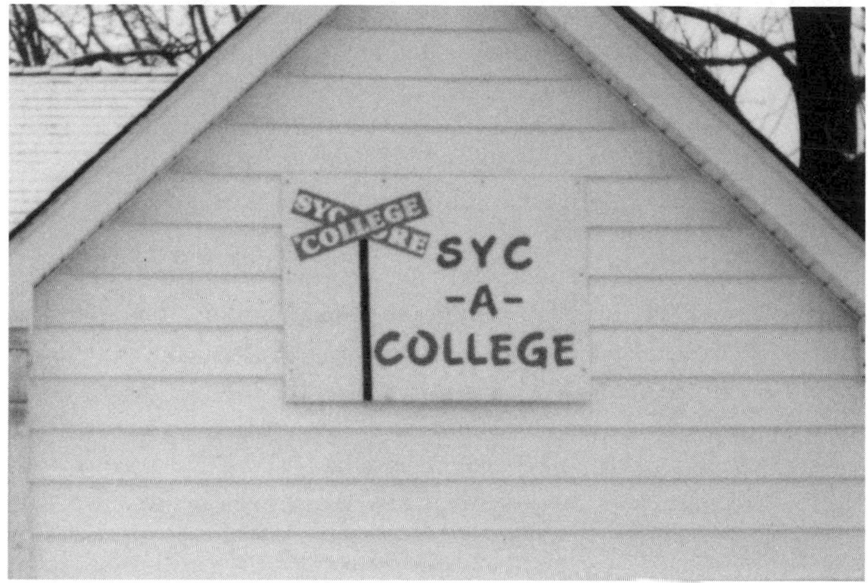

FIGURE 1.1. Syc-A-College

> Puff," "Fuzz-Buzz"), theme parties, engagement and marriage rituals (passing a candle around a group of sorority women to announce an engagement), clothing and personal-decoration variations (especially at sports events and at graduation), and the use of obscene songs as unofficial expressions of membership in clubs, fraternities, sororities, and sports teams (especially rugby). (1996, 3)

House signs support Toelken's argument in the sense that more house names are devoted to alcohol and sex than to the trials of academic life.

The work of folklorists and sociolinguists attests to the overabundance of lore and slang surrounding anxieties about the loss of virginity, the consequences of sex on a date, or the consequences of drinking too much or experimenting with drugs.[4] Not all of this lore involves college students, but colleges have often been places where previously forbidden activities become more available and tempting. For example, many of the slang terms offered by thirty or more students in Eble's surveys from 1972 to 1993 are oriented to such concerns. She reports "dweeb," "geek," and "turkey," glossed as "socially inept person"; "wasted," "catch a buzz," and "trashed," glossed as "drunk"; "chill" and "veg," glossed as "relax"; "grub" and "hook up," glossed as "kiss passionately"; "hot," glossed as "attractive"; "fox/foxy," glossed as "attractive person"; "jam," glossed as "have a good time"; "diss," glossed as "insult"; "clueless," glossed as "out of touch"; and "scope," glossed as "pursue for sex" (1996, 138–39). Inebriation seems to heighten sexual exploration, but in a way that is communal and often determined by orchestrated chance, as in the classic game Spin the Bottle. It is not difficult to imagine the tension underlying the titillating play that these games facilitate. One of the functions of slang, according to Eble and Munro, is to diffuse such tension and render it laughable or at least not serious.

Slang terms are like house signs in that they focus on aspects of life relatively new and perhaps problematic. A few slang terms and house signs are directed to the academic world, but many more are directed to the world of social relations wherein alcohol and sex have a significant presence. Ultimately, however, house signs are unlike slang because they are the names of specific locations and can be used to refer to houses' residents. House signs are physical objects that can depict an old name using new imagery, and they can be stolen or retired.

Historical Shifts in Collegiate Fun

Having fun is one of the most central and enduring concerns of life at U.S. colleges and universities, playing a major part in the definition of the student as a type of person, but like any social phenomenon, having fun is a moving target. The relationships between having fun and other aspects of student life have changed over the years in multiple ways, as have definitions of fun and ways of having fun. As universities have grown in number and size, the makeup of the student body has changed, and all of these transformations have occurred in tandem with changes in political and economic life in the United States.

Fun played a major part in a differentiation of students' dispositions toward the institution, particularly the faculty, from the earliest days of colleges' existence in the United States. Early enrollments circa 1800 represented a mere 2 percent of young men, the youngest coming from wealthy families and the older from more modest farming backgrounds. Out of this division emerged what Helen Horowitz calls "college men" and "outsiders." The former were characterized by hedonism involving violence, drinking, and sex across social class boundaries, all toward the creation of loyalty, secrecy, and a collective rejection of the authority of the institution. The latter sought development and growth within the curriculum and the guidance and approval of faculty, often in preparation for a life in the church. "College men" derided "outsiders" with terms such as "grind," "fisherman," and "brownnose" (Horowitz 1987, 13). The Greek system became a rather powerful instrument for the exclusion of "outsiders." Indeed, Horowitz uses a metaphor based in drink to describe the early power of "college men": "In the nineteenth century the sober students had no clear public voice" (1987, 68).

The proliferation of types of students complexly inflected by notions of fun was made possible by massive transformations in higher education at the turn of the twentieth century. Laurence Vesey calls the institution emerging then "the new university." No longer would a tiny minority of Americans attend college. The student population became larger and also less homogeneous. By 1900, "the urban universities of the East began to attract small numbers of Catholics and Jews and, very sporadically, a few Negroes" (Vesey 1965, 271). Trends that began with the rise of the new university included an increasing perception that the university afforded the possibility of socioeconomic advancement and the increasing rationalization of university affairs within a business model. Many would lament the rise of enrollments, athletics, and more academic departments as signs of "further loss of coherent meaning" (1965, 436). New students, however, would provide an "other" to an emerging image of a gentleman student couched in terms that did not overtly state their racist design. Harold Wechsler (1977), for example, has shown that Columbia University's curriculum and credentials were increasingly attractive to some of New York City's Jewish residents in the early twentieth century. Some administrators and admissions strategies tried to stem Jewish enrollment by treating widely dispersed geographic origins of a class and student traits such as "character" and "personality" as desirable qualities. These admissions considerations took their place alongside the testing in which Jews had done so well.

The growth of every aspect of the university was accompanied by the increasing rationalization of their functions. Part of this rationalization was aimed at accepting and even co-opting some of the energies of "college men," and extracurricular development became an increasingly important aspect of college life. Horowitz notes that the stark antagonism between "college men" and the institution diminished around the beginning of the period of rapid growth. Vesey writes of the institution after this transition: "It [campus] was to become a place prominently devoted to non-abstractive good fun: to singing and cheering, to the rituals of club life and 'appropriate' oratory; it was to be a place where the easy, infectious harmonies of brass band and stamping feet found few toes unwilling at least faintly to tap in time" (1965, 441). With increasing integration, the hedonistic debauchery of "college men" continued, of course, but had less to do with rejection of the authority of the institution. John Thelin, following Vesey, notes "an important social development between 1890 and 1910 was that the American public became fascinated with undergraduate college life" (2004, 157).

The expanding institution saw the emergence of new types of students. Horowitz notes that "rebels" were students oriented to the institution neither like "college men" nor "outsiders." "Rebels" were iconoclastic more than hedonistic, and challenged many of the divisions that underpinned the division between "college men" and "outsiders." For example, they sought some fulfillment outside the institution, in the world of politics. We associate the 1960s with the interests of such students, but the 1930s saw a greater proportion of college students involved in radical politics than any other decade (Horowitz 1987, 82–97).

While "rebels" emerged as a new type of student in the 1930s and the 1960s, this period also saw the dominance of fraternities and sororities in college life. Rules of residential life and Greek traditions mediated the social and sexual communication between "college men" and an increasing number of "college women." Nicholas Syrett explains that although only 11.74 percent of college men in the 1920s joined fraternities, the organizations had already come to be "recognized throughout the nation as being the ultimate fulfillment of the college ideal" (2009, 189). Stark separation of the sexes in their living arrangements was necessary to ensure the parental trust that would draw more women to college, and the arrangement of the sexes in the Greek system structured the ability to get dates and prestige.[5] Fraternities came to play such a prominent role in campus sexual life because fraternities had private accommodations, fraternity men were likely to have money for entertainment, and fraternity men isolated themselves from women and thus met them primarily on dates (Syrett 2009, 221–22).

Collegiate fun—the apex of which was Greek life—rested on a charged and unequal relationship between the sexes (DeSantis 2007 and Sanday 2007). Historian Beth Bailey (1988, 80) explains that "'petting' and 'necking' were the major conventions youth contributed to courtship in the years between World War I and the 1960s. (A significant percentage of young people had premarital intercourse during this period, but it did not become 'conventional' behavior among youth until the mid-1960s.)" Bailey notes that women bore most of the burden of respectability through minimizing sexual activity with males. Responsibility for avoiding sex fell so entirely on women that a woman was often blamed if her date was successful at seducing (or even raping) her. Reflecting on commentary and guidebooks on dating published between the 1920s and 1960s, the heyday of dating, Bailey concludes, "If the man took sexual advantage (which, in very early days, might mean only hand-holding but might extend to rape), or even tried to do so, the woman must not have *really* been a lady. She must have, somehow, invited or encouraged him" (1988, 90). College women's reputations came to depend on what they were and were not willing to do with college men, just as college men, especially those belonging to fraternities, increasingly sought pleasure and personal development within the institution rather than outside of it, even if not in its curriculum (Horowitz 1987).

Further transformations in relationships between student identities, students' relationships to the college or university, and collegiate fun occurred during the period from 1945 to 1975, what Arthur Cohen calls American higher education's "golden age." The number of students expanded massively in the three decades, from 1,677,000 to 11,185,000 (1998, 176). The baby boom after World War II allowed the convergence of two phenomena, more students in a time of unprecedented economic prosperity: "Economic expansion led to disposable income and to a delay in the time when young people had to enter the workforce, both contributing to the massive increases in college enrollments" (Cohen 1998, 178). The growing specialization and professionalization of labor during this period found in higher education a place where credentials could be sought, and the educational institutions responded to the opportunities for growth.

As more students flooded extant and new institutions, those institutions largely abandoned their role as *in loco parentis* (in lieu of parents). The rationalization that commenced with the rise of "the new university" played a major part during the "golden age" in the abandonment of the parental role. None of the duties of the new office of "student affairs" dealt directly with the moral development of students so common to the institution before its expansion. Ernest Boyer ties the decline of the institution's concern over the moral life of the student to the institution's increasingly bureaucratic structure: "Undergraduates enjoyed almost unlimited freedom in personal and social matters, and responsibility for residence hall living was delegated far down the administrative ladder, with resident assistants on the front lines of supervision" (1993, 323). With freedom came a decoupling of collective entertainment from the institution as well as a decline in dating as the primary means of sanctioned sexual activity.

The increased dynamism between the curriculum and the labor market coupled with the abandonment of *in loco parentis* set the stage for the emergence of another type of student, what Horowitz calls "the new outsider." Distinctions between "college men" and "outsiders" marked by hedonism further blurred during the 1970s. Horowitz claims that the "new outsiders" came to dominate college and university life in the 1970s, interjecting competition, anxiety, and ambition for class advancement like never before. Fun, dispersed around and off campus in bars, in coeducational residential arrangements, and in groups of friends (rather than in pairs on dates), seemed less a part of students' lives. Horowitz argues that some of the intense competition of the early 1970s has lessened somewhat. But what she calls the "new outsider," the student oriented toward studies and grades as preparation and credentialing for a later profession or professional education, has come to be the dominant presence on college and university campuses. Decreasing government support and the increasing need for employment during school, especially for minority students, has only made the identity of the "new outsider" more diffuse (Horowitz 1987, 263–88).

The period from 1975 to the present has seen the continuation of many of the trends that began after World War II. Institutions of higher education have taken yet more notice of the students they would serve, especially after the demographic decline that followed the baby boomer generation. This is the same period in which different kinds of institutions such as the community college and the junior college began to increase in number and size. The notion of the college experience—or even a college experience—has become less clear: "Undergraduate students are bifurcated into increasingly separate ethnic and racial enclaves. . . . With many students working while studying and most more concerned with private concerns than with community issues, there is no center to campus life" (Altbach 1993, 219). A growing collusion between an emphasis on the student's use of time toward self-management and preparedness for work, on the one hand, and the fracturing of coordinated activities, on the other hand, has emerged to encourage students to see fun as important but elusive.

Horowitz sums up what has been lost: "As limiting as it was, traditional college life did create a time and place away from home where young men and women could try to define themselves. Distinctive dress marked the collegian; hedonism offered new experiences; rejection of professional standards allowed a sublimated form of adolescent rebellion; and, for some, struggle among peers opened new opportunities" (1987, 271). Horowitz uses the past tense to write about traditional college life because the "new outsider" has come to see one's time in college to be so causally linked to what follows that college has ceased to be as distinct a period as it once was.

Ethnography of Collegiate Fun

Michael Moffatt argues that Horowitz overstates the degree to which students have excised having fun in the pursuit of high grades and credentials for later professional life. Students whom Moffatt came to know in the dorm where he lived during research at Rutgers University had indeed abandoned most of the organized extracurricular activities that held sway before the emergence of Horowitz's "new outsiders." Nevertheless, they replaced such organized engagement with fun that was "closer and closer to their private lives" (1989, 38). From casual observations in the dorm and from essays written by his students, Moffatt discovered that private fun reached its zenith in sexual experimentation:

> If relaxed, friendly fun was the private pleasure to which students devoted most of their free time in the late twentieth century, sexual and erotic fun were the even-more-private pleasures that they found most intensely interesting and enjoyable. (1989, 48)

The best situation for the realization of private fun is the party, an event whose very flexibility mirrors the increasingly unstructured nature of social life of late twentieth century college students:

> A party could be a scheduled event with a time and a place. Or it could be anytime that a few students gathered together with the necessary ingredients: liquor, music, and members of the opposite sex—or of the same sex, for homosexuals—who were not "just friends," who were erotically interested in one another. (1989, 49)

No longer as influential were the bawdy song sessions, games, or dating habits of the college folklore of an earlier era that had structured relations between the sexes, on the one hand, and erotic dynamics, on the other hand.

Alcohol and sex pervade the fun had in less organized, more diffuse arrangements of entertainment. Susan Blum notes the ways in which alcohol pervades campus life and its student types, confounding the categories from the time when allegiance to the institution carried such stigma:

> Students have been drinking on college campuses for decades, if not centuries. What is different now, it seems to me, is that at places like Saint U. [Blum's pseudonym for a large private university], drinking has become a scheduled activity in its own right, participated in by even the best students, and perhaps by the majority of undergraduates. (2009, 134)

Students do study and prepare for class and exams, of course, but the weekly academic calendar has come to accommodate partying with the curtailing of Friday classes, and students have come to accommodate "socializing and relaxing" with their academic scheduling (Blum 2009, 124).

While alcohol use has pervaded campus life, dating, the ritualized coupling that entails participation in an entertainment activity and the possibility of more or less quickly accelerating sexual exploration, has gone the way of large-scale communal fun. Bailey points out that sex is nothing new in the life of American youths, but the ways in which it has been envisioned, even named, has changed drastically (1999, 77). Dating, the demise of which began in the late 1960s, has largely given way to "hooking up" as the norm in college life whereby the decision to engage in sexual relations is relatively spontaneous, specific sexual activities are not predetermined, and there is no feeling that another encounter should happen: "Rather than formally planning dates [as they used to], many students go to parties in groups, joking about 'hooking up' (anything from kissing to more intimate activity)" (Tucker 2007, 117). Indeed, "hooking up" itself is a rather vague expression because it can refer to any sort of sexual activity, from light petting to intercourse: "you cannot be sure precisely what someone means when he or she reports having 'hooked up' unless you ask a follow-up question to see how much sexual activity took place" (Bogle 2008, 25). Whereas Moffatt shows that parties in the late 1970s came to replace dates as the primary context in which college students might seek sexual experimentation, Bogle shows that by the 1990s, youth were using the expression "hooking up" to refer to nothing in particular, allowing a vagueness, but also an extreme casualness, to characterize the description of sexual activity. Bogle argues that the consumption of alcohol at parties fuels the possibility of "hooking up." With their relative absence of predetermined couples paired with a supply of alcohol, parties provide the ideal setting for "hooking up."

Rebekah Nathan argues that "in 2003, 'fun' continued to be one of the most ubiquitous words in college discourse. . . . 'Fun' as a concept is associated with spontaneity, sociability, laughter, and behavior (including sexuality) that is unconstrained" (2005, 23). She explains that while students often talked about fun in a dorm in which she lived at a relatively large regional state university, actual enactments of such fun emerged even less frequently in communal places and situations than in Moffatt's earlier research. Generally speaking, students' schedules were incredibly complicated and responsible to an enormous number and variety of duties and activities. These included class schedules, work schedules, extracurricular activities advertised by the school, ROTC, and activities that take place off-campus. Nathan concludes, "It is hard to create community when the sheer number of options in college life generate a system in which no one is in the same place at the same time" (2005, 38). Even activities devoted to "community involvement" such as "Movie Night," a dormitory talent show, and what Nathan calls a "'How to Make Edible Underwear' program around Valentine's Day" created "an even greater proliferation of choices and fragmentation of the whole" (2005, 46–47). She describes getting together with others as a real effort, both logistically and ideologically, since students "resist claims that community makes on their schedule and resources in the name of individualism, spontaneity, freedom, and choice" (2005, 47).

Nathan took special note of visual expressions that appeared in the dormitory in which she lived because they reflected the pervasive, fractured, individualized notion of fun described by students. Using a combination of images (most frequently, "martini glasses, palm trees, cowboys, guitars, flowers, bikinis, hearts, Hawaii, belly dancers, [and] beaches") and phrases ("Bare Your Butt," "Young and Royal," "Las Vegas," "A Colorful Character," "Once upon a Mattress," and "The Next Best Thing to Naked"), residents in the dorm conveyed a sense of themselves that included qualities like "friendliness, youth, freedom, sexiness, sociability, irreverence, fun, humor, intensity, eccentricity, lack of limits, [and] spontaneity" (2005, 24–26). While displays emergent from what Nathan calls the formal culture of the dorm, erected by RAs in public places, stressed the dangerous aspects of "drinking, smoking, drugs, and sexuality," the informal displays celebrated them (2005, 25).[6] The formal and informal culture of the dorm thus provided mirror images of the same phenomenon, partying. The students did not celebrate these activities in concert, as in the past, but rather used them to create representations of themselves engaged in unfettered fun.

Based on fieldwork at what she calls Midwest State University, Mary Grigsby describes the "collegiate" ideal type in terms familiar by now in this discussion:

> Collegiate culture emphasizes college athletics, heterosexual dating (Holland and Eisenhart 1990), socializing with peers more generally (Robbins 2004), and being recognized by others with a similar orientation as being a part of the group. Of particular importance are parties where drinking is central and themed parties, where all who attend dress in accordance with the theme, signaling their insider status and offering a venue for demonstrating to others the college fun in which one is taking part. (2009, 95)

Grigsby explains that the majority of the students she interviewed in fact did not consider themselves as belonging to the "collegiate" ideal type. Even so, like Moffatt, Blum, and Nathan, Grigsby argues that the "collegiate" ideal type is the most salient in college life, even to those whose orientations demand other uses of time:

> While the collegiate culture at Midwest is not truly hegemonic, making up only a little over 20 percent of the undergraduate population in terms of a primary orientation, . . . it continues to be perceived by most students at Midwest as the dominant culture, and many aspects of the generalized culture that gloss over differences among students in their cultural orientations are drawn from it in part because of the strong historical institutional ties that make it highly visible, and in part because of the popular culture that depicts it as dominant. (2009, 104)

The collegiate ideal type no longer provides a specific stance toward the institution, as in the past, but has come to inform college life generally:

> Having fun is viewed by virtually all college students as an important responsibility that they must fulfill in order to claim the genuine college student experience. For some students, having fun involves drinking and going out to bars and parties. The emphasis on partying, drinking, and sex and the hooking up that goes along with these activities is linked to popular culture depictions of college life that most students can readily call up when asked about the dominant student culture. For other students, having fun involves being with people

> with whom they are comfortable and hanging out in residence halls, watching television together, or going to a movie. (2009, 86)

New communicative technologies are being used to reinforce the perception that what Grigsby calls the "collegiate" orientation is the dominant one on campus. Each party, she explains, provides students with an opportunity to take pictures of having fun for posting on Facebook.

Facebook has come to play a number of roles in the mediation of the fractured notion of student fun and the parties that fuel it. A website maintained at Indiana University entitled Folklore of Student Life includes student reports of the importance of Facebook and the internet more generally to the organization of parties and the depiction of fun had at them. One report states:

> Facebook is one of the newest crazes among college students. It is a networking website originally for college students to make friends or keep in touch with old ones. The website is made up of user profiles and many applications linking each profile to thousands of activities, events, clubs, common interest groups, etc. One way in which this site has become a huge network for the party scene is the development of an online invitation system. Users can create an event, which is usually some type of party, and provide a description of the location, time, place, and often theme. Facebook allows the party "host" to send out these notifications on a large scale, often to entire groups of friends within their networks. Usually some type of outrageous picture is included in the invitation to [give] guests a preview of what will be taking place. (McDowell 2008)

One's network of Facebook friends and the various networks to which they all might belong provide a means of inviting people to parties and a means for depicting themes as well as what might happen at parties.

Not only can students send out invitations for parties, but people at such parties can use Facebook to depict what happens at them. Another report on the Folklore of Student Life website states:

> Facebook is not only a major place for students to go to create party invitations, but it is an even bigger place students go to post pictures from outrageous parties they have attended. Thousands of photo albums, consisting of every type of party-going activity you could imagine are posted every day. These albums are a way for friends to share stories with others about their "wild" night out with friends. Many of these pictures are seen as "inappropriate" to be publically dis-

> played, and as a result Facebook has made it possible for users to limit which people can see which pictures on their profile. Don't want teachers seeing you in your Halloween "naughty nurse" outfit doing a beer bong? No problem . . . Facebook has your privacy settings covered. (McDowell 2008)

The student of folklore goes on to report, however, that some employers have begun to use Facebook in their hiring decisions, and athletic programs are checking Facebook to see whether athletes are abusing alcohol or drugs. The access to ostensibly private domains by people who are not students has cast into greater relief the consequences after college of depictions of college life.

While house signs do reflect the pervasiveness of alcohol and sex noted by ethnographers who attest to the prominence of fun in college life, it is important to note that they do not mediate notions of fun and the events that take place at parties in the same ways that Facebook does. The next chapter will demonstrate the ways in which house signs' form plays a crucial part in the ways in which students use house signs, reflect on their uses, and link them to the disposition of students. Nathan's description of the collages adorning dorm room doors and Grigsby's mention of Facebook, however, merit a brief comparison with house signs. House signs are much more like the collages adorning the dorm doors because the words and images appear on the residence of the people who put them up. They are more like the posts to Facebook, however, because their existence is almost entirely oriented to partying. House signs are, in the end, like neither the collages nor Facebook because their messages are short and constitute a name, and their images never depict anyone in particular.[7] All three domains, nevertheless, demonstrate the pervasiveness of fun and partying in contemporary college life.

Mass Media and Youth

House signs such as Animal House Knowledge Is Good, Home Alone, and Uptown Girls illustrate the degree to which the media have offered students a resource for the creation of folklore. Not only have the media shaped a space ripe with the possibilities of youthful consumption and expression embodied in the different ways described above by dorm door decorations, Facebook, and house signs. They have also offered depictions of youth themselves. And just as the composition of student bodies and their disposition to institutions of higher education have changed along with the growth and increasing complexity of the institutions, the disposition of youths to media has changed along with forms of media and their representations. Those representations are often of youths.[8]

While Horowitz has shown that the image of the rebellious youth has been around for as long as institutions of higher education have existed, advertising and commercial activity became particularly relevant in the mid-twentieth century in the creation of "a distinct, national subculture" that consisted of "the new age group of adolescents, which expanded in both directions (toward preteens and toward the early twenties)" (Fass 2008, 41). Thomas Frank argues that the 1960s saw the rise of an advertising and media industry in which the notion of rebellious youth became a value widely applicable to consumption.[9] Frank explains that the 1960s was "an era that saw both the rise of market segmentation and a shift from a management culture that revered hierarchy and efficiency to one that emphasized individualism and creativity" (1998, 25).[10] This certainly recalls Rebekah Nathan's description of the dorm room doors on which students have assembled fragments of mass-produced images, often lewd and edgy, toward the creation of a persona. Facebook joins personalized templates—ones very much like the dorm room doors described by Nathan—and offers the possibility of privacy by way of limiting access to a network of friends.

Often the roles and scenarios depicted by images—such as those that might appear on the dormitory doors described by Nathan—come ready-made. Released in 2001, "Merchants of Cool," a documentary in the Public Broadcasting Service's series *Frontline*, explores a number of ways in which media conglomerates, television shows, brands, celebrities, and consumers work together toward the production of images of youth. Their products are far more coordinated than the time in which *Animal House* emerged. "Cool hunters," for example, are a business unto themselves. They seek vanguard styles and sell images of them to larger corporate entities. Those entities, in turn, depict youth in myriad ways. For example, the documentary notes that a pair of personages, the "mook" and the "midriff," are recent depictions of young men and women. The "mook" is a hopelessly immature male whose grotesque and inappropriate antics are celebrated for their transgressions, whereas the "midriff" is a female sexualized beyond her years whose emotional immaturity makes her ripe for inclusion of fantasies of sexual exploration. This pairing, the documentary shows, is useful for the depiction of all manner of scripted scenes, but also for the representation of moments of unfettered pleasure in the lives of actual youth. The documentary depicts scenes from MTV's spring break specials to make the point. Youths enact the roles of "mooks" and "midriffs" at actual spring break locations to be filmed and advertised for the next spring break.

But college students do not just play the parts scripted for them in mass media venues. Sometimes they take elements of mass media productions and combine them in such a way that challenges the viewer to find anything that can be taken seriously (or decried morally). An issue of the *Daily Bull*, a broadsheet distributed at the small liberal arts college where I now teach, provides one illustration of the use of popular culture from multiple forms of media toward the creation of a new form. The back of the sheet has as a banner message, "GROUCHO MARX THOUGHT BETTER OF YOU." Underneath it is a "Lost & Found" section with a description of a missing iPod and contact information, and a "For Sale" section with a description of an aquarium and the seller's email address. The message below the two sections reads: "A request from your editors: We implore you, write for the DAILY BULL! As Richard M. Nixon once articulated, 'There is no such thing as bad publicity' (Tru 'dat, mo'fucka'). We want your work in our paper!" The seal of the broadsheet depicts an eagle clutching a tablet on which is written, "TRUTH, JUSTICE, PUBLIC SERVICE," behind which is a banner that reads, "Keystone of the Hearst Newspapers." Below are the (real) names of the officers with the titles "Editor-in-Chief," "Resident R. W. Emerson Scholar," "Use-a-loofah," and "The Boss."

On the front of the broadsheet is the title, "The Daily Bull," and the volume, number, and date. An image next to the title is taken from the film *Raging Bull*, and an image from an Elvis film is inserted in a hodgepodge of images below. There one also finds a picture of a mural depicting Frank Zappa, a picture of a boy band, pictures of people talking on the phone, talking to each other in a restaurant, or taking pictures of themselves. A bottle of malt liquor is positioned above the crotch of a reclining man. A picture of bikers, a woman kissing a statue, youth at a nightclub, a close-up of a face, a sleeping bus passenger, and a cat with a snow cone makes one clamor (helplessly) for a theme. Also included are a picture of the cover of a pulp novel entitled *There's an Owl in the Shower*, a man giving the camera (and now the reader) "the finger," and a picture of Australian singer James Blunt with Hulk Hogan. The whole is entitled "Summer Scrapbook—09." The mix of images taken from past and contemporary mass media, pictures taken of students at the college, images (and text on the back of the broadsheet) of incompatible styles including high-brow publishing, punk, biker, pop, retro, and urban (with hints of the involvement of racial difference in "Tru 'dat, mo'fucka'"), and depictions of relaxation and play present an image of youthful fun divorced from any hint of the serious.

The example of the broadsheet is only one of seemingly countless activities of youth that draw on the mass media for their display. I found the broadsheet particularly useful for discussion because it draws on and juxtaposes so many styles, celebrities, and brands, but there are, of course, many more. For example, the broadsheet is devoid of images of hip-hop, one of the most pervasive musical, sartorial, and performative styles to emerge in the United States in the last three decades or so. Both the broadsheet's incorporation of so many different and incompatible styles and its exclusion of others show that the relationship between images of youth produced by the mass media and the engagement with such media by youth (and others) is incredibly complex and particular at the same time. Mary Bucholtz, for example, explains:

> Youth culture is not a top-down phenomenon. Regardless of the number or source of available linguistic resources, speakers still use language creatively in specific local contexts to achieve particular social and interactional goals, and in the process both language and culture are reshaped to fit new, locally meaningful identities. (2000a, 282)

Youth cultural production involves a complex interplay of the widespread (though hardly boundless) circulation of images and the appropriation (and sometimes combination) of elements of those images in particular social contexts toward the production of a persona.

The rapid circulatory possibilities of media often foster the impression (in my students, for example) that the production and consumption of media images are boundless such that only the old and outdated need to be avoided (or repositioned as classic, retro, or kitsch). Oxford's world of house signs shows us that the production and consumption of mass media images are not boundless and are rather tied to the context of reproduction. For example, the house names in Table 1.1, like the issue of the *Daily Bull*, exclude more manifestations of style in music, clothing, film, television, and language in the United States than they include. And the specificity of the reproduction of house signs does not end there. I discovered just how much the production of house signs rests on particular contexts, even among college students, when I used house signs in a lecture about language and community in a course in a regional state university in New England. My students there had trouble understanding what was so special and even exciting about house signs. Some of my students said that they were too old to live with so many other people in a situation wherein so many parties would be thrown. Others explained that some of the clubs and bars in the city center catered to them and often advertised theme parties based on the now ubiquitous dichotomy of aggressive males and sexualized females. Yet others said that the regional state university lacked students from middle-class backgrounds able to pay rent without working at a time-consuming job, and lacked a residential area where students could live in close proximity.

Although they are particular and require, for example, a certain social class position, house signs and their relationship to ideas about fun reflect many of the shifts noted by scholars of college life in the United States reviewed above. Fun has generally become more dispersed in its enactment while imagined increasingly to be an omnipresent potential. A house sign indicates that parties occur within the house, but apart from the rare display of a party announcement, residents do not specify when they occur. The question of who is invited is left unanswered, even when banners do announce a party. This vagueness, as we will see in the coming chapters, contributes to the feeling that the entirety of Oxford's Mile Square and Ghetto offer a giant, continuous party, or at least hints of one everywhere. The feeling of insouciance surrounding ideas about how house signs should be read contributes to the vagueness surrounding the link between house signs and actual occurrences of parties or partying. The claim by some house residents that they were too lazy to coin a clever name reinforces this lack of connection.

Fun is less organized by institutional affiliations and less shaped by groups defined as anything other than "friends." Unlike fraternity and sorority organizations, for example, a house name is used to refer to a single house and its inhabitants. While some house residents do seek to ensure that the house name will be preserved by the next residents, the practice is hardly universal. The only requirements for living in a named house is that one is "friends" with others in the house and that one pays one's rent. Just how close one is to others in the house or what friendship entails is quite variable. In the overview of house signs presented in the introduction, for example, house residents claim that sports brought some residents together to live in a house. On the other hand, some residents see no significance in the sports motif present in their house sign. There will be examples later in the book of residents for whom the house name itself was motivation to move in with others. None of these possibilities is representative. Residence in a named house, therefore, seems less purposeful than membership in a fraternity or sorority where rituals are meant to create a bond between oneself and prior members.

Underpinning the lack of care about how house signs should be read is the notion that fun is less directed toward an opposition to authority, especially that of the institution of the school. Only a few house signs lampoon aspects of academic life while a great many involve the world of music, literature, and film produced by the mass media and available for consumption. They use less permanent media to welcome parents and thank them for their financial support. Indeed, very few house signs launch a critique of or lampoon a figure of authority, and in the coming chapters, residents of named houses will argue that searching for such significance obviates the pleasure one might derive from reading house signs. In short, to find significance in house signs is to read them incorrectly because they are tokens of fun in themselves. They hint at what makes parties fun: alcohol, sex, and—less often—drugs, and indicate where such fun can be had. They display this to all passersby, whether partygoers or not.

In sum, house signs reflect an increasingly salient trend noted by ethnographers of contemporary college life: the purpose of college life is to have fun with minimal constraints on one's already overbooked self. What better way can one imagine the fulfillment of this notion than in quick jolts of pleasure obtained from clever punning and double entendre behind which one can imagine the probability of a forthcoming party with minimal requirements of affiliation and minimal obligations toward future relationships, sexual or otherwise.

House Signs as Metaculture

Noting that house signs reflect many transformations in how college students have fun leaves an essential question unanswered: how do we relate specific practices through which students have fun to reflections on those practices by the students involved?[11] Informing the approach of this book is an insight of recent work in cultural anthropology: a reflection on a practice is a practice, too. We can learn much about what kind of assumptions, expectations, and social dispositions are necessary for the creation of culture by examining reflections on culture. Greg Urban (2001) in particular has called cultural productions that describe or situate other cultural productions "metaculture." Metaculture is that cultural production that gives evidence that human beings engage in more or less orchestrated routines as they respond to or introduce cultural production in their lives.

An example will help to illustrate the relation between a metacultural production and the cultural production toward which it is directed. A book review is an example of metaculture directed toward a book and situates that book as belonging to a category of books in a particular way:

> Book reviews . . . are a well-defined metacultural genre that bring a book to our attention by reflecting upon it and characterizing it as an exemplar of a certain type of recognizable cultural form—books of a particular genre, for example. (Wirtz 2007, 7)

We might thus learn much about distinctions between types of books by reading a book review. Does the book review name the group to which the book belongs? Does the book review name other groups of books? We might turn to other book reviews to find out whether all books get reviewed. We might begin to think about what other metacultural activity is directed toward a book. These might include such types of communication as conversations, lectures, and advertisements. They might teach us much more about the ways in which a book is recognized as a cultural production.

The discussion thus far has offered many examples of metaculture directed toward collegiate fun. The films, novels, websites, and examples of folklore mentioned throughout the discussion, for example, are oriented toward college fun in particular ways. Some provide character development by selecting from and reinforcing a limited set of roles. For example, some borrow and reinforce the pair constituted by an aggressive male and a hypersexualized female. The metacultural forms of films, novels, websites, and folklore selectively represent college as a cultural entity, just as the metacultural set of roles in them selectively represent the possibilities for cultural categories of persons on campus.

One reason that representations of culture are so important to consider is that a metacultural rendering of a recognizable cultural form can seem remarkable or even off the mark. College students who view *Animal House* for the first time might find that certain expressions, styles, or events in the movie are not familiar to them. This is not so much due to the fact that the viewers did not actually experience what happens in the movie. It is rather that certain cultural elements being represented by metacultural elements in the movie do not exist for the viewers. People will often produce metaculture that attests to the fact, deriding a representation as dated, stupid, or flawed.

Should the viewers of *Animal House* begin to appreciate the metacultural rendering, they might begin to regret that their own world is not similar. They will thus see college life in a different way from those for whom the movie evokes nostalgia. Taking note of the relationships between metacultural and cultural production thus provides important lessons about what gets represented, how it gets represented, and how people engage with the representation.

One of the most valuable reasons for thinking about the particular relationships between metaculture and culture is the realization that they can vary radically between contexts of cultural production. Indeed, the relationship between house signs and partying differs from the metacultural orientation to culture of a much better known example. Literary critic and philosopher Mikhail Bakhtin's *Rabelais and His World,* submitted as a dissertation in 1941 but not published until 1965, is an exploration of two sixteenth-century novels by François Rabelais, *Gargantua* and *Pantagruel.* Richard Bauman has claimed Bakhtin's book to be "among the most stimulating and illuminating ethnographies of an expressive system ever written" (1982, 8–9). Bauman praises the book because Bakhtin was able to recognize and describe the ways in which Rabelais drew on the language of the sixteenth-century marketplace and carnival to craft his novels. For our purposes, Bakhtin's book is valuable because there are multiple relationships between metaculture and culture in it, and the relationships differ so radically from those that exist in house signs.

Bakhtin did not follow his predecessors in considering Rabelais a satirist. Rather, Bakhtin built the case for seeing Rabelais as an author who was engaged with and appreciative of the world from which his novels drew their means of expression. That is to say, Rabelais's work is a metacultural reflection on the sixteenth-century marketplace and carnival that represents that world by incorporating its language. Bakhtin shows that Rabelais drew from three sources to achieve his representation:

1. *Ritual spectacles:* carnival pageants, comic shows of the marketplace.
2. *Comic verbal compositions:* parodies both oral and written, in Latin and in the vernacular.
3. *Various genres of billingsgate:* curses, oaths, popular blazons. (1984, 5)

The mastery of Rabelais's novels, Bakhtin contended, lies in the ability of Rabelais to draw on these sources of folk culture toward the (re-)creation of a "boundless world of humorous forms and manifestations" (1984, 4). The appreciation of Rabelais's incorporation of the language of the marketplace and the carnival allowed Bakhtin to treat the novels as a "key to the immense treasury of folk humor which as yet has been scarcely understood or analyzed" (1984, 4).

The house sign is a metacultural production related to partying in a very different way than Rabelais's novels were related to the sixteenth-century marketplace. On the one hand, a house sign might not be considered metacultural with respect to a party because house signs do not describe the parties or what happens in them. Furthermore, house signs are visible during daylight, whether a party is actually occurring or not. But house signs can be considered metacultural with respect to parties because students who live in named houses understand that the signs indicate the occurrence of parties and even believe that the signs mimic the qualities of parties, including a laid-back disposition and a lack of care. On a few occasions during interviews, I mentioned that some house signs do seem to describe events that might be understood to occur at parties, such as Boot 'N Rally, Fill 'er Up, or Hangover Here. In making this assertion, I was arguing that residents of named houses could be seen to represent the parties occurring in named houses very much like the novels of Rabelais represent the sixteenth-century marketplace and carnival. Residents of named houses in Oxford invariably dismissed my examples by explaining that I was "missing the point of house signs" because I was "taking them too seriously" and "reading too much into them."

House signs do not re-create what happens at parties, nor do they even pretend to, whereas Rabelais's novels revel in the quotation of the language of the marketplace. I offer a diagram illustrating this difference in Figure 1.2. The "mode of representation" in the upper half of the diagram contrasts the incorporation of the language of the sixteenth-century carnival and marketplace in Rabelais's work (on the left) with the lack of residents' incorporation of the language of parties on house signs (on the right). But there is another difference between metaculture and culture in Bakhtin's book and mine. The "means of access" in the lower half of the diagram contrasts Bakhtin's access to Rabelais's work solely through his novels with my students' and my access to house signs, but also to their creators, by way of interviews. It was in the context of interviews that my students and I discovered that residents of named houses understand that the house sign should not be taken seriously. Indeed, residents of named houses did not use the occasion of the interview to reflect on parties, whether through description or re-creation through dialogue.

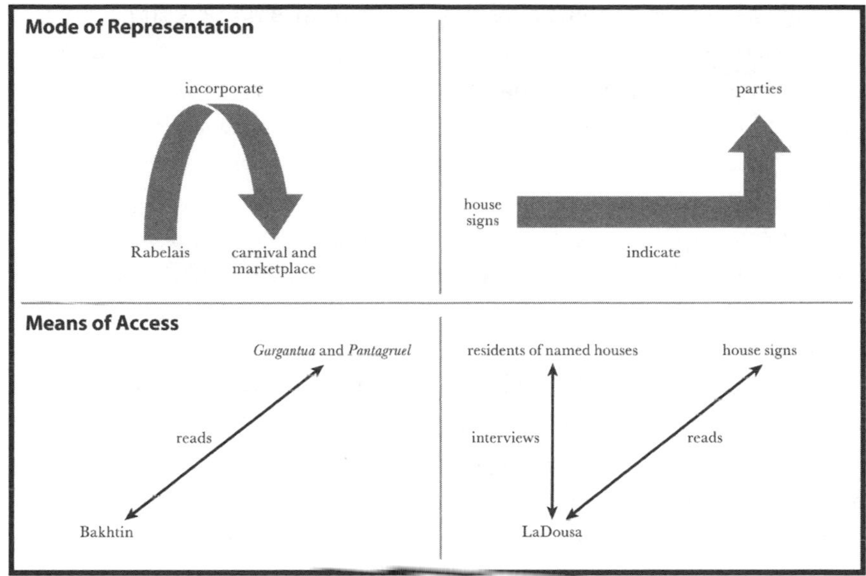

FIGURE 1.2. Culture and Metaculture in Bakhtin and This Study

Bakhtin famously argued that Rabelais's novels are so special because they show that there was a time and place when laughter was achieved within a "whole comic world" (1984, 88). Bakhtin contended that the humor evident in Rabelais's novels differed from that of the preceding medieval world in which "a strict dividing line is drawn between the pious and the grotesque" (1984, 96) and that of the encroaching modern world in which "humor is deprived of its historical color" and relegated to "a trivial private way of life" (1984, 101). Bakhtin argued that Rabelais uses the body, especially "the open mouth, the genital organs, the breasts, the phallus, the potbelly, the nose," to show the world as an unending and limitless set of processes and transformations (1984, 26). The ability of the body to transform the low to high Bakhtin called "gay relativity," an idea at the center of Bakhtin's understanding of Rabelais and the world about which he wrote. Bakhtin described the "gay relativity" made possible through uses of the body "deeply positive" for its lack of an individual, private perspective. Indeed, Rabelais's novels illustrate a world inflected by "the gay and festive character of all images of bodily life" (1984, 19).[12]

My view of house signs is very different from Bakhtin's stance toward Rabelais's novels. I cannot claim that students produce house signs as metacultural reflections that describe or even quote what happens at parties, nor can I claim that students produce much metacultural reflection on parties via house signs in interviews. Some house signs do celebrate the body's lower functions in their punning (Asspen, Boot 'N Rally, Liquor Up Front, Poker in the Rear), or invoke non-normative, topsy-turvy sexual practices (Girls on Top, Top or Bottom?), and I was certainly tempted to see in such signs the reversals and transformative possibilities that Bakhtin found so inspiring in Rabelais's novels. But residents of named houses hardly embrace and celebrate such signs. Rather, they argue that house signs' lack of sincerity and larger importance is an essential part of what makes them enjoyable. In the coming chapters, some residents of named houses will find enjoyment in mentioning and reflecting on house names they find to be salacious. However, they will consistently do so at a remove, in a qualified manner.

Thus, while Rabelais's literary works might be understood as metacultural reflections of the carnival and the marketplace that draw maximally on the tropes, metaphors, and images of the carnival and the marketplace to depict them, students who erect or maintain house signs argue that the short, rather transparent cleverness of names mimics the laid-back, carefree atmosphere of the parties that occur within houses. Perhaps such a relationship between culture and metaculture in Oxford's world of house signs is not surprising given that residents of named houses most often and consistently claim that "one should not take house signs too seriously." Though no student ever articulated the point in interviews, perhaps understanding house signs to be a representation of parties, and not simply as an indication of them, would run counter to a central metacultural means of reflecting on house signs. One might argue that Rabelais draws a world into his novels whereas residents of named houses have house signs stand in for a world.

When viewed from a time when collegiate fun was realized in activities that involved whole campuses or large constituencies within them, a house sign seems to be relegated to very few people, the residents of a named house. House signs' connection to the parties and partying they are said to represent allows for house signs to make collegiate fun seem omnipresent at the same time that specific ways in which house signs might advertise parties are absent. The seemingly universal availability of fun stands in stark contrast to the ways in which house signs presuppose a social class disposition and exclude much more in the way of popular culture than they include. Finally, the very activities of collegiate fun for which house signs are supposed to stand are less structured by dating or organizational affiliation.

House signs represent in particular ways. House signs are said to indicate parties and partying generally, but they do not re-create or describe what happens at such parties. One might say that house signs indicate the possibility of a party, whereas Rabelais's novels strive to bring the represented world (the sixteenth-century marketplace and carnival) into the representing one (Rabelais's sixteenth-century novels). The larger significance of house signs' relationship to parties and partying will emerge as crucial in relation to what various kinds of people see in house signs.

CHAPTER TWO

Witty House Name: The Textual Lives of House Signs

> Since a man generally named his own plantation, there arose a variety and originality such as New England lacked—a touch of wit or irony, a pun, an alliteration. So came Chaplin's Choice and Jordan's Journey, Flower dieu Hundred, Argall's Gift, and Martin's Brandon. Thus the Virginians brought to the New World a touch of Elizabethan fancy.
>
> —GEORGE R. STEWART, *Names on the Land*

Whatever else house signs are—pieces of wood, metal, or plastic—they are texts. The notion of text is a staple of scholarship in anthropology and folklore. Textuality, the quality that makes a text a text, might be imagined as something like a force that emerges from the interrelatedness of elements in unfolding discourse, whether spoken, sung, heard, read, remembered, or otherwise, that lends continuity. Describing textuality as something like a force is harder to conceptualize than the popular notion that texts are written or printed on the page or are easily recognizable, often named, instances of discourse such as the Gettysburg Address or *My Fair Lady*. Describing textuality as something like a force has the advantage of distancing us from our ready-made notions of texts so that we can see that we are more often engaged with texts than we might realize and that we often alter them as we reproduce them. Textuality is so pervasive because it is found in multiple aspects of discourse, sometimes simultaneously; aspects of discourse that give evidence of textuality include repetition, parallel constructions, and formulaic literary devices that can occur at any level of acoustic, linguistic, or pictorial complexity.

How, then, do we conceptualize texts as they actually take shape such that we recognize them more or less easily? When aspects of discourse lead one to expect a certain kind of text, the text belongs to a genre. A particularly salient example is "once upon a time . . ." for which there is the genre name "fairy tale." The ensuing text might also be called a fairy tale or might have a name of its own like "Snow White." The people who name or produce the texts belonging to a genre do not always have a name for the genre. My grandfather and many men of his generation, for example, often told stories about commandeering vegetables during their teenage years from fields guarded by men who had replaced the shot in their shells with rock salt. I never knew a name for these tales, nor did the men who told them, yet I could recognize one as soon as the teller began to tell it. Though I have no recorded examples to draw from, my recollection does make it possible to fit the stories into one kind of genre rather than another. For example, the man told the story from his own point of view, he told the story as if he had experienced the dramatic events, the story's setting was in the rural South during the Depression, and the action included screaming kids running with rock salt in their backsides. These aspects made the stories more like personal narratives than tall tales, for example (Dundes 1971).

Given all that can create textuality, how do we begin to recognize the aspects of house signs that indicate they belong to a genre? First, we need to explore the properties that give them form and substance as a genre, focusing on three aspects of texts: the formal, thematic, and pragmatic. Second, we need to consider the fact that the genre of house signs, like all genres, rests on the experience of those who encounter them and thus can prompt different evaluations of significance, purpose, and morality that can tell us much about the genre's social life.

Formal Properties

Texts might be identified by their formal properties. Bauman explains, "The formal properties of texts have to do with how they are made, their formal constituents and organizing principles, what it is that marks them off from their discursive surround and renders them internally cohesive—in a word, their poetics" (2008, 31).

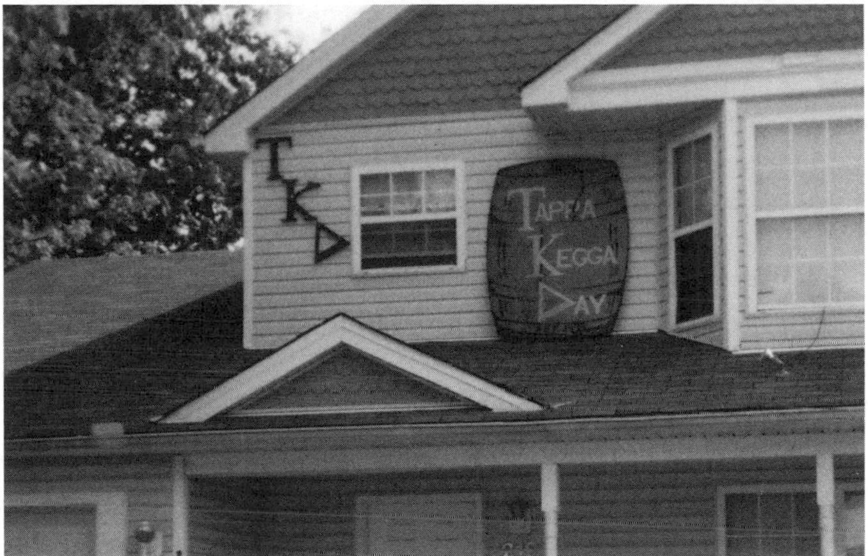

FIGURE 2.1. TKΔ

Minimally, a house sign consists of a board with a name on it. Sometimes the surface forms the outline of the name itself. AA, for example, consists of two pieces of plywood, four feet high, cut in identical shapes. The AA house sign distinguishes itself from most others by not using much paint. In some cases, the board forms the outline of a design. The board on which Precinct 109 has been painted, for example, was cut to resemble a police badge. Beech Bunnies has been cut to look like the Playboy Bunny. The sign for TKΔ, Tappa Kegga Day, is cut and painted to look like a beer keg.

One sign is a pair of plywood cutouts, one in the shape of a bottle and one in the shape of a fish, without text (save the XXX on the bottle). One of my students learned that the house was called Chubby Bungalow. A chubby is an alcoholic beverage that is concealed in a soft drink bottle for secret consumption in public places. The house sign utilizes an old way of indicating a beer's strength, labeling the bottle "XXX," and shows a fish consuming the contents. In a manner typical of house signs, lurking alongside the meaning of a chubby as a concealed alcoholic beverage, there is another possible meaning: an erection.[1] The fish's exaggerated lips are sexually suggestive, too. Many formal properties of house signs emerge when we pay attention to the ways in which language and images contribute to the production of humor. The formal properties that emerge help to constitute signs as texts.

Most house signs are rectangular, thus confirming Simon Bronner's observation: "In America, we don't expect paintings or arguments to be circular and we don't expect our rooms to be so. Whether a bed or a coffin, a rectangle frames our bodies from birth to grave" (1986, 16). A particularly interesting case of a rectangular house sign is Bored of Education. Lines and dashes marking their midpoints mimic a blackboard. In most cases, the backboard plays no part in the design itself. The city of Oxford passed an ordinance in 2005 requiring house signs to be no bigger than six square feet, grandfathering in signs displayed prior to the ordinance. The town ordinance reflects the fact that Chubby Bungalow is an unusual house sign because of its nonrectangular backboard. Its surface area would be difficult to measure indeed.

There is no reason to imagine that the boards on which signs are displayed could not accommodate more words, but two factors help to explain their brevity. First, they are meant to be seen from the street and to be read easily. Second, they announce names and do not offer the viewer much in the way of propositional content. Propositional content refers to a message's claim about some state of affairs that can be judged true or false. For example, "the cat is on the cot" describes a state of affairs. Its poetic quality, the repetition of [k] in "cat" and "cot," for instance, does not.

An example illustrating the difference between a house sign and its message and a sign with propositional content is Figure 2.4. The house name, The Heisman, can be found in two places, on the sign above and on the fabric banner below. On the banner, it serves as a signatory to the wish, "Happy 21st Laura." The wish rests on the proposition "it is Laura's 21st birthday," and its validity depends on whether it is indeed Laura's twenty-first birthday. The banner displayed by the residents of The Heisman includes propositional content in the manner of residents offering birthday wishes, welcoming parents, or announcing a specific party. There are examples of propositional claims on signs themselves, but they appear as a subtitle to the primary name of the house. Thus "Knowledge Is Good" serves as a subtitle of Animal House, "Rules Were Meant to Be Broken" serves as a subtitle of Champagne Room, and "We Shoot. We Score" serves as a subtitle of Game On. Although they are not strictly propositional, "'We'll Leave the Light On for You'" serves as a subtitle for Ho-Tel 6, and "'Spread 'Em'" serves as the subtitle for Precinct 109 (figure 2.10). The quotation marks in "'We'll Leave the Light On for You'" seem to be in recognition that the house sign quotes a company's motto. I render the stars as quotation marks in "'Spread 'Em'" because the sign seems to indicate the issue of a command.

FIGURE 2.2. Chubby Bungalow

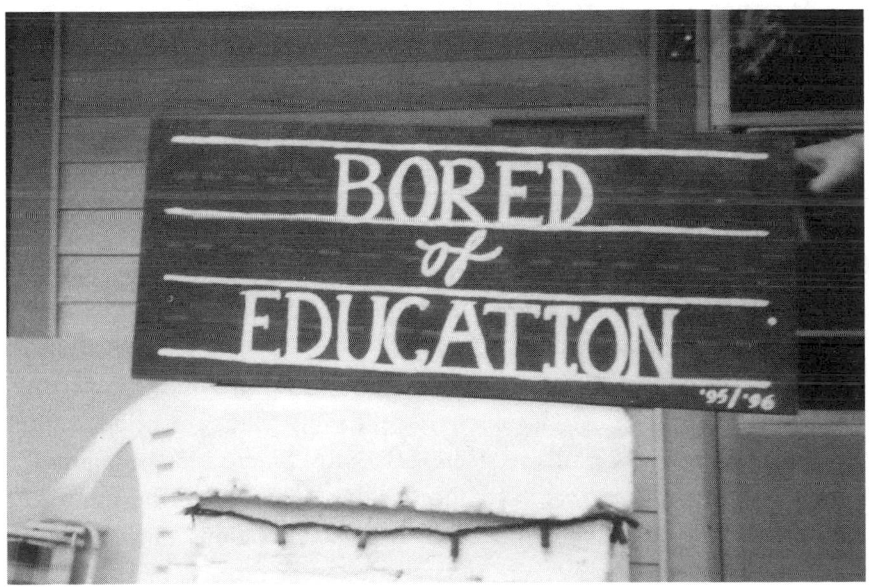

FIGURE 2.3. Bored of Education

FIGURE 2.4. The Heisman

Most house names are noun phrases, sometimes of a single word (Che, Jaundice, and Moist), sometimes with an article (The Dresden, The Heisman, and the Ivy League), sometimes with a modifier (Absolut Chaos, Alcoholics Unanimous, and Church Key), and sometimes of a longer string with or without articles (3 Chicks and a Cock, Ghetto Super Stars, and Good + Plenty). Another class of messages is formed by a past participle and its phrase (Bored of Education, Crammed Inn, Fully Loaded, and Rolling Stoned). A present participial phrase is included in Raisin' Hell and Startin' Early. A prepositional phrase is At Church and Almost High. A handful contain verb phrases (Boot 'N Rally, Come-N-Go, and Set Sail). A sign that includes a verb in the imperative form is Gimme Shelter. The category of imperative verbs can be expanded significantly if the following names are included: Boot 'N Rally, Come-N-Go, Hangover Here, Hit & Run, Liquor Juggs, Liquor Up Front, Poker in the Rear, Set Sail, Stop Making Sense, and the subtitle of TKΔ, Tappa Kegga Day. Some house signs are abbreviations. The last sign in the list in addition to one other use Greek letters reminiscent of the names for fraternity organizations. Whereas TKΔ is expanded as Tappa Kegga Day, what AΣΣ stands for is left to the imagination. Since its letters spell a word if

Σ is replaced with "s," perhaps AΣΣ doesn't require the kind of elaboration given TKΔ.

These examples show that even though house sign messages are short, in many cases their formal features include assonance and alliteration. Assonance refers to repetition in vowel sounds that results in rhyming, whereas alliteration refers to repetition in consonant sounds that begin words. Thus we find the following examples of assonance: Dysfunction Junction, Crib of the Rib, Hell's Belles, The No-Tell Motel, Slow Idaho, The Boom Boom Room, The Panty Shanty, and Waste of Space. Yabba Grabba Brew is particularly complex with respect to its assonance because it rhymes with a familiar—if nonsensical—expression ('yabba dabba doo"). Alliteration is even more common. Examples include Band of Brothers, Bed Booze & Beyond, Beech Bunnies, Betty Boops, Bamm Bamm, Copa-Cabana, Dirty Dozen, Girls Gone Ghetto, Girls Gone Wild, Hangover Here, Hut Hut, Pitcher Perfect, Set Sail, Sugar Shack, Team Ram-Rod, and The Boom Boom Room. Some examples of assonance and alliteration already exist in the names borrowed from popular culture. But most are of residents' invention.

The fact that house signs offer little in the way of propositional content, coupled with the fact that they indulge in assonance and alliteration, suggests that they are a form of speech play. Barbara Kirshenblatt-Gimblett and Joel Sherzer have noted that "speech play . . . represents a radical alternative to the tyranny of propositional meaning and instrumentality" (1976, 10). Mahadev Apte sees in speech play—what he calls "linguistic humor"—"the twisting of the relationship between form and meaning, the reinterpretation of familiar words and phrases, and the overall misuse of language" (1985, 179). John McDowell explains that part of what allows speech play to draw attention away from language's ability to refer is that it "fastens on the 'wrinkles' in the linguistic code, its points of overlap, inconsistency, ambiguity, and anomaly" (1992, 139). Even more common than assonance and alliteration in house names are puns and double entendres, both of which indulge in "ambiguity and anomaly."

Joel Sherzer provides a definition helpful for considering a major feature of house signs' formal properties, punning: "In the most general terms, a pun is a form of speech play in which a word or a phrase unexpectedly and simultaneously combines two unrelated meanings" (2002, 29). Puns thus have a family resemblance to jokes because both thrive on ambiguity: "Joke texts are ambiguous; they are usually capable of bearing more than a single inter-

Table 2.1. Features of Punning of Selected House Names

	Sound Patterns	Morphology and Lexicon	Syntax and Semantics	Pragmatics
· Alco Hall		Alco Hall vs. alcohol	name vs. noun	university naming pattern
· Boutique Hall	k final vs. k initial	Boutique Hall vs. Booty Call	name vs. noun	university naming pattern
· Di-Vine	v vs. w [pictured with wine bottle]	Di as The?—v/wine vs. divine	noun vs. adjective	house on Vine Street
· Hangover Here		hangover vs. hang over	noun vs. verb	
· Looks Te-quil-ya		Te-quil-ya suggests to kill you and tequila	noun	
· Miss B. Haven	en vs. ing	Miss B. Haven vs. misbehaving	name vs. verb	
· Syc-A-College	A vs. of		adjective	house on Sycamore and College Streets
· Tipsy Chicks	t vs. d and p vs. k(x)	Tipsy vs. Dixie	adjective vs. name	popular band

pretation" (Elliott Oring 1996, 375). Sherzer claims that "puns are speech play par excellence" and can be a major part of "social-interactional strategies and competition; verbal deftness and quickness; social, cultural, and linguistic manipulations; and the creative pleasure of saying, hearing, and seeing what language can do" (2002, 36). Sherzer is thus arguing that punning draws on and contributes to what Roman Jakobson called "poeticity," the poetic quality of a text. Jakobson explains that poeticity "is present when the word is felt as a word and not a mere representation of the object being named or an outburst of emotion, when words and their composition, their meaning, their external and internal form acquire a weight and value of their own instead of referring indifferently to reality" (1976, 174). Sherzer explains that punning can be accomplished at many linguistic levels including sound patterns, morphology and lexicon, syntax and semantics, and pragmatics (1978). Additionally, puns can play with features of multiple languages at these various levels. The levels are not mutually exclusive, and one house name can pun at various levels simultaneously. The pervasive use of puns in house signs would seem to make punning germane to the entire genre.

Puns are achieved in several ways in house names. Sometimes, manipulations of the visual representation of sound create the pun. Thus, "ya" suggests "you" and "Te-quil" approximates "to kill," but also allows the suggestion of "tequila." "Syc-A" is left as an incomplete manifestation of "Sycamore" so that the possibility of its understanding as "sick of" can be achieved. The form of a name is initiated with "Miss," which is followed by a letter of abbreviation of a middle name and a surname. The whole, however, results in a gerund, one rendered as one might actually speak, without the pronunciation of the final "g." Thus manipulations of the visual representation of house names often involve morphological, lexical, and pragmatic shifts. Alco Hall, written as a university place-name, is identical with "alcohol" when spoken. The shift from visual to oral representation brings about a grammatical change emergent at the level of syntax and pragmatics. The use of the house name in the domain suggested by the house sign would be silly. Imagine the question, "Could you tell me which building is alcohol?" Yet the board on which the house name is displayed reinforces this possibility. The board had been cut so that it has a scroll at the top and has been painted white. This is similar to the design of signs for buildings on campus. The figure shows that punning in signs not only generates coinages such as Alco Hall but sometimes invokes recognizable words or phrases without which the coinage would be nonsensical. Imagine, for example, someone exclaiming, "You're just too Poplar for the Ghetto," without "popular" as a word in the lexicon to make the pun work.

In the case of house signs, the punning element can occur at any of the linguistic levels that Sherzer mentions, but as a whole, the formal features of house signs make them distinct from other more widely known genres in which punning occurs. Sherzer gives an example of punning from the work of Sigmund Freud: "Two Jews met in the neighborhood of the bath-house. 'Have you taken a bath?' asked one of them. 'What?' asked the other in return. 'Is there one missing?'" (Freud 1905, 58, quoted in Sherzer 2002, 31). In this example, Sherzer presents us with a pun imbedded within a kind of text easily recognizable as a joke. Its structural features include the presentation of two people in the past whose mundane—perhaps too mundane—dialogue is interrupted, so to speak, by the shift to a literal notion of "to take." The length of house signs does not allow for texts required for the kind of punning found in Freud's joke.

Sherzer, however, gives us this road sign indicating workers on the road: "Working for you. Give us a brake" (2002, 31). The pun works by virtue of the homonyms "brake" and "break." Textually, the example reminds one of house signs on which puns operate within the confines of a few words, typically fewer than in Sherzer's shortest example. Thus the textuality of house signs rests on an extremely brief message, the puns of which are not couched in a set-up, as in a joke, or even in a simple distinction of pronouns as is in the case of Sherzer's example: "[We're] Working for *you*. [You] Give *us* a brake."

If the punning is broadened to double entendres, still more house signs must be included in examples of speech play. Most of the double entendres involve puns. "Asspen" is a pun in that it rests on the name "Aspen," a popular vacation destination. The depiction of two snow-covered mountaintops, each topped with a red flag, reinforces the allusion. "Asspen" is also a double entendre because it might be understood as a place, a "pen," where there is the availability of a sexual partner, or in popular parlance, the attainment of a "piece of ass." "Collgirls" suggests "call girls," a popular euphemism for expensive sex workers, but preserves the spelling of the street name, College, on which the house is located. "Morning Wood" is a popular double entendre that is borrowed without any punning transformation. It is a euphemism for waking with an erection. "The 'O' Face" is a sign that borrows from the movie *Office Space*. In the movie, "the 'oh' face" describes one's facial expression during orgasm. The "O" on the house sign is complemented by two dots and a line, suggesting a face. "The Rusty Trombone" is borrowed without transformation from popular parlance, wherein "rusty" and "trombone" are both

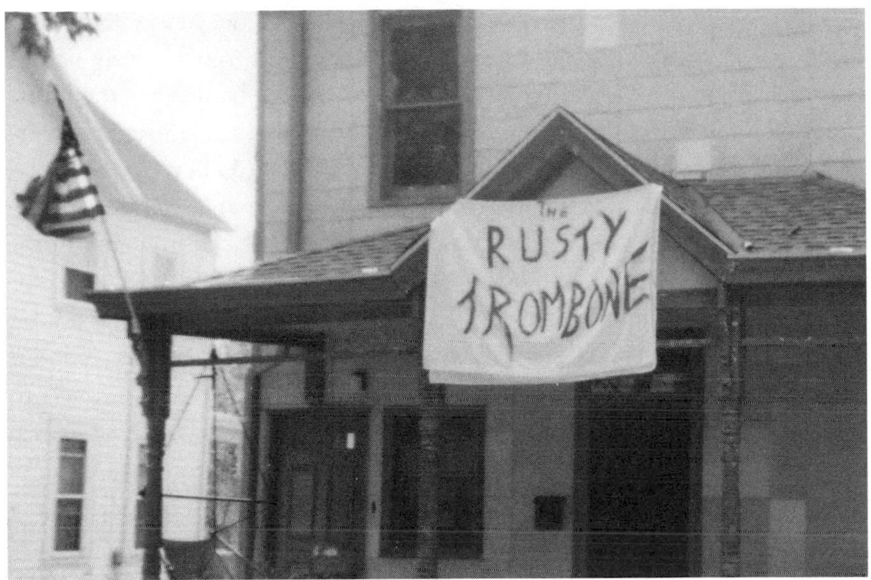

FIGURE 2.5. The Rusty Trombone 1

FIGURE 2.6. The Rusty Trombone 2

double entendres. The expression refers to a sexual practice in which the anus and penis serve as the bases of "rusty" and "trombone," respectively. This is the only example in which the residents used a cloth banner for the house sign itself. This might have been due to the vulgarity behind the euphemism. In another year, the residents simply affixed an actual trombone to the house, paralleling Chubby Bungalow in a lack of a spelled-out name. Tuna Sandwich is a house of male residents whose neighbors on either side are female. The name relies on fish standing in for female genitalia. Well Hung Over combines "well hung" and "hung over." The first expression is a common double entendre that is used to describe a person with a large penis. The second is a common expression for illness felt on the day after drinking too much alcohol. The name "6 Pack" is a double entendre for an abdomen on which muscles are apparent and attractive. It is also a name for a common number of cans or bottles of some beverage packaged for sale, and it corresponds to the number of residents in the house.

Thematics

This consideration of puns and double entendres inevitably leads to the second aspect of textuality mentioned by Bauman, the thematic dimension of a text. Bauman explains, "Thematics, by contrast [with the formal properties of texts], has to do with the referential or propositional content of texts, their way of representing the world" (Bauman 2008, 31). Because the texts found on house signs are names, one might argue that the propositional content is inconsequential. Such an argument might point out that a house's name simply enables one to refer to a house and that as long as there is little possibility of redundancy in names, any name might do just as well as any other. One can imagine, for example, that Church Key, Keg Stand, or The "O" Face might do just as well in the utterance "[house's name] is a rather pretty house," as long as the name picks out the actual house one is describing.

Elizabeth Mertz's work on personal names, however, shows that they can invoke cultural categories that cut across individual acts of referring. Examples that Mertz offers from her fieldwork among residents of the Cape Breton community in Nova Scotia include Holy Malcom and his sons Holy Charlie, Dannie Holy, and Murdoch Holy. Holy Malcom got his name because of his saintly character. Thus, in order to understand the thematics of naming in Cape Breton, one must understand that the name Holy Malcom rests on more than the ability to refer to the man named Holy Malcom. Saintliness is a cultural category that must transcend the particular behavior of Holy Malcom, and the thematics of personal names in the Cape Breton community partly rely on this category. Long John MacInnis is particularly tall. Angus Chaisemaker and Donald Painter are engaged in occupations from which their names have been derived. People living at a distance from the community will sometimes have the name of the distant place incorporated into their names. Thus, DJ Rocky was born and lives in Rocky Side, some distance from the community (Mertz 1983, 62).[2]

House signs give evidence that their thematics are hardly random or inconsequential. Indeed, they are highly organized by cultural distinctions. Figure 2.2 illustrates that a good number of house signs can be grouped together by their thematics and that a house name can fall into two or more groups. Sometimes the sign's pun on some recognizable name creates the possibility of multiple thematic group membership. Thus Tipsy Chicks alters the band name Dixie Chicks. The band name already presents the possibility of reflecting the house residents' gender, but Tipsy Chicks allows for the additional theme of alcohol. Genital Hospital puns on the soap opera *General Hospital*. The house is near the city's primary hospital, and the pun extends the house's name to the theme of sexuality. Yabba Grabba Brew puns on Fred Flintstone's popular exclamation in order to invoke the theme of alcohol.

House names do not always manipulate names taken from the world of film, literature, music, or television. Sometimes they use well known names, such as 4 Non-Blondes, Band of Brothers, Cheers, Girls Gone Wild, Miami Vice, Octopussy, Risky Business, Strangers with Candy, Where the Sidewalk Ends, and Where the Wild Things Are. Without any further punning, some of these allow membership in more than one group. Cheers is the name of a television series but also the name of a bar depicted in the series. Octopussy, named for a James Bond movie, joins signs that include—in some way or another—the number of people who live in the house, as well as the group of signs that include sexuality.

Membership in multiple groupings of house name themes is not confined to widely recognizable names taken from the world of media and literature. Many signs make up a group, for example, because they all include the word "inn" in their names. Some depict "inn" as a separate word, one with its usual meaning (Booze Inn) and several that can be read as "in" (12 Feet Inn, Cornered Inn, Inn Pursuit, Stagger Inn, and Stop Inn). Inncoherent takes the basis of its punning, "incoherent," and renders it more like the other house names that include "inn." Finally, The Chick-Inn incorporates "inn" in such

Table 2.2. Thematic Categories for Selected House Names

Theme	Cluster of House Signs		
* * *			
Alcohol	*6 Pack*	*AA*	Absolut Angels
	Absolut Chaos	*Alco Hall*	*Alcoholics Unanimous*
	Bed Booze & Beyond	Beer Goggles	*Betty Ford Clinic*
	Boot 'N Rally	*Booze Inn*	Bottoms Up
	Brew-Ski	*Champagne Room*	*Cheers*
	Church Key	*Cocktail*	*Cocktales*
	Cosmopolitan	*David Hasselhoffbrauhaus*	Dirty Martini
	Di-Vine	Fully Loaded	Hangover Here
	Happy Hour	Hit & Run	Immaculate Consumption
	Inncoherent	Jäger Städium	Keg Stand
	Last Call	*Liquor Juggs*	*Liquor Up Front, Poker in the Rear*
	Looks Te-quil-ya	Pitcher Perfect	Pour House
	Pucker Up	Red Stripe	*Sex on the Beech*
	Stagger Inn	Startin' Early	Subject to Blackout . . .
	Sugar Shack	*TKΔ*	*Tipsy Chicks*
	Tom Collins	*Well Hung Over*	West High Life
	Whine Cellar	*Yabba Grabba Brew*	
* * *			
Pun Contains "Inn"	*12 Feet Inn*	*Booze Inn*	Cornered Inn
	Crammed Inn	*Inncoherent*	Inn Pursuit
	Stagger Inn	Stop Inn	The Chick-Inn
* * *			
Institution	*AA*	*ΑΣΣ*	*Alco Hall*
	Alcoholics Unanimous	*Bed Booze & Beyond*	*Betty Ford Clinic*

	Boutique Hall	Copa-Cabana	Dis-Graceland
	Ho-Tel 6	*Hootersville*	Precinct 109
	TKΔ	The Ivy League	*The Playm~~ate~~eight Mansion*
	Unplanned Parenthood	*Wendy's Backyard*	White Castle
* * *			
Media (Film, Literature, Music, and Television)	*4 Non-Blondes*	Animal House	Bamm Bamm
	Band of Brothers	Betty Boops	*Blue Lagoon*
	Boogie Nights	Casa Blanca	Catch 22
	Cheers	Copa-Cabana	Cruel Intentions
	David Hasselhoffbrauhaus	*Deez Nutz*	Deuces Wild
	Dirty Dozen	Dirty South	Dude, Where's My House?
	Gary Coleman Fan Club	*Genital Hospital*	*Girls Gone Wild*
	Goodfellas	Green Machine	Home Alone
	Hotel California	Leave It to Beaver	Little Women
	Miami Vice	*Octopussy*	Pee-wee's Playhouse
	Risky Business	Rolling Stoned	Scooby
	Scrappy	Stop Making Sense	*Strangers with Candy*
	The Big Kahuna	*The Land of Odds*	*The "O" Face*
	The Usual Suspects	*Three's Company*	*Tipsy Chicks*
	Tony Danza	Uptown Girls	Where the Sidewalk Ends
	Where the Wild Things Are	*Yabba Grabba Brew*	Yellow Submarine
	Young and Restless		
* * *			
Street Name (Beech)	Beech Bunnies	Pebble Beech	*Sex on the Beech*
	South Beech	Spoiled Beeches	

Continued on the next page

Theme	Cluster of House Signs		
(Church)	At Church and Almost High	*Church Key*	
(Poplar)	*Poplar Cherry*	*Poplar with the Ladies*	*Pop-N-Wood*
	Too Poplar for the Ghetto		
* * *			
Number of Residents	*3 Chicks and a Cock*	*4 Non-Blondes*	*6 Pack*
	:10 Spot	*12 Feet Inn*	*Casual Six*
	Dirty Dozen	*Four Play*	*Ho-Tell 6*
	Octoballs	*Octopussy*	*Six Appeal*
	Six Geese a Layin'	*The Land of Oddz*	*The Playm~~ate~~eight Mansion*
	Three's Company	Unisix	
* * *			
Sexuality	*3 Chicks and a Cock*	*6 Pack*	*ΑΣΣ*
	Asspen	*Bed Booze & Beyond*	*Blue Lagoon*
	Boogie Nights	*Boutique Hall*	*Casual Six*
	Champagne Room	Clothing Optional	*Cocktail*
	Cocktales	Collgirls	Come-N-Go
	Deez Nutz	Dillywhop	*Four Play*
	Girls Gone Wild	Girls on Top	Gutter Balls
	Hoe Down	*Hooter~~s~~ville*	Kinkytown
	Liquor Juggs	*Liquor Up Front, Poker in the Rear*	Live Bait
	Morning Wood	*Octoballs*	*Octopussy*
	Pheromones	*Poplar Cherry*	*Poplar with the Ladies*
	Pop-N-Wood	*Risky Business*	*Sex on the Beech*

Six Appeal	*Six Geese a Lay'n'*	*Strangers with Candy*
The Boobie Trap	The No-Tell Motel	*The "O" Face*
The Panty Shanty	The Petting Zoo	*The Playm~~ate~~eight Mansion*
The Rusty Trombone	Top or Bottom?	Tuna Sandwich
Unbuckled	*Unplanned Parenthood*	Up Your Alley
Well Hung Over	*Wendy's Backyard*	

Note: Italicized names appear in two or more thematic categories.

a way as to yield the word "chicken." In this last case, it would seem possible that the word created by the joining of "chick" and "inn" is a by-product of the punning of the name and not productive of a theme into which the pun might place it. Indeed, the example gives evidence of Sherzer's claim that the inability to separate a pun's use of formal properties and thematics is what makes it an especially important example of speech play.

If house signs that fit into a single theme are added, the number of names that do not include a pun increases greatly. Cosmopolitan, Dirty Martini, Last Call, Precinct 109, The Ivy League, and White Castle are all examples. In some of these cases, one might begin to question whether house names reflect themes. In others, one can identify a theme, but the small number of relevant signs and the lack of a clear relationship between the theme and other themes make one wonder whether the theme is actually relevant to house signs' thematics. For example, while many house signs involve alcohol in their names, only a few involve food. These include Good + Plenty, Peeps, Tuna Sandwich, Wendy's Backyard, and White Castle. One might wonder whether two groupings emerge from the small theme. Good + Plenty, Peeps, and Tuna Sandwich are food items, the first two brand-names and the third a generic description, whereas Wendy's and White Castle are commercial establishments. Does the fact that the latter are commercial establishments make the signs that contain them resemble Cheers, Copa-Cabana, and Hootersville, all three of which contain the name of an establishment that offers an item for consumption? Booze Inn, Stagger Inn, and Stop Inn are some of the signs that suggest the same kind of commercial establishment. Deuces Wild invokes a specific card while Liquor Up Front, Poker in the Rear invokes a card game at one level of meaning. The Boom Boom Room includes a depiction of cards and poker chips on its sign. Drugs might be seen as a theme in At Church and Almost High and Rolling Stoned. Scooby and Scrappy are named after characters in the cartoon series *Scooby Doo,* wherein the character Shaggy has been glorified by many as a stoner, someone who enjoys marijuana and an associated laid-back lifestyle. Scooby is Shaggy's dog, and Scrappy is Scooby's nephew. In these cases, one is left wondering whether the ways in which house names resemble one another in the themes that they invoke are salient to the thematics of house signs as a whole. Themes like alcohol and sexuality seem to be quite salient indeed, but themes like food, cards, and drugs seem comparatively rare.

Finally, some signs evade membership in a thematic category altogether. The single most mysterious sign for the classes I taught was Moist. No other sign invoked a quality devoid of any tie to popular media, institutions, objects, or places, much less to the themes tying together other house signs. Some students wondered whether the word "Moist" might be sexual. Others wondered whether the house might have a damp basement. Someone mused that perhaps residents liked their brownies moist, perhaps baked with marijuana. We were at a loss, however, when it came to finding ties between the name and any sort of theme found in another sign. Dysfunction Junction was mysterious as to theme membership just as it was one of the most poetic names for its formal features. We mused that the name might have been coined after *Schoolhouse Rock*'s "Conjunction Junction," a cartoon skit demonstrating conjunctions as grammatically interesting words. The cartoon likened "and," "but," and "or" to train cars useful for joining other cars, and even included a pun depicting "or" as a car filled with ore. Dillywhop struck us as a bit isolated from the themes of other signs. We were surprised frankly that the sign had lasted as long as it did given that a drawing of a penis formed part of the sign. If Dillywhop is taken to be a euphemism for a penis, the house name might be grouped with Morning Wood wherein "wood" suggests an erection. The class could not identify any thematic participation by Melee. Finally, we could not find a theme with which to link Jaundice to another sign, nor did it incorporate a celebrity, place, or item of wide currency. I wondered whether this name might have to do with damage to the liver associated with heavy drinking or hepatitis that has been sexually transmitted, but these could only remain guesses. Neither alcohol nor sexuality is explicitly invoked by the name. These five house names were the few of over two hundred that did not seem to participate in a theme or borrow from a source, whether by simple incorporation or by punning manipulation.

Pragmatics

The ambiguity of some of the signs with regard to themes should give pause to someone who might argue that a sole focus on house signs' thematics can be used to understand them. Indeed, such ambiguity leads us to consider the third dimension of textuality described by Bauman, who argues that "the pragmatic dimension of texts pertains to their modes of presentation and use, how they serve as resources for the accomplishment of social ends" (2008, 31). The three aspects of texts that Bauman describes—formal, thematic, and pragmatic—are intertwined, of course, but the third demands attention to the situation of texts in contexts. That is, the pragmatic dimension of texts raises questions about who might find texts useful or meaningful, in what capacity, and toward what ends. And transformations in the relationships between texts and contexts can be at issue. The pragmatic dimension of textuality draws attention to what happens to texts as they are taken from one context and given life in another.

Context can be explored as a factor in the pragmatic dimension of textuality through the theory of signs developed in the late nineteenth century by the philosopher Charles Sanders Peirce.

> There are three kinds of signs. Firstly, there are *likenesses,* or icons; which serve to convey ideas of the things they represent simply by imitating them. Secondly, there are *indications,* or indices; which show something about things, on account of their being physically connected with them. Such is a guidepost, which points down the road to be taken, or a relative pronoun, which is placed just after the name of the thing intended to be denoted, or a vocative exclamation, as "Hi! there," which acts on the nerves of the person addressed and forces his attention. Thirdly, there are *symbols,* or general signs; which have become associated with their meanings by usage. Such are most words, and phrases, and speeches, and books, and libraries. (1998, 5)

"Indications," more commonly called "indexes," rest on the relationship between a sign and its object of representation that calls attention to context. While the examples that Peirce offers in the quote depend on an actual physical or temporal connection for their indexical properties, Peirce argues that indexicality can rely on an existential connection between a sign and its object of representation. It is such a connection that allows the following of Peirce's examples to exhibit an indexical relationship between a sign and its object of representation:

> I see a man with a rolling gait. This is a probable indication that he is a sailor. I see a bowlegged man in corduroys, gaiters, and a jacket. These are probable indications that he is a jockey or something of the sort. (1998, 8)

Unlike the iconic relationship between a sign and its object (such as a blueprint and those aspects of a building it resembles), or the symbolic one (such as the sound "cat" and that which the sound denotes), both of which do not rely on contextual positioning for their ground of representation, the gait or the legs and dress mentioned in Peirce's example rely on relationships between these aspects of movement or physical features that have accrued to sailors or jockeys, respectively. Unlike icons, the examples do not signify by imitation, and unlike symbols, the examples do not signify by an arbitrary relationship between sign and object.[3] On this last point, try the experiment wherein you say a word to yourself quickly and repeatedly. You will find that the relationship between sign (the sound) and object (the denotational value of the sound) "comes apart" after some time. What you are experiencing is the realization of the arbitrariness of the relationship between sign and object characteristic of the symbolic aspect of semiosis.

Oxford's house signs indulge in all three of the semiotic relationships proposed by Peirce. For example, the sign The Ivy League is painted green in iconic imitation of ivy. The sign Stop Inn contains the depiction of a stop sign. In some sense, this is an artistic rendering or idealization and does not match the dimensions, color, lettering, or material construction of a real stop sign. One could imagine the students using a real stop sign. Peirce notes this sort of distinction elsewhere in his theory of signs, but for our purposes, the octagonal red form represents a stop sign by an iconic resemblance. On the sign Di-Vine, the residents have depicted a bottle. Note that the depiction of a bottle has a very different relationship to its object of representation than the word "bottle" has to it. The latter relationship between sign, the sound "bottle," and object, the denotative value of the sound "bottle," is symbolic. There is nothing in the sound—unlike in the image—that provides a ground for representing the object of the sign.

House signs indulge in symbolic relationships between signs and objects, not just in iconic ones, in two senses. First, the words have denotative values. Nothing in the sound or the form of the word contributes to the way the word or form relates to its object of representation. Symbols are thus arbitrary in a way that icons are not. Indeed, many of the puns encourage the realization of multiple possibilities in the relationship between sign and object. For example, house signs that use "inn" promote the realization of "inn" or "in" because their spoken forms are identical. Second, many of the images on house signs have an arbitrary relationship to their objects of representation. For example, the residents of the house Inn Pursuit explained that the "t" in the name is a cross. The relationship between perpendicular lines and a cross on which the crucifixion of Christ took place is imitative and iconic, but the relationship between a cross and Christianity is symbolic. The same might be said for the fact that the "t" of pursuit is golden in color and is understood, by the residents at least, to represent Christianity. And while the green color of

The Ivy League rests on an imitative relationship to the green of ivy, the relationship between the golden color of the "t" and Christianity is arbitrary and therefore symbolic.

In an early application of semiotics to folklore, Petr Bogatyrev, attributing their origins to Vološinov, provides examples of material objects differentiated by indexical and symbolic relationships to that which they represent:

> If we take a stone, paint it white, and then place it between two fields, something . . . happens. . . . It will become a marker, that is, a sign with a particular and variously usable meaning. A sign for what purpose? A sign to mark the border between two plots of ground. Similarly, when we see the crossed hammer and sickle prominently displayed, they represent for us not merely tools, a picture of tools, but a symbol of the U.S.S.R. (1976, 13, excerpting Vološinov 1930, 45)

The painted stone represents the border by its connection to it. In the case of the painted stone, context is crucial to the stone's representation of the border. In the second example, the crossed hammer and sickle represent the Soviet Union through convention. The relationship is neither iconically nor contextually dependent and is symbolic. Thus the two examples may be seen to rest on very different relationships to their objects of representation.

All textuality is in the end related to its pragmatic dimension in the sense that all manifestations of semiotic relationships in the world involve indexicality. Indexicality is so pervasive because it is not confined to the spatial disposition of objects and sounds, but also calls our attention to the seemingly limitless possibilities for sociocultural framing of persons, places, activities, styles, and so on (Blommaert 2005). A short vignette illustrates the ways in which iconic, indexical, and symbolic relationships between signs and their objects pervade our world. A few months ago I drove to New York City from Utica, New York. I entered the Bronx on the Major Deegan Expressway. A large digital sign on wheels announced, "A car is stalled on the RFK. Expect delays." The RFK? I didn't know what it was. This mattered because an exit to the Cross Bronx Expressway faced me and I wondered which highway the stalled car might affect. I remained on the Deegan and suffered for an hour or so in traffic, not knowing whether the traffic was better or worse on the Cross Bronx Expressway. On the way out of town, I saw a sign on FDR Drive, this time printed green and white and mounted permanently, that read, "The Triborough Bridge has been renamed the RFK Bridge."

The example shows some ways in which language and objects, as they are produced and encountered, are reliant on and productive of indexicality. In other words, the example illustrates the important part context plays in understanding texts as part of the world. For example, that the first message I saw was displayed on a large digital signboard was indexical of some temporal situatedness of the message. In the case mentioned here, I derived the temporal dimension from the tense used in the utterance "is stalled" and from the fact that it was displayed on a digital screen likely to disappear or change at some point.[4] Such temporal relevance was absent in the second sign I saw. Its green and white design, relatively permanent rendering, and relatively fixed placement on the side of the highway are all three signs related to their objects of representation in an indexical fashion. The green and white design is iconic of signs erected by the city's government and can be taken to be indexical of its authority. The permanent rendering is indexical of a state of affairs in which the temporal dimension of the message's relevance might not be focal. The fixed placement on the side of the highway is indexical of the focus of attention of motorists. Thus the indexical possibilities of the two signs are not identical.[5]

Which relationships between sign and object might emerge as a focus of attention depends on the experience of the viewer, and that is always changing. In my own case, the first sign did not confuse me because of any of the possible indexical values rendered thus far in my explanation of the two signs. I am reasonably competent when it comes to understanding road signs. But I was not familiar with a recent change in the name of one of New York City's landmarks, one particularly relevant to traffic. For me, the second sign clarified the indexical value of RFK Bridge. The second sign rebaptized something I recognized, the Triborough Bridge, the RFK Bridge. I was then able to think to myself, "They've renamed the Triborough? No wonder I had such traffic on the Major Deegan!"

A few scholars have begun to work outside of a traditional emphasis on verbal communication by considering the ways in which the textuality of visual language largely rests on indexicality.[6] The same scholars point out—but largely leave it to others to ponder—that a singular interest in such indexical relations and the contexts they require begs the question of how people engage with them and what that says about those people as part of larger groups.[7] For example, anyone brought up in the United States probably knows that RFK is an abbreviation, and such abbreviations are very common in naming landmarks. One might then proceed to find that landmarks are named

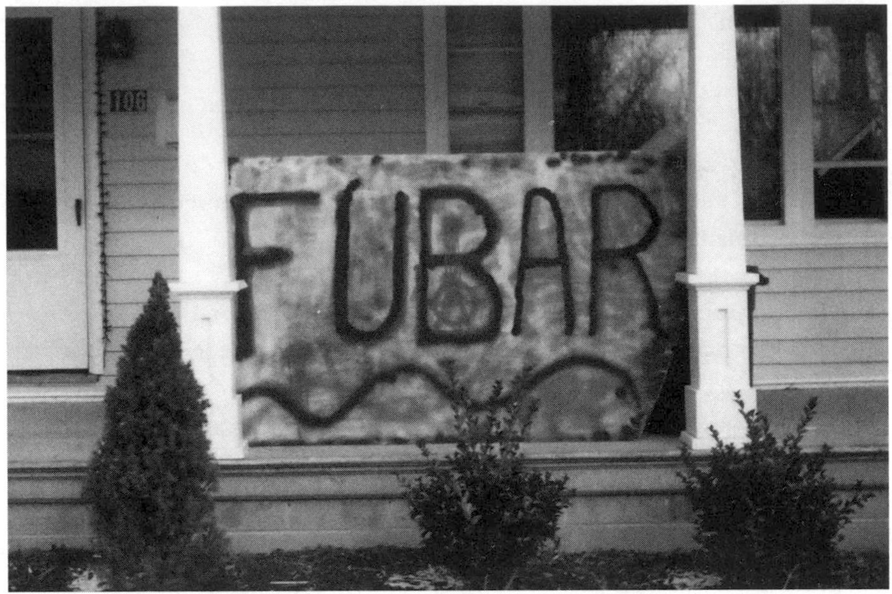

FIGURE 2.7. FUBAR

for people or groups important in the history of a town, county, state, or nation.[8] Notice that house signs, with very few exceptions, do not share this feature of textuality. The one house sign that takes an abbreviation for its name not discussed so far is FUBAR. The abbreviation stands for "fucked up beyond all repair." There are many variants, especially on the last word of the phrase, but none of them stands for the name of any public figure. Indeed, naming conventions in the United States would not allow FUBAR to abbreviate someone's name because names are not usually five words long. The abbreviation of well-known names is thus an index of landmarks but not of house signs. This could become relevant to the ways that one understands (or fails to understand) a house sign.

Attention to the production and display of objects and language, situated in the lives of those who make them meaningful, whether they are practitioners, admirers, or disinterested onlookers, has become known as a practice approach: "For cultural study, praxis [practice] is activity resulting in the production, and I would add consumption, of an object, but one where the doing, the processes involved and the conditions present, rather than solely the end, is paramount" (Bronner 1986, 19–20). House signs are objects, of course, but one should keep in mind that their linguistic aspects are relevant to practice, too.

When the interpretation and/or habits of production and display of language and objects can be located socially in a group, this has come to be called a "community of practice."[9] Practice operates at the nexus of context, activity, and orientation toward consequences: "Practice encompasses three elements: social context, which both constrains and enables the practice; social consequences, which can be intended or unintended; and the practice itself, which is influenced by context and oriented toward consequences" (Berger and Del Negro 2004, 25–26). The fact that practice is "oriented toward consequences" suggests the existence of intersubjective alignments that can become indexical in myriad ways. For example, in the vignette about driving, one can imagine that someone might have as much trouble with any one of the (semiotic) signs mentioned as I had with the indexical relationship between RFK and its object of representation, were that person unpracticed in driving on U.S. interstate highways.

Indeed, one of the surest ways to discover that a community of practice is involved in the production and consumption of material and linguistic folklore is to feel yourself being made an outsider by the ways in which you reflect on it. This can happen when one becomes confused by indexical values or when others point out that one's understanding is incorrect. Given their different experiences with the community in question, people might vary quite widely in their apprehension of indexical phenomena involved in some practice.[10] Someone thus might be unfamiliar with any combination of the semiotic signs involved in some practice as in the vignette about driving. Someone might come to index themselves as participants in or strangers to the community of practice in question depending on how the first point plays a part in communicative interaction. Thus the concept of indexicality can be used to trace membership in communities of practice by showing that the lack of intersubjective alignments can become a foregrounded issue when the construal of indexical phenomena differs (Urciuoli 1995).

An example of my own initial excitement and subsequent shock about a house sign provides an example of an interpretation's emergence in interaction opening up a social gap between the residents of a named house and me. Early on in the first year of the project, several colleagues were intrigued by Che, understanding the name to refer to Che Guevara. They told me with skepticism that they were hopeful that the sign indexed a revolutionary spirit

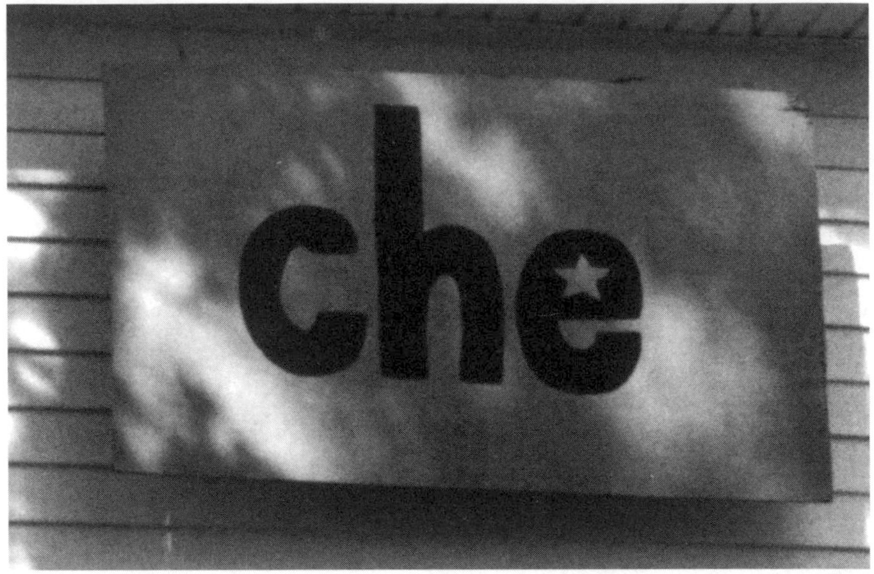

FIGURE 2.8. Che 1

coupled with a socialist political-economic disposition within the student body, however limited in number the imagined young leftists might be. During interviews, neither the residents of Che nor the residents of several other houses to whom the name was mentioned were familiar with the historical figure. We were told that we "did not understand" house signs because we were "taking them too seriously." I grew increasingly dismayed when the residents of Che explained that the previous year's residents named the house after a "drunk Mexican man" they met while transferring buses in Buffalo, New York, during spring break. The current residents wanted to keep the name, thereby maintaining its "tradition," but also to make it "our own." So they decided to change the pronunciation from "chay" to "chee."

Only very gradually did we begin to appreciate the fact that if we wanted to understand the pragmatic dimension of textuality in house signs, we should pay attention to that aspect of folklore illustrated in the description of our encounter with the residents of Che: metafolklore. In a seminal article, Alan Dundes pointed out that folklorists could learn much about folklore by considering "folkloristic statements about folklore" (1966, 509). Dan Ben-Amos remarked, "In addition to naming . . . folklore, people [everywhere] talk about it . . . folklore forms are, in and of themselves, the subject of folklore, much the

FIGURE 2.9. Che 2

same way other aspects of culture, society, and nature are" (1974, 5, as cited in Babcock 1984, 62). As the discussion of Che demonstrates, much can be learned by paying careful attention to folklore about folklore because metafolklore contains clues as to "an interpretive frame within which the messages being communicated are to be understood" (Bauman 1984, 9). The relationship between folklore and metafolklore recalls the relationship between culture and metaculture. Indeed, all folklore is culture just as all metafolklore is metaculture. Metafolklore, like metaculture, provides clues as to how people interpret folklore.

Residents of Che dismissed our reflection on the house name. This indicated that our metafolkloric explanations seemed wrongheaded to them. Indeed, once they discovered that we were trying to connect the house name to a historical figure, they indicated that we had failed to read the house sign properly. In their idiom, we had "taken the house sign too seriously." Thus our interpretation of the house sign indexed our exclusion from the group who reflect on house signs in a less problematic way. At the same time, we learned that our assumption that Che Guevara was involved required adjustment.

Later on, we would learn that other people—indeed, most other people—living in named houses thought Che an unusual and undesirable house name.

This shows that people can be members of a community of practice without making particularly good contributions. The residents of other named houses concurred with the residents of Che by pointing out that my colleagues' and my interpretation of the house involving Che Guevara was off the mark. Such an interpretation prompted metafolklore that showed that my colleagues and I did not know how to read house signs.

Barbara Babcock writes comments about metacommunication that apply just as well to metafolklore and metaculture: "Metacommunication in narrative performance may be described as any element of communication which calls attention to the speech event as a performance and to the relationship which obtains between the narrator and his audience vis-à-vis the narrative message" (1984, 66). As we have seen, the "narrative message" involves a text on a house sign. As people produce metafolklore about house signs, they reposition the audience from being a potential viewer of a sign to being a listener of the sign's name, and they change the sign's status from material object to sound. Put most simply, when texts are taken out of a context and placed in another, the pragmatic dimension of textuality is brought into play. Scholars have called the first action "decontextualization" and the second action "recontextualization." Because house signs are names, and their formal properties show that most are noun phrases, a few are verb phrases, and a handful are abbreviations (sometimes forming a word), they can be grammatically incorporated very easily for the production of metafolklore. When one does so, one is engaging in recontextualization. One is taking the house name from its place on the house sign and interjecting it into a new context.

Sometimes the recontextualization of text happens quite literally. The introduction, for example, explained that some house signs have been "retired" to a bar in Oxford where they can be viewed by patrons. That a bar is the place where signs are retired is hardly inconsequential to signs' textuality. Indeed, the idea that these signs have a special relationship to some of the activities that go on in a bar will turn out to be quite salient later in the discussion. We can say that signs' physical recontextualization in the bar is indexical of their relationship to consuming alcohol in a social setting.

Other forms of recontextualization occur. Quotes from newspaper stories will recontextualize the names of house signs, rendering them with typographical regularity and depriving them of their stylistic and pictographic flair. I have been doing this since the first page of this book. When anyone talks about house signs and invokes a house name, they recontextualize it, changing its visual form to an acoustic one. When I quote such a person, I recontextualize the name yet again, converting it back into a visual form and changing its relationship to surrounding text, potentially radically. The formation of a text through such processes is what scholars have called entextualization.

Through the processes of entextualization, certain interests, ideas, or goals can come to shape texts and make them particularly appropriate or inappropriate for certain contexts. Whenever texts are recontextualized, new entextualizations are possible, and these are shot through with the possibility of changing dynamics of interpretation and power. Charles Briggs and Richard Bauman explain:

> By choosing to make certain features [of a genre] explicit (and particularly by foregrounding some elements through repetition and metapragmatic framing), producers of discourse actively (re)construct and reconfigure genres. Note the great similarity between the discourse practices associated with the use of genre in shaping entextualization, on the one hand, and the scholarly practices of linguistic anthropologists, literary critics, and the like, on the other: both entail creating classes of texts, selecting and abstracting features, and using this process in creating textual authority. (1992, 148)

Briggs and Bauman see the processes they describe as relevant to every context in which recontextualization occurs, from talk between friends, to interaction that is explicitly staged as a performance, to the representation of folklore in print, whether for lay or scholarly audiences.

Cristina Bacchilega, for example, shows that colonial officials in Hawai'i set about renaming many places, disrupting the indexical relationships between former names and events and historical figures, and entextualizing a post-conquest means of referring to place. Their recontextualizations of place-names were particularly overt—even drastic—in their formal features because they involve a change in language, and in thematics because they grossly simplified the place-names they recontextualized. Bacchilega explains, "In many cases, they [Hawaiian place-names] have been replaced by names that tell or evoke a shorter version of history: Pūowaina has become known as Punchbowl, Pu'uloa has been turned into Pearl Harbor, Āliapa'akai has been converted to the generic salt lake" (2007, 43). What results is that the new names are based on a textual pragmatics of conquest that serves as an index of the colonial event of renaming. Bacchilega acknowledges that simply reverting to former place-names would not bring back pre-conquest Hawai'i, but it would, in her words, "help to challenge and shake settlers' hegemonic approach to land, place, and history in Hawai'i" (2007, 43). What Bacchilega means by hegemonic is that settlers rename places without hesitation because the world encoded by extant place-names is not salient to them.

When a text indexes another text, one speaks of intertextuality. Intertextuality can play an especially important role in entextualization. The indexical relationships between signs and their objects of representation shift when extextualization occurs, and tracing such changes can tell us a great deal about the pragmatic dimension of textuality. What Bacchilega chronicles in the examples above is the disruption of what intertextuality existed between place-names in the past by the replacement of them with much simpler ones in another language. A new intertextuality emerges just as a new way of referring to places in the world is entextualized on the back of the old.

It would be absurd to claim that house signs suffer the same sort of abuse when recontextualized as place-names in Hawai'i. But tracing processes of recontextualization and the discursive interaction that unfolds will tell us a great deal about boundaries and distinctions that separate the house sign community of practice from other people who reflect on house signs as well as within the house sign community of practice.

A return to the example of Che will illustrate the importance of considering technical terms like "decontextualization," "recontextualization," and "entextualization." My colleagues and I became so excited about Che because we believed that the residents had recontextualized the name of Che Guevara, entextualizing the possibility that house signs index residents' leftist revolutionary disposition. The residents had not done so. They had recontextualized the name of the house as they found it, indexing the change in residents with the change in pronunciation from "chay" to "chee." The former house name was already a recontextualization of the name of a man known to the house's residents by a shared experience. In hearing the metafolklore provided by residents, we were learning that our understanding of the house sign as the recontextualization of Che Guevara's name indexed my colleagues and me as very different readers of house signs from the residents of Che. Indeed, after hearing the residents' explanation of the name, one of my students conducting the interview wondered aloud whether anyone not living in the house might understand the context (the bus station in Buffalo) from which the name was recontextualized. In later discussion, we will find out that the answer is no and that the answer is reflected in one of the typical ways in which residents of named houses pronounce judgment on other signs.

Only long after the interview with the residents of Che, however, did it occur to me that the thematic textuality of house signs helps to explain the strangeness of Che. When house names (rendered here in parentheses) contain the names of real people, they are television celebrities such as Gary Coleman, who played Arnold on *Diff'rent Strokes* (Gary Coleman Fan Club), David Hasselhoff, who starred in *Baywatch* (David Hasselhoffbrauhaus), and Pee-wee Herman, a character played by Paul Reubens (Pee-wee's Playhouse). These actors' involvement with the media, especially in roles that have been the butt of many jokes, contrasts with the political involvement of Che Guevara. In addition, the celebrities' names are complemented with descriptors. Thus "fan club" accompanies the mention of Gary Coleman, David Hasselhoff's name serves as the basis for a pun involving a place to consume beer, and the "playhouse" of Pee-wee's show's name is borrowed wholesale. Nevertheless, thematics should not be taken to be a key to understanding house signs. Indeed, themes could not explain the existence of "Che," just its strangeness and lack of resonance beyond its walls. Yet it exists.

Three Entextualizations of House Signs

As my students and I worked through the steps of the project, we began to reflect on our own procedures and understand them in terms of theoretical notions derived from scholarship on the aspects of textuality and on the semiotic properties of language and culture introduced above. Those concepts, when applied to our methods of approaching house signs as meaningful elements of folklore, provided a sense of dynamism in the relationship between our understandings of signs and the changing contexts through which we gained understanding. We came to learn that the relationship between theory and method in field-based research evolves and does so in unanticipated ways. We would realize this most fully only after talking with residents of named houses. But the basis for realizing how a change in context from seminar room to interview situation would be so important to issues of entextualization was formed early on.

After photographing the house signs, we brainstormed about what they might be about. Themes such as those grouping house names in Table 2.2 quickly emerged. In fact, what we were doing was creating a community of practice of our own, generating our own metafolklore and entextualizing the signs in our own particular way. We enjoyed finding intertextual links. To do this required what Dan Ben-Amos noted about the process of decontextualization entailed in the collection of folklore:

> The collection of things requires a methodological abstraction of objects from their actual context. No doubt this can be done; often it is essential for research purposes. Nevertheless, this abstraction is only methodological and should not be confused with, or substituted for, the true nature of the entities. (1972, 9)

Perhaps we did not pay a great deal of attention to the fact that we were engaged in the process Ben-Amos describes because we believed that we must share the community of practice of the residents of named houses.

One might ask how it was that we could make such an assumption given that we did not live in named houses ourselves. We noted that many signs are themselves intertextual with texts that we had no problem identifying. These texts, in fact, made up part of our world as much as they made up the world of those living in named houses. For example, we were familiar with features of a small American town and Oxford in particular. We were also familiar with much of the media and product titles used in the signs. As a result, we knew that West High Life corresponded with Miller beer and the western side of Oxford, Poplar Cherry drew on its location on Poplar Street and invoked a sexual double entendre dealing with virginity, and Precinct 109 "Spread 'Em" invoked a police station with its name and picture of a police badge.

As the number of such associations we were able to identify grew, we became confident we could understand house signs as texts by noting that they provide a physical space on which messages and images index different locations or practices, some emergent from the students' lifeworlds of renting houses, attending college, or throwing parties, and others emergent from the more mundane lifeworlds of street names, policing the town, or cautioning motorists and pedestrians. We reasoned that because we largely shared that lifeworld, we could assume that the residents saw their signs as indexing that lifeworld in the same ways we did. We were confident that the ways in which we were entextualizing the signs—such that themes emerged as their most significant feature—were similar to the ways in which residents entextualized them. That is to say, we came to see the themes as house signs' most important pragmatic dimension. Confined to the seminar room, we agreed that residents of named houses put up their signs to display and create intertextual linkages between themes.

Before describing the next stage of the project in which we began to interview residents, it is important to note how a few others have entextualized

FIGURE 2.10. Precinct 109

house signs. Two more examples show that entextualization can vary radically such that signs can live different lives in different contexts. Just before moving away from Oxford, I visited friends who worked in the university's bookstore. They showed me a copy of a book published by its author, Reginald D. Olson. The book's title was *Please Sign In (A Study of Oxford House Signs: Pointing to Students' Values)*. Olson identified fifteen themes.

Olson's themes are listed in reverse order of preponderance. From 1998 to 2000, for example, he notes that 0.6 percent of house signs belonged to an "Undetermined Theme" and 15 percent of house signs belonged to "Sexual Relationships." Thus Olson joined us in finding themes to be an especially salient aspect of house signs. Indeed, his creation of categories and sorting methods were more exhaustive than our own (2000).

A less prominent aspect of Olson's publication is a survey that he sent to students and nonstudents (2000, 13). He devotes a mere page to the survey, but its importance to exploring the pragmatic dimension of textuality of house signs is enormous. He reports receiving 108 responses of which 16 were male students, 56 female students, 1 student of unspecified gender, 18 male nonstudents, 10 female nonstudents, and 7 nonstudents of unspecified gender. Olson reports, "Our survey respondents were asked why students put up house

Table 2.3. Themes and the First Six Examples from Reginald Olson's *Please Sign In*

Theme	Examples
· Undetermined	Blue Nerpis, Lesotho, Railroad Brakeman
· Restaurants	Precinct, Wigwam, Shadynook, Distractions, Waffle House, White Castle
· Relaxation	Lazy Daze, Halfway House, Paid Vacation, Chill Inn, Sleep Inn, Main Event
· Educational	Pleiades, Unfinished Business, Undecided, Ivy League, Procrastinate Inn, Inncoherent
· Religious	At Church and Almost High, Casa del Soul, Refuge, Sanctuary, Steeple Chase, Vineyard
· Women	Chick Inn, Fox Den, Petticoat, Little Women, Tiny Size Chicklets, Hooterville
· Television or Movies	Dirty Dozen, South of the Border, Casa del Soul, Treasure Island, Castle Grayskull, Casa Blanca
· Music	After Midnight, Boardwalk, Boogie Nights, Copa-Cabana, 8 Daze a Week, Gimme Shelter
· Location	At Church and Almost High, Beech Pit, Da Vine House, Drinkmore, Home Plate, Main Event
· Living Quarters	Boxed Inn, Buzz Inn, Chick Inn, Chill Inn, Come Back Inn, Crammed Inn
· Recreation	Reckless Abandon, Dogg Pound, End Zone, Game On, Hut Hut, Heisman
· Feature of the House or the Lot	Blue Lagoon, Blue Moon, Casa Blanca, Castle Grayskull, Jade Lounge, Jaundice
· Mental State	Adult, Cosmopolitan, Dogg Pound, High Maintenance, Inn Pursuit, Ivy League
· Alcohol and Drug Usage	Absolut Angels, Absolut Chaos, Alka Hall, Blue Moon, Bourbon County, Champagne
· Sexual Relationships	Boogie Nights, Bottoms Up, Come Back Inn, Face Time, Four Play, Game On

signs." He lists the answers of 10 respondents, but does not mention how these were selected. The results are as follows with the respondent number followed by that respondent's answers:

> (1): tells what tenants are like, because of insecurity, for amusement, because they are bored, builds pride, they can't read house numbers, territoriality "as a dog uses a fire hydrant," for a party theme, as an act of rebellion; (2): to appeal to opposite sex, for bagel or pizza delivery, so they can get robbed; (4): gets attention; (6): for group identity and cohesion; (8): mark of character, personalized; (19): for tradition; (21): no answer given; (23): to be creative; (31): to be fun, humorous, cute, cool; and (48): to identify (help find) house. (Olson 2000, 14)

Given the importance of context in considerations of the pragmatic dimension of textuality, one might want to know more about the responses than Olson tells us. For example, knowing which of the respondents was a student and which a nonstudent might be very helpful. I had the sense, for example, that all of the respondents whose answers have been listed are not students. Number one uses words like "tenants," "insecurity," "amusement," "territoriality," and "rebellion" that index a stance that is not in keeping with what we heard in interviews. Perhaps, in some cases, when asked to fill out a questionnaire, students used a different set of descriptors because they felt that literacy demanded a different means of expression—what scholars of language call a register—than an interview context. One just cannot be sure given the information that Olson provides.

Even more important to the larger argument about textuality, however, is that the notion of theme nearly fades from view in the responses. Much more important in the answers are the uses of house signs to prompt or assist in social interactions such as having parties, facilitating food delivery, and finding a house. Other possibilities are related to the signs' ability to focus the attention of others, whether for the subversive effects of "an act of rebellion" or the pleasing effects of attracting "the opposite sex." Yet other possibilities reflect an aesthetic achievement on the part of those displaying the sign including being "creative" and being "fun, humorous, cute, cool." The only answer that invokes a theme qualifies the theme's relevance to a social occasion, a party. According to Olson's questionnaire results, themes seem to be relatively unimportant when students and nonstudents are asked why residents put up house signs. Olson's questionnaire results, while comparatively neglected in his book, actually reflect many of the uses of signs that students claim to be important in the interviews.

A third way in which Olson characterizes house signs is by arguing that they reflect values deemed to be typical of freshmen. Drawing from the survey conducted by the Cooperative Institutional Research Program of the American Council on Education entitled *The American Freshman: National Norms for Fall 1998,* Olson argues that house signs reflect many of the values identified in the study. He finds that the content of house signs reflects the following values on the part of residents of named houses: entertainment and recreational stimulation, relaxation, playing the adult role, bonding with others, sense of location, sense of certainty, and attainment of education. He goes on to argue that the acts of designing, producing, erecting, and defending of house signs reflect the following values: conformity, creativity, identity, preservation, rebellion against authority, civic responsibility, and mainstreaming (2000, 70).

Olson thus entextualizes house signs in three ways based on themes, responses to a questionnaire, and values. Each of these emerges in an intertextual relationship with a different text. The intertextual partner of themes is the house signs and all the items of local and popular culture with which they engage intertextually. The intertextual partner of the question "why do students put up house signs?" is the results of the questionnaire. The intertextual partner of values expressed by the signs is the survey conducted by the Cooperative Institutional Research Program. These intertextual sources make it rather obvious that the three entextualizations involve different perspectives, means of interpretation, and people.

Olson's study does teach us something extremely valuable that we would learn only after leaving the seminar room: when residents of named houses reflect on house signs, themes do not emerge as their most prominent aspect. Unfortunately, however, one is not told how to understand the relationships between the three ways of configuring house signs. We have already noted that themes, Olson's first entextualization of house signs, cannot account for the ways in which students and nonstudents reflect on the importance of house signs, Olson's second entextualization. Some of the values offered, Olson's third entextualization, seem relevant indeed, but one is left wondering what part they play in the production and display of house signs. Some are so broad that nearly any human activity might fit. When interviews are considered below, most of the values will disappear entirely. Yet another objection to attributing values to house signs is that the term "values" is a word relatively alien to our interviews. Words culled from Olson's questionnaire such as "fun," "cute," and "cool" are more at home. The term "values" itself indexes its source as being distant from the context described. Indeed, at the end of his book, Olson is explicit that his project is to rectify an image of students as "valueless." If the context of themes is the house sign and the context of responses is the questionnaire, the context of values seems to be Olson's own polemical desire to redeem students and their signs. He concludes: "We have reviewed some of the values which house signs demonstrate. Who said that students don't have any values?" (2000, 71). Olson does not provide an answer to this question or tell us why it might be important. That students should have values is left as a foregone conclusion.

I came to know a third entextualization of house signs while conducting the project. Some colleagues approached me after a public presentation to tell me it had given them the idea of integrating the project on house signs into the freshman orientation program. Missing the point entirely, I observed that students generally do not move into named houses until after their second year. My colleagues explained that they were not concerned with the particulars of who names the houses, but rather had found many of the signs to be racist or sexist, and they thought that contemplating the signs might help freshmen understand the prevalence and dangers of racism and sexism.

I expressed my reticence, explaining that our institutional review board approval stated that house residents would be assured that we would not be judging them in terms of whether their signs were racist or sexist. It then occurred to me to mention that faculty members could make their case without the kind of research that brought us into students' homes. Finally, it dawned on me to ask the question that I should have asked initially: "Which signs strike you as particularly racist or sexist?" They replied that Plantation is racist and Octopussy is sexist.

I explained that we too had taken special note of these two signs but that I would be very uncomfortable vilifying the residents in an organized orientation activity. I explained that in many interviews, students had claimed that Plantation simply reflected the way the house looked but that I was skeptical. We had not yet interviewed the residents. I did tell them, however, that we had interviewed the residents of Octopussy and that I had been surprised to discover that they were women. The colleagues were aghast, and one of the women asked, "Why would any woman want to do that to herself?" I replied that one of the points of the course I was teaching was that one cannot rely solely on a name, an expression, or any chunk of discourse without attending to its context, including the ways in which those who would interpret it are situated in relationship to it. I had the feeling that my colleagues felt that I was being evasive and would not take a stand on the issue.

Indeed, I am not trying to argue that house signs are free of racism or sexism. But I do want to point out that my colleagues had entextualized these signs in a particular way such that discovering that the residents of Octopussy were women came as a shock. This simple discovery was enough to disrupt my colleagues' understanding of the sign as sexist. That is why I was unwilling to submit our classes' experience with house signs to the effort my colleagues had in mind.

Interviews: Moving into the House Sign Community of Practice

The example of Che and the responses to Reginald Olson's questionnaire about house signs show that members of the house sign community of practice do not primarily focus on themes when reflecting on the meanings of house signs. What do people living in named houses find important about house signs? Answering this question, of course, necessitates an analytic shift from semiotic relations presented within visual language to interpretive practices by which subjects render signs meaningful. The example of my colleagues' understanding of the house sign for Che demonstrates that practices and beliefs taken by just any onlooker to be indexed by a house sign are unreliable indicators of the "interpretive frames" that made signs salient to the house sign community of practice in our interviews (Hanks 1993, 130). Put another way, residents of named houses rarely invoked construals such as those presented in Table 2.2 to interpret house signs, confirming Joseph Errington's 1985 observation that speakers' reflections on a phenomenon consistently fail to include the full range of its indexical relationships. My colleagues' understanding of Che shows that some people can find significance in a house sign in a manner far afield of what members of the community of practice find. In turn, the interpretations that members of the community of practice recount show that they do not include the full range of what is found on house signs.

Just as people produce metafolklore when they characterize folklore or interject it into some new context, people produce metapragmatic reflection when they characterize the pragmatic dimension of some phenomenon, in this case folklore. Across interviews, residents consistently claimed that house signs should be or do a limited number of things. In the parlance of Michael Silverstein (1993), the ways in which residents claim that house signs should be read or found significant are "overtly metapragmatic," because they describe the effects that house signs ought to accomplish. Jeff Titon asserts that the metapragmatic dimension of folklore is salient in current scholarship. He explains that scholars are no longer just interested in the texts collected by and generated in the study of folklore because "questions having to do with the uses of tradition, with tradition-bearers' own ideas about folklore, with folklore as it is experienced in human consciousness are the more interesting questions today" (2003, 81). When brought to the residents of Oxford's named houses, Titon's emphasis on "tradition-bearers' own ideas" reveals three concerns.

First, students consistently explained that referring to a house's name is much easier than referring to its address. A practice that occurred in every interview was a student's mention of an actual address of the student's own or some other house or a student's typification of an address (e.g., 123 So-and-so Street). Subsequently, the student would explain that the use of the house name was an easier or more efficient way of referring to a house than using its address. When one of the interviewers would ask about typical scenarios in which such references occur, residents offered the identification of their places of residence, the invitation to others to visit, and the identification of the location of a party.

A resident of Oxford Circus reflects on the practice:

SUE: I mean you never say we're going to Fou::r Twe::lve East Main, because people will say where the heck's that at, but if you say the house name they know

A resident of Hot Box explains that referring to house names is more entertaining than simply using an address:

BRENDA: I just think it's better to have a na::me for a hou::se than be like, I'm going to 20 East Spring or whatever, as opposed to I'm going to Hot Box or, pick a name

The residents of Freshmen O Rientation claim to be a landmark.

JIM: so like every weekend, we're **around** our house you know, having fun, and yeah, people stop by and it's like, **we'll** have a party just about like every Friday and Saturday night

BETH: I have to admit **I've** sat on that corner waiting for people, it's like oh yeah, meet me at Freshmen O Rientation, on the corner, yeah

BOB: we're a landmark

ALL: #

BETH: you **are** a landmark(3) do you think there's other houses around town that people think are landmarks

JIM: well I definitely think Ivy League's a landmark 'cause I know at the beginning of the year that's how we told people where our house is, yeah we live down right across from Ivy League

Beth, the interviewer, offers her own experience of referring to the residents' house name as a location to coordinate her activities with others. The residents use the term "landmark" to incorporate her short example into a wider claim of being well known. The residents of Freshmen O Rientation go on to explain that initially they used The Ivy League, a house predating their own, to explain where their house was. The implication is that they no longer have to do this as they too have become a landmark.

Second, residents of named houses judged house signs to be either clever or dumb. It was impossible to determine why residents judged some signs to be clever. Many interviewees explained that their approval was due to personal preference. Much more consistent was the rationale for declaring a house sign to be dumb, weird, or gay. On several occasions, interviewers asked for an explanation of "gay." Respondents claimed that the term means strange and, therefore, has no relationship to sexual identity. Residents consistently remarked that dumb, weird, or gay signs are those whose cleverness must be a private joke shared among its house's residents. This characterization, in turn, fits nicely with the way that many residents elaborated on the universal "clever." Typical elaborations included "you know, they're funny," "they are just fun," and "the trick is not to take it too seriously."

The residents of Inncoherent know little about who coined the house name, but explain that they have kept the sign because it is clever. John asks about the origin of the house's name:

JOHN: did you guys pick the name Inncoherent

KELLY: no

JOHN: so it was handed down to you guys

KELLY: yes

JOHN: um, do you know why they made it up

KELLY: do you know why [addressing another resident]

JANE: I think it just sticks because it's clever, because of the "inn," **you know** just . . .

JOHN: do you know how lo::ng it's been the name

KELLY: I think for a while
CHERYL: yeah, I think for about five years
KELLY: I'd say even more than that(3)
JANE: so we don't know how long, it's going to be a guys' house next year

The residents explain that the longevity and cleverness of the sign go hand in hand. Indeed, the two qualities emerged in many interviews, and the relationship between age and cleverness was taken to be self-explanatory.

The residents of Deez Nutz explain that they did not change their name when they moved in because of their own lack of cleverness. Thus they confirm the idea that a house sign should be clever by explaining that they lack the quality that might lead to a change in their sign. Sam begins in a typical way by asking about its origins:

SAM: OK. alright, we::ll, your guys', sign is, Deez Nutz, uh. first of all where did it, where did it come from. d'you guys know.
NICK: uh, I think it's actually been in uh . . . it's been **named** this for almost ten years, I think . . . it was about when The Chronic came up by Dr. Dre, I would assu::me, the name's taken from and it's just been pa::ssed o::n ever since, it's kind of a unique name so. We actually thought about changing it last year but it didn't happen 'cause everybody already knew where it was 'n stuff like that so it was **ea**sily recognizable
SAM: yeah, what were you guys thinking about changing it to::, any ideas
NICK: ⌈u::h, not really, that was another reason why we didn't change. uh, a lot of the good ones are taken 'n we're not clever, so we couldn't really think of anything funny to come up with, so we decided to stick with what we ha::d
ALL: ⌊#
BILL: stick with what we had . . .

Though they can trace the name to a specific musical source and can name the performer and album from which the song title came, the origin does not seem to be particularly important to the current residents. Nick claims the knowledge indirectly with the use of the verb "assume." Most important to the fact that the house name has a specific origin seems to be that it is unique. In other words, no one else has used it. This and the fact that the name is venerable and well known seem to be its most valuable qualities to the residents.

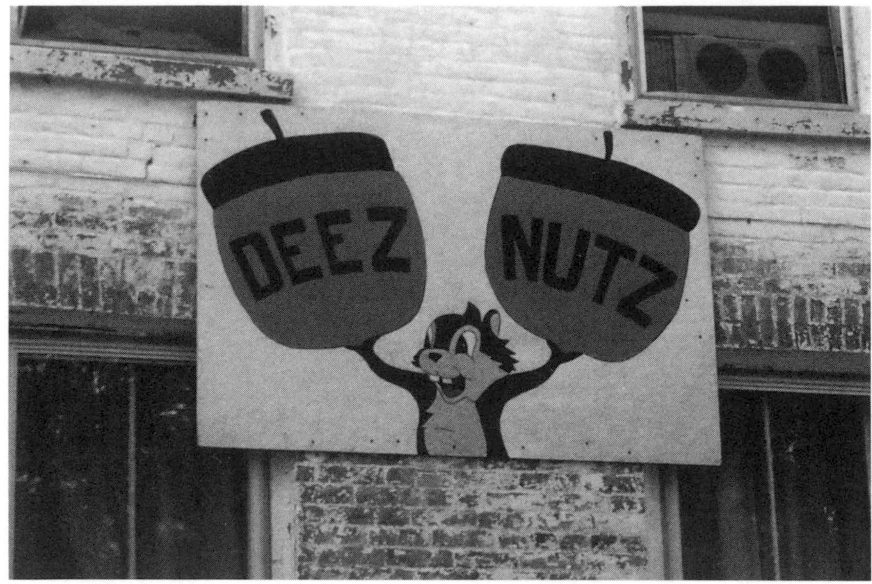

FIGURE 2.11. Deez Nutz

When the interviewer asks about the double entendre of the sign, the residents further distance themselves from its thematic possibilities.

SAM: u::h hm . . . uh the **name** Deez Nutz isn't talkin' about acorns actually. ⌈ what's behind that name
BILL: ⌊#
NICK: just that we don't really care about anything. I d'know. we're not like. we're just . . . I mean not that we don't care about anything but it's kind of just like, it's a very lai::d-ba::ck attitude around here all the ti::me, nobody gets really uptight or worried about anything, I mean we're here for **school** 'n everything bu::t. there's a lot more to college besides classes and everything, we try to make the best out of what we do::

Rather than addressing the issue of the double entendre, Nick talks about the more general point that the residents "don't really care about anything." Nick quickly qualifies this point, seemingly recognizing that such a strong and absolute statement is indeed indicative of a strong stance and in conflict with the statement itself. What emerges is an opposition between "laid-back," on the one hand, and "uptight" and "worried," on the other. The house sign, according to this explanation, indexes the laid-back ambience of the house and its residents. It would seem that the description, in some sense, is a response to the interviewer's question about the possibilities of the double entendre. Perhaps calling attention to the house name differentiates one from the resident who does not get uptight and worried enough to notice.[11]

In the interview with Beech Bunnies, the residents contrast the house sign's potential to be "cheesy" with the risk of its indication that the residents are sexually promiscuous.

BARB: we thought Beech Bunnies, and we don't want to just put a bunny on our house
CASS: like an Easter bunny
BARB: yeah, that would be real cheesy, so . . .
BONNIE: Barb thought of Beech Bunnies and Cass thought let's put a Playboy bunny on the sign(3)
ELLA: and Colleen Bonnie and Ella were a little nervous at first
ALL: #
ELLA: about people thinking we might be prostitutes of some sort, but then we decided that it was just cute and funny so . . .
COLLEEN: uh, how do you like, how do you think sexuality played a part in this. was that really an issue or just . . .
ELLA: I think right at first I was kind of nervous about that, but then I thought that was just silly because it's just for fun

The residents explain that after some reflection they found that the cute and funny qualities of the house sign obviated the sign's potential to index their own sexual behavior. The image of the Playboy bunny and its double entendre's potential to be cute and funny outweighed the Easter bunny's potential to be cheesy.

BARB: yeah 'cause we all thought, should we really show this to our grandparents, but we all think it's cute so it's just, we're in college and . . .
CASS: some people say oh you live in the Playboy house, and we say, well it's ⌈not
ALL: ⌊#
CASS: the Playboy house, and then other people say oh that's really cute, so, I don't know, some people may think it's stupid that we have a Playboy bunny, but . . .

COLLEEN: do your parents have an attitude about the sign
BONNIE: we don't care
CASS: it's not offensive, no
BONNIE: they don't worry about it, they know where it's at, my dad actually made the sign

Cass does differentiate understandings of the sign as "the Playboy house" versus "cute." One might be tempted to understand Cass's statement to invoke a differentiation of sexuality and cuteness, perhaps a lack of seriousness. But Cass invokes the notion that signs are clever or dumb when she explains, "Some people may think it's stupid that we have a Playboy bunny." Colleen reintroduces kin in order to ask about the effects of signs on particular onlookers, but Bonnie and Cass claim a laissez-faire stance. Bonnie then surprises Colleen with the claim that her father manufactured the sign.

Residents singled out The Dresden in several interviews, adding such comments as "I just don't get it" and "it's weird." When we interviewed The Dresden residents, I discovered firsthand what it is to be an outsider of the house sign community of practice. I asked them whether the matchbook pictured on the sign intersected the linguistic elements "Dresden" and "Night" (of "Get a Night Life") to create an index to the bombing of the German city during World War II (Figure 2.12). They responded that the house sign had "nothing to do" with the war. The house's name was inspired by a popular movie, *Swingers,* wherein various characters frequent a bar called The Dresden. In addition to the sign they have anchored to the house, the residents have hung a large commercial poster in their living room that depicts the movie's bar scene. Each member of the house has found a character in the movie with which his habits—especially his favorite drinks—resonate. Residents reported that sometimes they employ their roommates' movie names, especially when talking about upcoming parties or favorite beverages. In keeping with the notion that house sign activity must be considered as emergent from a community of practice, one might explain it thus: residents of other houses do not understand the basis upon which The Dresden might be judged as creative.

And third, residents consistently characterized the messages displayed by house signs to be about sex, drugs, and alcohol. Several interviewees invoked one house sign in particular, Witty House Name (Preferably with a Drug, Sex, and/or Alcohol Reference). One resident explained that the sign was referring to other house signs.

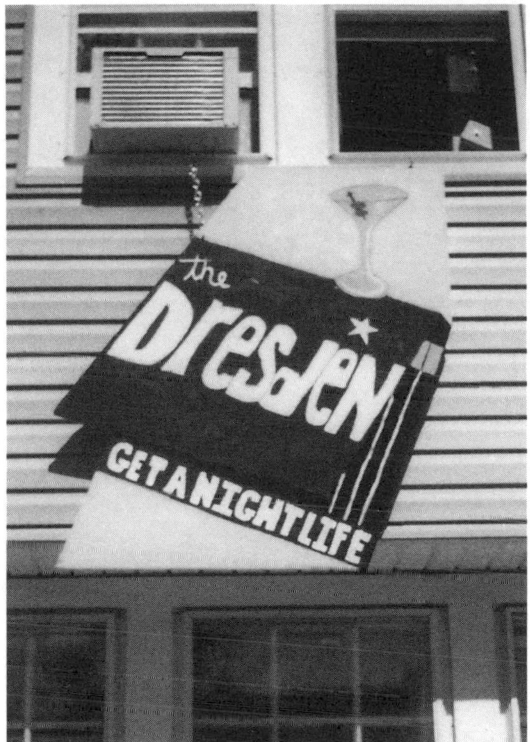

FIGURE 2.12. The Dresden

JOE: I think that we're trying to . . . just make fun of house names, all other house names. yeah, just the formula they use to **name** the houses, yep . . .

SEAN: I think it's coo::l because it just brings attention to the **structure** that everybody uses to create their house sign, the drinking and sex

PETE: well, do you think, kind of in not using the same structure you define the formula, as you said, for creating the house sign

MIKE: the way **I** look at it is that we've just stripped it down, to::, like what their formula, like what's on our sign **is** the formula. for a house name

SEAN: except in terms of some pop culture

PETE: yeah, a little variation

SEAN: but it's the same structure

FIGURE 2.13. Witty House Name

Even so, partying was offered across interviews to cover the ubiquitous mention of sex, drugs, and alcohol. By using words like "formula" and "structure" to characterize their house sign relative to others, the residents of Witty House Name make obvious their house's metacultural disposition. The words seem to invoke a register of analysis. Indeed, Sean even notes that the sign ignores pop culture.

Pat, a resident of Boutique Hall, uses house signs as ice breakers in conversation and an index of the proclivity of house residents to party:

> PAT: I don't think you judge the people based on their house sign, but you get an idea of what kind of people they're like or how much they party, what they're into, what their sense of humor's like.

The residents of Come-N-Go make the connection between a house and the proclivity to party more assertively:

> STEPH: I would say that people with signs tend to **have** more parties than people who **don't** have signs
>
> RACHEL: yeah
>
> STEPH: except, maybe people in apartment complexes(5)

STEVEN: do you guys feel this has anything to do with the image, that having a sign on your house, portrays, like, you know, like you always think of a house sign, a party house, do you think that also reinforces the fact that they **have** parties

CINDY: I think it has to do with personality, like I think people that, are **mo::re** like(2) outgo . . . not necessarily like more outgoing, like, the more like, people tend to throw parties, and the same people have to, like have the personality, and(2) whether it be outgoing or(2) drugs or alc . . . I mean, whatever, like, I think

STEPH: I think all you got to do is have a house sign, have a party, and(2) there you go

CINDY: a party reputation is born that way

RACHEL: I would say it's like the outgoing thing, but at the same time, if you're not outgoing at all and you're incredibly lazy and you move into a house that's already named, you're not like, you're not outgoing, but you're too lazy to take it down, so

CINDY: like I look at a house that has a sign as the norm, not like the minority of the houses, and like, I go to a house that doesn't have a sign, and like, I go where's your sign. don't you want to have fun

STEPH: are you guys planning to have a party

RACHEL: that's the norm

An Extended Example

The residents of For Sale differ from others, including those living in Che and The Dresden, because they seem very dissatisfied with the name of their own house. Furthermore, they are dismissive of the inclusion on house signs of the two major elements said to comprise a party: sex and alcohol. Many of the residents' ideas diverge from notions taken for granted in other interviews. Yet, despite these differences, the residents of For Sale orient their comments toward many of the same ideas held by others. Indeed, they make explicit that they have entangled themselves in a number of contradictions. The interview shows that the residents who have atypical opinions about what makes a good house sign largely agree with everyone else about the ways in which the signs should be interpreted.

The residents of For Sale give answers that diverge from those typical in interviews with residents of named houses.

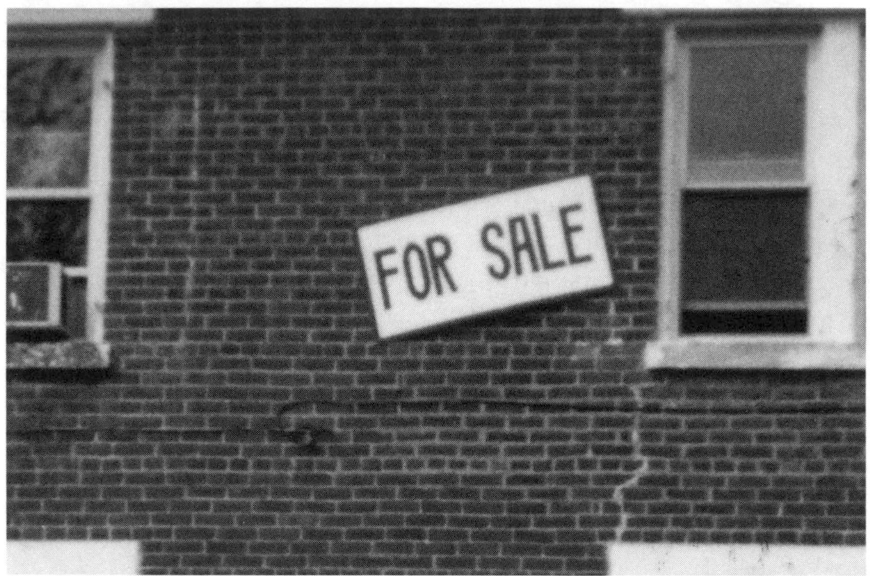

FIGURE 2.14. For Sale

CHRIS: and what was the house's name when you guys moved here

TIM: what was . . . it was previously known as Usual Suspects after the movie(5)

CHRIS: and why did you change the name

TIM: Mr. X [euphemism coined by Tim to address Matt without using his name]

MATT: oh, I'm answering it

TIM: yeah.

MATT: we thought it was very unoriginal. you can't just take a . . . a hou . . . a like a like a mo::vie

TIM: unless it's like a . . . a famous name of a house, like for example Morning Wood seems like a ⌈house

MATT: ⌊no no no no that's what I'm saying, that's not a movie title

TIM: ⌈OK

MATT: ⌊that's not a movie title, you shouldn't use a movie title 'cause it's not very original. so we went for something that didn't make us look like big lo::sers

DALE: or perverts(5)

MATT: yeah and it was kind of funny mainly because our house is a giant piece of **shi::t**, so we thought this was appropriate 'cause it looks like it should be **sold** or **torn down**(3)

Tim indicates that Matt has particularly strong opinions about the former house name by assigning him a turn to answer Chris's second question. Matt's answer comes as a surprise. In many interviews, residents explained that a good way to be clever or funny without relegating a house's name to an inside joke was to borrow or pun on a movie title. Octopussy, for example, was frequently offered in response to questions about a favorite name. Yet Matt argues that the name Usual Suspects was not original precisely because its origin was a movie title. Tim adds a clumsy rejoinder, countering that the fame of the house name might trump the lack of originality. When Tim gives an example, however, the name's origin is not a movie title. Matt points this out and intimates that using a movie title for a house name makes the residents look like "big losers." Dale, silent until now, adds, "Or perverts." The descriptor seems to follow Tim's lead of offering Morning Wood with its sexual basis. Matt explains that the sign complements the house's dilapidated condition.

Chris then asks what house name would indicate that the residents were perverts or alcoholics. Chris's addition is interesting in that the theme of alcohol had not been raised in the interview prior to his introducing it. Chris was, no doubt, completing the pair always mentioned in interviews when residents described a party. I believe that Chris's introduction of alcoholics was in recognition of a widespread means of characterizing parties rather than a gratuitous change in the subject of the interview because of what ensues after he introduces the term.

CHRIS: what kind of name d'you think would render you:: perverts or alcoholics(2)

DALE: u::h there's a number of names on campus that are pretty ridiculous I think. anything relating to:: sexual organs, genita::lia, positions. anything that relates to like, hooking up with freshme::n. the stuff that's just kind of like alright guys that's just not very like, very like fu::ny(2) it's kind of like going over the top(2)

MATT: such as, **Li::quor Juggs**

DALE: yeah, Liquor Juggs

TIM: not saying that it's bad, that's one that's really funny, I still walk by and laugh

DALE: I just kind of think it's, I don't know I think it's kind of weird, so . . .

MATT: I just don't want to be known as that, like cree::py guy.

DALE: or Moi::st for example

MATT: there's a house called Moist

DALE: there's a house called Moist

MATT: I like it

DALE: I just think it's . . . it's just stupid

MATT: **so**, we've kind of matured by, by now.

This is the second time that the house's residents present themselves as an exception to residents of most named houses. Dale seems to fail to feel that the humor in the sign itself or the lighthearted disposition of its reader trumps the sign's sexual nature. In fact, he makes explicit that sexual signs are not funny. He invokes the metaphor of "going over the top" to characterize transgression. Matt complements Dale's explanation by offering an example that Dale reiterates. Tim contradicts Dale's explanation, however, intimating that the sign is funny and therefore not bad. Dale and Matt proceed to tie the name to the idea that a sign can reflect its inhabitants' perversion by arguing that the name is weird and makes a resident "that . . . creepy guy." Generally in interviews, "weird" served as a synonym for "dumb" or "gay" and not "creepy." Dale offers Moist as another example, but this time Matt replies, "I like it." Whether he means to disagree or means to be sarcastic is not evident. When Dale claims that Moist is stupid, Matt introduces the notion that the residents of For Sale have matured.

Chris picks up the idea of maturity and uses it as the basis of his next question.

CHRIS: and as freshmen what did you think of the signs(4)

MATT: I think some of them were interesting, I mean I actually didn't give a lot of thought to it. but if a house had a good name like I'd chuckle a bit

DALE: I thought they were even funnier than I do now 'cause I was a freshman, and I thought everything was like really coo::l and funny

ALL: #

CHRIS: what's your favorite house sign on campus(4)

MATT: aw man, I can't even . . . nothing comes to mind actually
DALE: um(5)
TIM: I think Morning Wood, I think that's pretty funny, and I know that falls into the sexual category . . . but there's something funny about it.
DALE: I like the Dee::z Nutz house with the squirrel holding up two giant acorns. yeah, that's ⌈one of my . . .
TIM: ⌊I guess we're like contradicting ourselves
DALE: I I I still think it's ⌈funny
TIM: ⌊yeah . . . **I just wouldn't** I wouldn't want to be associated with that house
DALE: I think it's, yeah, I think it's funny, I think it's creative but I wouldn't want to be associated with that ⌈house
MATT: ⌊ri::ght
DALE: but Dee::z Nutz isn't really bad
MATT: right
DALE: I think, I think it's funny. I don't know I don't know
TIM: most of the houses on campus have some sort of **sexual** innuendo, so . . .
DALE: except for ours
MATT: except For Sale
DALE: except For Sale(4)

In response to Chris's question about the impressions of house signs as freshmen, Matt is noncommittal while Dale lampoons the enthusiasm of freshmen. When he states, "I thought everything was like really cool and funny," he lengthens "cool" significantly. By thinking thus about everything, he presents his past self as overeager. Everyone present finds this claim funny. When Chris asks about the residents' favorite sign on campus, they are initially silent. Tim offers a sexual sign and notes the fact, and Dale follows with another. Tim notes the contradiction between their earlier dismissal of sexual signs and their offer of the same as funny. Tim differentiates finding a house's sign funny and residing in the house, claiming that he would not want the latter. Dale concurs. Dale then claims that Deez Nutz isn't really bad, and Matt concurs, but neither explains why. Tim claims that most house signs involve sex when Dale and Matt mention For Sale as an exception. This seems to follow the earlier-stated aversion to living in a house with a sexual sign.

The third way in which the residents of For Sale differ from most residents of named houses emerges when Chris focuses attention on the perception of others. No one else interviewed claimed to hate a sign, especially their own. Indeed, such an opinion conflicts with the lighthearted attitude that is supposed to judge the merits or lack thereof of signs. They should emerge as clever or dumb; one should not love or hate them.

CHRIS: how do you think other people perceive your house name
DALE: I think everyone **hates** the name of our house personally. including my**self**
TIM: personally I never **wanted** this house ⌈name
DALE: ⌊yeah I for one, also . . . we had a **vote** to see what the house name would be. I voted agai::nst it thou::gh
TIM: what what I mean what was your ⌈third house name
DALE: ⌊I don't know, I don't know what it was
TIM: **mine** was . . .
MATT: it would be, it would be too hard, you would actually have to have a ⌈visual understanding of it
DALE: ⌊ri::ght
MATT: ⌈that's right
TIM: ⌊but it was, well it was(2) it was going to be uh(3) uh called Alcohol(2) but it was going to be one of those signs you see around the freshmen dorms like Morris Hall, Reed Hall but it was going to be called Alco space Hall and I thought it would be creative, yet clever, but it would make us look like a bunch of drunks. I'm not saying I'm **not**(2) but maybe I shouldn't . . .
MATT: that's another ⌈thing
TIM: ⌊I don't know how my parents would feel ⌈about it
DALE: ⌊I uh, I uh think the sign **is** a creative idea, but at the same time I think not only is sexual innu . . . innuen . . . innuendo uh . . . houses kind of get on my nerves after a while. also houses that imply how drunk people are in the house also **really** bother me. just like **look how crazy we are**, we get drunk **a::ll** the time. we're **cra::zy**
TIM: **woo::**

DALE: you know, and it's like, oh that's great
MATT: like name your house Inebriated
DALE: yeah, it's . . . sometimes you're like . . . it's . . .

Chris then asks about a common notion across interviews that has been subverted in various parts of his interview with For Sale. The residents immediately contradict many of the notions they have been arguing thus far and fall into line with typical residents.

CHRIS: do you think the house sign should correspond to the people inside of it
MATT: nah
TIM: no, it's really not that big of a deal as long as it's kind of funny(2)
DALE: I think it's just a tradition at school. I don't think anyone in their right mind should give too much thought about it.
TIM: also, I live with so many weird fucks that I don't think we could find one sign that matches all of our personalities
DALE: speak for yourself
TIM: I want you to use that quote. I live with so many weird fucks(5)
CHRIS: # what were some of the other names that were being tossed around that you guys considered
MATT: oh, Dale(3) is one, uh, um(2) what else was there
DALE: I can't . . . oh Lo::ck Bo::x.
MATT: Lock Box # that would make a pretty ⌈good . . .
DALE: ⌊what else
TIM: see what I actually wanted to call our house was For Sale, but under it put By Boner instead of By Owner
DALE: yeah
TIM: I thought that would be funny, but then then then comes in the sexual meaning though. just to have boner on the sign I think would be good(3)
DALE: um, I can't remember the suggestions. there was a . . . there was a big array, we kind of like brainstormed for a while on paper. we kind of had preliminary voting rounds. it came down to like three or four final decisions

The interview with the residents of For Sale is particularly important because they contradict many of the typical ways that residents claim signs should be read. They seem to differ from residents of other houses, and be an anomaly. Yet, as they talk, they either orient themselves toward or simply come to align themselves with typical ideas. They decry the use of movie titles, but acknowledge that signs should be clever. Though it is not a movie title, the offer of "lock box" has its origins in the media world. They decry the presence of sex and alcohol on signs, but claim to like Liquor Juggs, a sign involving both sex and alcohol. They make a distinction between looking at a sign and living in a named house, but proceed to argue that a house sign's play blocks its potential to reflect the actions and attitudes of house residents. The idea that house signs are funny, especially sexual ones, emerges to render the residents of For Sale to be fairly typical.

The textuality of house signs can be explored in three ways. Each informs the others. Houses have names, and these names are short and full of punning and double entendres. These names do cluster into recognizable themes, but many lie outside of those themes. When the uses of house signs are considered, house names become entangled in patterns of interpretation and activity practiced differently by person and/or group. Signs, for example, can be indicative of the fact that students have values or that many signs are racist and sexist. When the people who created or inherited signs are asked, they explain that signs are easier to use than an address, that they are either "clever" or "dumb," and that they indicate the proclivity to party. Does this exhaust what house signs do or how they might be read? Addressing this question is the task of the rest of this book.

CHAPTER THREE

Inn Pursuit . . . of Christ: The Unevenness of Agency

> The right to bestow names is a right which signifies that the namer has power. That said, it is not always the case that individuals who are given the right to bestow names are the most powerful in more general terms across society.
>
> —VALERIE ALIA, *Names and Nunavut*

Though the argument thus far has been that residents of named houses are unanimous in their belief that house signs should be clever, are easier to remember than the house's street address, and indicate activities within that can be summed up as "partying," there are more subtle boundaries between groups of residents delimited by what they hope their signs will (or won't) achieve vis-à-vis an onlooker. Interviews reveal that those residents who understand their signs to involve a sexual element dismiss its effects on onlookers. On the other hand, interviews conducted with residents of another set of named houses reveal that the residents use signs to indicate their Christian faith and to offer an invitation to the onlooker. The groups of residents identified by these boundaries are not equal in their ability to realize their goals of participation in Oxford's world of signs. This realization requires analytic moves that engage with increasingly sophisticated understandings in folklore and linguistic anthropology of the ways that participants in an expressive practice can share certain understandings of the practice at the same time that only the goals of some will be realized. Thus agency, what Laura Ahearn defines as "the socioculturally mediated capacity to act" (2001c, 112), is distributed unevenly across residents such that only some of their signs express what they want them to.

Webb Keane points out that an interpretive practice can expose its practitioner to risk by virtue of the fact that she or he is embedded (and can become entangled) in larger fields of practice: "Language is both intimately bound up with the subjectivity of its speakers and consists of linguistic forms and pragmatic conventions not fully of their own making" (1997a, 676).[1] The "hazards of representation," in Keane's terms (1997b), are involved when indexical connections between a house name and its residents' Christian faith are subjected to the interpretive practices embodying the larger house sign community. While residents of houses with Christian signs have elaborate and passionate understandings of what they hope that their signs will achieve, their participation in Oxford's world of signs subjects their signs to interpretations out of their control. Thus the conceptualization of agency requires attention to—but cannot be limited to—the ways that visual language is embedded in context and the ways that social actors engage with visual language through interpretive habits. Indeed, the concept of agency prompts questions about whose meaning-making activity is able to cross the boundaries of interpretive habits and whose is not.

Folklore studies have shown how tradition (Handler and Linnekin 1984), nationalism (Abrahams 1993; Bauman 1993; Bendix 1992; Coe 1999; Herzfeld 1982), authenticity (Bendix 1997; Stewart 1991), textuality (Bauman 1995; Bauman and Briggs 2003; Briggs 1993; Briggs and Bauman 1999), heritage (Kirshenblatt-Gimblett 1998), and notions of the local (Shuman 1993) have provided organizing tropes by which people, sometimes participating in powerful institutions such as states, museums, schools, and scholarly publishing, have constructed and attempted to control means of ethnographic representation and interpretation. In the words of Amy Shuman and Charles Briggs, "Folklore is always already (in Derrida's terms) a politics of culture" (1993, 112). Indeed, the aforementioned scholars engage the notion of agency because they demonstrate the ways that habits of interpretation can selectively enable people to define, interpret, authorize, decry, discount, or forget some practice.

Such processes are germane to practices that give social life to house signs. They emerge between residents' reflections on their own motives of the display of signs and their notions about how onlookers interpret them. Within this dialectic, there exists the risk of having one's motives subverted or the luxury of having one's motives realized. We have already seen the example of residents stating the ways in which house names should be interpreted while disregarding a great deal of meaning and activity. In every interview, residents engaged in the three habits of interpreting signs that included the notions that house names are easy to remember, signs are either clever or dumb, and that signs are about partying. Rarely did residents reflect on the complex negotiations involved in the decision to maintain or change the house's previous name. By consistently invoking only the three habits of interpreting signs, residents engaged in what Gal and Irvine (1995) and Irvine and Gal (2000) call "semiotic erasure," wherein beliefs about linguistic practice make certain linguistic practices invisible. Indeed, the three interpretive habits erased the complex parameters of constraint and possibility faced by a house's residents when they are in the process of naming their house.

An important question is raised: How can some ideas about how house signs are used be erased when residents of named houses are largely in agreement about the ways that signs should be interpreted, especially the notion that signs should be understood as "just for fun." Oxford's world presents the study of expressive culture with the opportunity to show the relevance of agency to a practice wherein there is an absence of a will to power, authority, or even description of alterity, because the selective subversion of interpretive desires happens outside the conscious awareness of participants. In other words, residents do not seem to be aware that different motives of display might lie behind the presentation of signs, just as they subvert those motives with their interpretive practices.

The exploration of whose underlying goals of participation in a practice are most easily recognized requires an understanding of the relationship between motives of display or performance and the ways that they relate to interpretive practices circulating in the larger community. Consider an example. The idea that house signs involve sex, drugs, and alcohol was ubiquitous in the interviews we conducted. But when one considers the house names presented in Table 1.1, it becomes obvious that not all house names have an indexical tie to sex, drugs, and alcohol. One cannot stop there, however. Through ethnographic exploration, we learned that the subjects of this chapter—those residents who understand their signs to involve a sexual element, on the one hand, and those residents who understand their signs to involve their Christian faith, on the other hand—emerge as distinct, in part, by their dispositions to the larger notion that signs involve sex, drugs, and alcohol at the same time that they share the notion.

(Excusing) Responsibility toward Onlookers: Agency and Its Denial

Residents who want their signs to indicate their Christian faith differ most from residents of houses with sexual names. This is due not so much to the content of the signs as to the residents' different dispositions toward their responsibility for the signs' display. Indeed, even when compared to residents of houses with other kinds of names, the degree to which residents of houses whose signs include references to sex decried their own culpability in their sign's display is extreme. In other words, interviews conducted with the residents of houses with names such as Deez Nutz ("nuts" being a euphemism for testicles), Hot Box ("box" also being a term for the vagina), Morning Wood (waking with an erection), Octopussy, and The Panty Shanty demonstrate that they feel the need to excuse the display of their signs, and are adept at doing so. The especially complex constructions of responsibility that emerged within interviews conducted with residents who understand their signs to contain a sexual element give evidence that there exists a community of practice within the larger whole wherein agency is particularly important to consider. Residents who understand their signs to indicate their Christian faith will be seen to have a different disposition to the issue of responsibility.

Alessandro Duranti provides a definition of agency useful for exploring the house sign community: "Agency is here understood as the property of those entities (i) that have some degree of control over their own behavior, (ii) whose actions in the world affect other entities' (and sometimes their own), and (iii) whose actions are the object of evaluation (e.g. in terms of their responsibility for a given outcome)" (2004, 453). When applied to the residents of named houses, Duranti's definition includes practice (residents' naming of houses and displaying of signs), habits of interpretation that make sense of practice (the three interpretive habits described above with which residents make sense of signs and that index them as a community of practice), and differences between residents of named houses in the ways they reflect on the relationship between the sign and the onlooker.

As the third, reflexive part of Duranti's definition, "actions are the object of evaluation," suggests, constructions of responsibility that underpin understandings of action and its effects are variable within the house sign community of practice. Laura Ahearn suggests the possibility that agency is mediated differently within different communities of practice when she poses the question, "What types of supra-individual agency might exist?" (2001a,

8). The answer depends on the nexus of interpretive habit and groupness, such that one answer emerges for the house sign community of practice as a whole but another answer emerges for the two groups marked by more delimited interpretive habits. For example, the interpretive habits of the house sign community as a whole help to create its boundaries because anyone who sees something other than convenience, cleverness, or partying in a sign indexes herself or himself as an outsider. Such a person becomes, in the rubric of the community of practice, someone who takes house names too seriously. Agency is at issue in such moments because the significance of someone's offer of unrecognized indexical connections between sign and social practice can be dismissed or ignored.

Residents of houses whose signs make a gesture to sexual matters constitute a group, in part, because they imagine and characterize specific types of onlookers when the issue of responsibility is raised (Hill and Irvine 1992). Bakhtin's notion of heteroglossia—his demonstration that language practice involves a complex interplay of language and perspective—is helpful in understanding why it is that certain types of people emerge when the issue of responsibility is raised in discussions with residents who understand their house names to involve a sexual element. Bakhtin notes, "Our speech, that is, all our utterances (including creative works), is filled with others' words, varying degrees of otherness or varying degrees of 'our-own-ness,' varying degrees of awareness and detachment. These words of others carry with them their own expression, their own evaluative tone, which we assimilate, rework, and re-accentuate" (1986, 89). At one level, all house signs are heteroglossic because they use language not their own.[2] For example, they borrow street names; the jargon of commercial activity; brand-names; or popular film, television, and music performers and titles. Deborah Kapchan and Pauline Turner Strong usefully warn that the notion of heteroglossia can "threaten to dissolve difference into a pool of homogenization" when scholars fail to pay careful attention to contextual features of interpretive practices (1999, 240). The discussion of the three interpretive habits helps to avoid the risk of homogenization because the habits show how the community of practice narrows the indexical possibilities of signs, on the one hand, and marks other interpretations to be those of nonmembers, on the other hand. In the parlance of Bakhtin, members of the community of practice "rework" house names within a relatively narrow regime of interpretation. But what of the heteroglossic possibilities that signs might present to people who (house residents sense) do not participate in the community of practice? Are the possible interpretations of nonparticipants rendered moot by the three interpretive habits? The three interpretive habits create, in part, the possibility of a Bakhtinian "other"—a figure who may or may not be present or explicitly addressed and to whom justifications are made in interviews. The awareness of such an other indicates that house residents sense that the three habits of interpretation might be insufficient to account for the interpretive habits of some viewers.

An interview with the residents of a house named Morning Wood illustrates that they sense exactly this possibility and that they have fairly clear notions about the types of people whose alternative perspectives might raise the issue of the residents' culpability. However, in the interview, the residents claim that such others lack access to the sign's meaning, lack access to the sign physically, or are simply ridiculous. In short, the residents of Morning Wood sense that some types of people might interpret the signs in such a way that suggests the house residents are doing harm, but the house residents make claims about such types of people, or comically imitate them, in a way that obviates any responsibility for the display of the sign.

I present an extended excerpt from the interview in order to demonstrate the complexity with which the residents of Morning Wood handled the notion of responsibility toward onlookers. Further below, I present a shorter excerpt from an interview with the residents of Octopussy in order to demonstrate the ways in which the same issue was handled in a house of women. The first interview segment begins with a response by the residents to a question posed by Jay, a student conducting the interview with me, about whether anyone "in the Oxford community" has "ever said anything" about Morning Wood. Although the residents respond negatively, the issue of responsibility hardly disappears.

BEN: no not that I've noticed
JAY: no like negative, criti⌈cism
CHUCK: ⌊not like directly to us, but I'm sure ⌈it exists
AL: ⌊**oh I**
mean like yeah, no one's ever directed like stuff **towards** us but
I'm sure it's been ta::lked about
ED: I'm sure Strangers with Candy that's right across the street ⌈from a
nursery school has more problems than ⌈us
CHUCK: ⌊that's
what I was thinking . . . ⌊**Strangers with Candy**(5)

FIGURE 3.1. Morning Wood 1

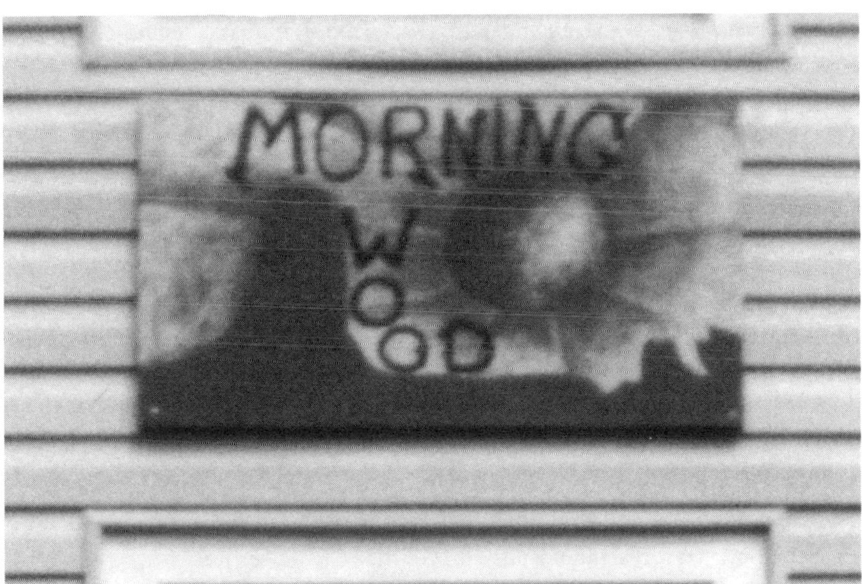

FIGURE 3.2. Morning Wood 2

BEN: I don't think it's too offensive. if you don't know what Morning Wood means which most of the kids don't, I mean, it's not really a big deal

ED: **yeah**, most townies, they probably don't know what Morning Wood is, they just. you know. ⌈I guess . . . **I mean the only time**, like i told you about that guy stopping his ⌈car

CHUCK: ⌊**hold it**

DAN: ⌊what **is** Morning Wood. I don't really know.

ED: I don't wanna give a definition of it, **pervert**

CHUCK: pe::rve::rt(4)

AL: u::m, yeah, I don't think, like nobody's given us, any grief about it I don't think

Ben answers Jay's question with a denial of ever hearing comments made about Morning Wood. When Jay makes explicit that he is asking about "negative criticism," Chuck and Al too assert personal ignorance but surmise that such criticism probably occurs. Rather than guessing what the talk of others might include, however, they deflect attention from their own sign by mentioning another. The mention of Strangers with Candy is particularly appropriate because the house sits opposite a school, making the house name's index of predatory activity that much more robust.

The implied victims of the "strangers" of Strangers with Candy are the focus of the next few lines as the residents of Morning Wood shift their focus from the names of houses to their viewers. They differentiate "kids" and "townies" from others and claim that the first group is incapable of understanding the sign. This is the first moment in the interview that the residents of Morning Wood identify who might be reading their sign, and they identify those groups that might invoke their culpability in and responsibility for the sign's display. Ben focuses on "kids," indexed previously by Strangers with Candy, and argues that the meaning of Morning Wood is probably opaque to them and thus insignificant. Ed expands the group from "kids" to "townies" and begins to recount a story told earlier in the interview that constitutes an example of a "townie" recognizing the meaning of the sign. Ed's mention of his earlier story is interesting because it provides evidence that "townies" do indeed have the ability to understand what Morning Wood means. Ed seems to sense this as he qualifies his reminder with "the only time." Ed's original tell-

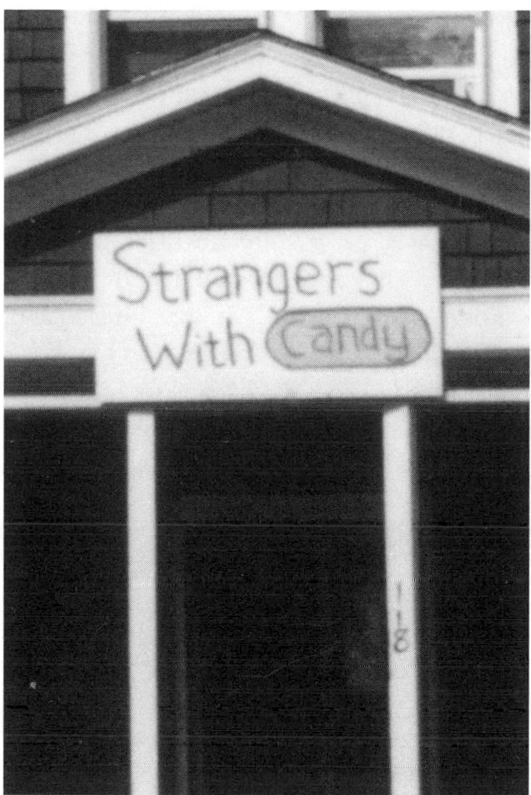

FIGURE 3.3. Strangers with Candy

ing in the interview drew the response from Chuck, "fucking townie," after which the focus was moved back to parties held at the house. In the excerpt presented here, Chuck likewise changes the frame of the discussion, contravening the presentation of exceptions.

Dan continues Chuck's interruption, inhabits the point of view of an onlooker, and initiates a momentary "breakthrough into performance" (Hymes 1981, 12) of a modeled conversation. Dan's question, "What is Morning Wood?" is "double voiced" in a Bakhtinian sense in that Dan takes up the perspective of a person who, unlike everyone present, cannot understand the sign (Bakhtin 1981). For example, Dan does not use "I" of "I don't really know" only to referentially index himself as a participant in the interview. Never made explicit is who Dan might be when asking the question, whether a "townie," another college student, or, as a reviewer intriguingly suggested, the engaged professor. In any case, there are several aspects of the interactions that ensue that indicate that they take place in a different frame than that of previous interaction and that, in this segment, Dan, Ed, and Chuck mean to be seen as not playing the role of members of the house sign community of practice. Rather than answer the question, Ed calls Dan a pervert simply for asking it. Ed's tone is indignant as he accuses the character Dan plays of being a pervert. Chuck returns interaction to its previous frame of students being interviewed with his laughter as he isolates "pervert" for repetition. The playful frame that double voicing makes possible allows Dan, Ed, and Chuck to invoke the capacity to offend, to raise the specter of its criticism, and to laugh off such criticism as ridiculous. Chuck's contribution affirms that the voices are overly sensitive and can be dismissed safely. Al confirms that no actual person enacted in the segment has existed as far as the residents know.

While in the previous excerpt the residents of Morning Wood focus on house names and their viewers and perform personae not their own, they shift in the next excerpt to focus on themselves. In arguing about whether they consider themselves to be part of the town of Oxford, the residents mitigate their own responsibility for the display of the sign yet again. Immediately following the previous excerpt, Jay asks whether some of the signs are "inappropriate," to which the residents respond:

DAN: na::h, 'cause I'm a college kid and I don't really ca::re
ALL: #
AL: yeah, I don't care
DAN: I mean, like yeah, this isn't really our, like ⌈my town
AL: ⌊**we don't really care**
BEN: I think that it kind of **is**, but I mean. it's a small town and all . . . just kids, walk by like big parties every day. and they're used to it . . .
CHUCK: well, **it's not like**, I don't think like **residents** are in, this, this **area** that much, I mean there are . . . the residential area's not really **he::re**, kids don't walk by here going to school(2)
AL: I know people from other schools that think it's really . . . I mean, I guess just **co::ol** that like, all the different houses around here have names, it's kinda funny
DAN: y'see, stuff on TV that's a hell of a lot worse than the sign on the front of the house anyway, so. I don't think we're really exposing them to too much more than anything else that, they can get

CHAISE: sure, I mean, was that part of the reason of making the sign
was ⌈to push boundaries
AL: ⌊**no**. ⌈not real . . .
BEN: ⌊kinda just part of tradition of, campus, I think it's
I think it's really cool, like other schools, they just know the
houses by address and stuff like that, I think it's a really cool
tradition they d::o.

The town of Oxford emerges in this excerpt as a location mediating relationships already identified in the interview, "kids" and "townies" on the one hand and people like the residents of Morning Wood on the other hand. Dan expands his status to that of "college kid," explaining that the category implies a general indifference. Al agrees. Dan then uses the possessive to argue that Oxford is not his "town," drawing a distinction between "college kid" and Oxford (and its "kids" and "townies"). In short, Dan and Al decry any displayer's responsibility for a sign because the students living in Oxford have no possessive investment in the place where they live.

Ben disagrees with Dan and Al but maintains a responsibility-mitigating stance while shifting its parameters. Ben envisions the residents to be part of Oxford but argues that "kids" have become used to the parties that take place there. The smallness of the town serves to habituate "kids" to signs through maximal exposure. Chuck, however, gives an explanation that is contradictory to Ben's in that it argues for the inaccessibility of Morning Wood to "residents" and "kids." Whereas the meaning of "kids" in Ben's usage could follow Dan's usage of "college kid," Chuck's usage refers specifically to children and youths who are younger than college students, indexed by "school." And rather than foreground desensitization, Chuck presupposes a contrast between the "residential area" where "kids walk to school" (and "townies" live) with "here" (where "college kids" live). Whereas Ben argues for desensitization through habitual exposure, Chuck argues that younger town residents have no immediate access to house parties (and signs) in the first place.

Al changes the parameters of discussion by shifting the referential index of "here" from the house to the town. Al thus takes the focus off of distinctions of people and places within Oxford and makes the existence of house signs stand in for the town as a whole. "People from other schools" find Oxford "cool" by virtue of its signs. Dan, however, explicitly reintroduces issues of culpability and responsibility to the interview. Dan repositions the phenomenon entirely by opening up a seemingly limitless frame of comparison, what one might see on television. In doing so, Dan invokes Susan Gal and Kathryn Woolard's idea that "The notion of public need not even rely on the idea of a concrete readership or spectatorship, but rather on the projection or imagination of groups or subjectivities in print or other mass media" (2001, 8). And notice that by saying, "We're exposing them," Dan represents the house residents as agents—in a grammatical sense—of an act, but one trumped by its ability to harm by a pervasive social phenomenon, the television.

It is worthwhile to note Dan's representation of the house residents as grammatical agents by offering "to push boundaries" as a characterization of the sign's display. The characterization is rejected immediately. Again, the residents use a number of techniques to reduce their own responsibility. Ben invokes "tradition" that inherently includes the residents of Morning Wood by his use of "campus." His use of the adjective "cool" invokes the interpretive habits whereby signs can be judged to be "clever." And the invocation of "tradition," when viewed from the standpoint of responsibility, is reminiscent of Bauman's claim that "when one views the item of folklore as the collective product and possession of society at large, the performer is reduced to the role of passive and anonymous mouthpiece or conduit for the collective tradition" (1986, 8). Ben has some trouble with the strategy that Bauman describes, however. His statement, "It's a really cool tradition they do," is slightly awkward because, ostensibly, he includes himself.

The final excerpt contains a surprise in light of the myriad responsibility- and culpability-reducing techniques that the residents of Morning Wood have engaged in so far. Initially, they maintain the stance of the previous excerpt:

CHUCK: we weren't, we weren't trying to push. boundaries,⌈just trying to be funny.
AL: ⌊**we just thought it was funny. yeah**, we just wanted to do this funny ⌈house thing
DAN:⌊as funny as ⌈possible
AL: ⌊yea::h we were going for the humor factor
CHUCK: a::h definitely
AL: no **boundaries** [sarcastically], i don't think we care about ⌈**boundaries** at a::ll
ALL:⌊#

BEN: I know people from other schools that think it's really, I mean, just **cool**,that like all the different houses around here have names.
AL: we took it over the edge
BEN: it's kind of funny . . .

Chuck begins by rejecting my description, "to push boundaries," and offers "to be funny" as an alternative. Al and Dan agree, casting the intentions of the house members with different uses of "funny." Al offers "the humor factor" as a gloss for "funny." Al then indexes my use of "boundaries" by employing it himself, but he revoices it with sarcastic intonation and dismisses the use in a way reminiscent of "pervert" in the first excerpt. In both cases, the revoicings serve to "rework," in the parlance of Bakhtin, the words of others such that they become injected with a severity that creates a ridiculous image. Their views then can be safely dismissed. As in the previous excerpt, Ben deflects attention from local surroundings when he invokes the point of view of college students elsewhere.

Al claims, "I don't think we care about boundaries at all," yet, just four lines later, he makes a strong claim of agency in the display of Morning Wood. Al's final comment, "We took it over the edge," is remarkable given its invocation of an image of boundary crossing and its contrast with his previous denial. What Al seems to accomplish in this segment is an index of register difference between the overly serious "boundary," to be mocked and dismissed, and the much "cooler" "over the edge," illustrating Asif Agha's observation that "registers are 'heteroglossic' phenomena, typically uniting several types of conventional pragmatic value" (1998, 154). Ben ends the segment with "funny," completing a set of descriptors—"cool," "over the edge," and "funny"—that contrast with "boundaries" and that cast it as overly serious.

Laura Ahearn (2001b) has pointed out that people can downplay or decry their own agency while they point to its expanding horizons. This bivalent process seems to pervade the interview segments presented above. The residents of Morning Wood engage in responsibility-reducing techniques for the display of the sign by pointing to another sign as worse than their own, arguing that "kids" and "townies" cannot understand it, lampooning as ridiculous any concerns about the meaning of their sign, removing themselves as "college kids" from the activity of the town, arguing that "kids" have become used to house signs, arguing that "kids" have no access to their sign, pointing to the positive feelings of students at other campuses about signs, calling the phenomenon a "tradition," and rejecting overt claims to be doing anything with their sign other than "being funny." The reduction of responsibility in the interview is a complicated affair indeed. At the same time, however, the residents of Morning Wood index the charged presence of their sign by invoking another sign's sinister index of children, by taking care to insure that such people have no cognitive or physical access to Morning Wood, and by noting overtly that they have pushed some unidentified practice "over the edge."

This Janus-faced phenomenon emerged in all of the interviews with residents of houses the names of which might be construed to involve a sexual element. Sally began an interview with the residents of Octopussy:

> SALLY: OK, did you all name your house.
>
> ALL: no
>
> AMY: from what we understa::nd
>
> ALL: #
>
> AMY: it was named that in the late seventies or the early eighties after the James **Bond** movie, *Octopussy*(2)
>
> SALLY: do you think that's the only reason they named the house that
>
> AMY: **n::o**
>
> BETH: **ei::ght gi::rls**. might've have had something to do with it

Other participants proceeded to explain that eight women have traditionally occupied the house. When Sally asked later in the interview whether the residents have ever been targeted with negative criticism, they explained that they have not and pointed to the James Bond film and the number of house residents to explain the meaning of the sign. Yet, at various points throughout the half-hour interview, one resident in particular interjected such exclamations as "It's hot in the pussy!" and "Party in the pussy!" Uproarious group laughter followed these outbursts. Thus the residents index a popular film and the circumstances of residence when imagining an onlooker of the sign and his or her interpretation, but they sometimes index the sexualized potential of the sign in its use. Indeed, I witnessed the overtly sexualized use of "Octopussy" (in which the movie title plays no part) outside of an interview context. Early one morning, I was having a cigarette in front of the building in which I was about to teach. A young man passed a young woman and exchanged greetings with her approximately fifty feet in front of me. I surmise that one

FIGURE 3.4. Octopussy

of their quick exchanges involved the night's plans because several seconds after their parting, the young man turned and screamed, "Party in the pussy tonight!" He then whooped, throwing a fist high in the air.

A Different Agency: House Signs as Invitations

In certain respects, students who live in houses with names such as Cornerstone, Crib of the Rib, Inn Pursuit, Paradise City, Green House, The Living WC ("with Christ"), and The Rock comprise yet another community of practice within the larger house sign community. While they share with all residents of named houses an appreciation for signs that evidence cleverness on the part of their creators, the belief that a house name is more convenient than an address, and the understanding that a sign entails a party, they differ from residents of houses such as Morning Wood, Che, and The Dresden because they intend for their house names to index an ethos characterizing the house's residents as a group. Among the first topics discussed in an interview with the residents of a house named Inn Pursuit was the ethos that the residents wish the house's name to reflect.

CHAISE: and what does the:: sign mean(2)
KIM: well, Hil . . . (3)
HIL: well, it's called Inn **Pur**suit, **and um,** basically I think everyone is in pursuit of something, um, if it's mo::ney:: po::we::r relationships, like everyone's looking for something, happiness. um, but ou::r inn Pursuit, is our friends' too, pursuit of Jesus Christ and a personal relationship with him. so that's what we're in pursuit of(5)
LYNN: you'll notice like, the **t** is a **cross**(4)
KIM: and in part it's just because it's a house and so we spell it with two *n*'s.
PEG: it's the little cute thing
ALL: #
LYNN: 'cause of the cross.
PEG: 'cause of the cross

The residents' appreciation of their own creativity or cleverness is evidenced by their remark about the spelling of the "Inn" in Inn Pursuit to be "the little cute thing." Such appreciation of creativity shows that, at one level, the residents of houses with names that denote Christian faith enact interpretive practices of the house sign community at large.

But the ways that the residents of Inn Pursuit imagine their name to correspond with an ethos marks them as a community of practice different from residents of houses such as Morning Wood, Che, or The Dresden. Hil uses the name to characterize the residents in a common activity. She also illustrates a handful of ways, held together in their differences by the house's name, in which other people might be different. Unlike the residents of Morning Wood and Octopussy, the residents of Inn Pursuit make no attempt to downplay or decry their responsibility for the existence of the sign or for its effects on onlookers.

In the next excerpt, the residents of Inn Pursuit show not only that they wish for their house name to index their Christian faith but also that they wish for the house name to index the offer of Christian community in the house. In other words, the residents of Inn Pursuit mean for their sign to serve as an invitation. Thus religious signs are underpinning their display in a more specialized form of agency than that underpinning the three interpretive practices of the house sign community generally (including residents who understand their signs to involve a sexual element). The specialized form of agency is captured by Charles Briggs and Clara Mantini-Briggs as "the capacity to act in accordance with a concrete plan" (2003, 22). The invocation of a "concrete plan" captures the way in which the house residents see their sign as an indication of their Christian faith and the way in which they hope that it will serve as an invitation to others.

CHAISE: did you choose ⌈your
HIL: ⌊we **did** choose our house because, it's like a nice house
CHAISE: ya::
HIL: it's a nice house, we've enjoyed it, and we knew the girls who had it before a::nd we just got it passed down to us and and(2) I don't think we chose it necessarily on the **basis** of its name, but it was just kind of an added bonus that it was this. y'know it was kind of **known** for being this house of like Christian women and . . . y'know we just really appreciate the community that we have within the house, there's ten of us total
CHAISE: oh my good⌈ness
HIL: ⌊and so, there's two downstairs three up here and five upstairs(2) and so . . . we just really appreciate the fellowship and the friendship that we have around here so . . .

Hil begins by asserting that the residents did choose Inn Pursuit but then blends representations of the house's residents as both agents and patients vis-à-vis the actions of (unnamed) others. For example, she explains, "We just got it passed down to us." She says that the current house residents take their place in a lineage of Christian women who have occupied the house previously. She uses three words to characterize the atmosphere within the house: "community," "fellowship," and "friendship." Among the three, "fellowship" indexes a whole host of possible practices and beliefs that specify that the house residents are Christians. The residents confirmed this, explaining that they come from a number of denominations. They also argued, however, that they had been able to transcend denominational difference by a focus on the Bible.

In the next excerpt, the perspective is shifted from looking into the house at its residents to looking out of the house at others.

LYNN: and even how we can use this house to like just minister to other people, and um reach other people, serve other people(2) what we desire to do.
CHAISE: what sorts of things does that include

LYNN: well, for example, a couple of weeks ago we had friends over and cooked them dinner, just little things like that

CHAISE: these are friends from college

LYNN: yeah(3)

KIM: um or just how, like our one, our one girl that we know doesn't really live in the best environment will sometimes just come over here to hang out and get away.

JAY: environment, like, how d . . . how d'ya mean, like what kind of environment

KIM: like she lives with peo . . . with like potheads basically

LYNN: she doesn't have a lot of fellowship

KIM: yeah, and so . . . so she comes here to get away from that(3)

LYNN: even just like, like, some of us lead Bible studies, and just being able to have them over he::re

Lynn shifts the disposition of this cluster of terms from within the house, shared among its members, to outside, shared, potentially, with anyone. Whereas Hil uses the nouns "community," "fellowship," and "friendship," Lynn uses the verbs "minister," "reach," and "serve" and envisions the house as a tool—"we can use this house"—to facilitate such activities. It is in this sense that, in the eyes of the residents of Inn Pursuit, the agency underpinning their display of the sign is part of a "concrete plan."

The residents of Inn Pursuit offer three examples wherein the house is a focal location of activity. Lynn states that the residents of Inn Pursuit had friends over for dinner, minimizing the example's gravity with "just little." Kim, however, projects the house as a refuge from places that are described, initially, in vague terms. When asked to clarify, Kim explains that the friend's roommates are "potheads," a gently derisive term for people who consume marijuana. Lynn describes such a scene to lack "fellowship," something previously stated to exist at Inn Pursuit. Kim again characterizes a trip to Inn Pursuit, this time as "to get away." Lynn offers a third and more generalized example: leading Bible studies.

Susan Harding has written about her encounter with a preacher who tried to persuade Harding to accept Jesus as her personal savior (2000, 40). The preacher built complex verbal tableaux of sacrifice meant to place Harding increasingly in a position of involvement. During the interview with Inn Pursuit, the residents never attempted to alter our roles (as interviewers and interviewees), nor did they give us the impression that they wished to attempt emotional conversions of the kind about which Harding has written. Nevertheless, they used transitive verbs to describe what they and their house offer. Furthermore, they created a picture of an environment from which there is the need of escape. The residents of Inn Pursuit envision their own sign to be like those whose house residents are like them and to be unlike those of others. The boundary between the two, after all, is what gives force to the offer of fellowship in Inn Pursuit.

House Signs, Group Boundaries, and Interpretive Ambivalence

The residents of Inn Pursuit reflect on the sign's ability to index them as a group that, in turn, is tied to residents of other houses sharing their Christian faith. Notice in the excerpt the use of "the groups we hang out with" to specify knowledge of the group-denoting ability of the sign.

KIM: withi::n, the groups we hang out with like everyone knows where Inn Pursuit is like even if they've never, seen it like, a lot of people have just heard of it, just with the girls that have lived here, the past couple years and then, the:: like people we know now, like they know where it is so, I would say the name's kno::wn definitely, but . . .

HIL: yeah like I met some girl once and she was describing to me where, she lived, or where she was going to be living next year, this was last year, and she was like well it's a great location it's right down the street, from The Rock and from Inn Pursuit, and I was like, I'm going to be **living** in Inn Pursuit # next year, so like among like our groups like it's kind of a well-known place. I guess more well known than the people that are gonna live in it 'cause she didn't even know, I lived in it.

KIM: and I don't even think our address is outsi::de, so ⌈just

LYNN: ⌊I think it ⌈is

KIM: ⌊the two thirty but not the, street name

HIL: yeah so, it's just easier to say, I live in Inn Pursuit(3)

Kim asserts that house names can circulate in conversations so that one can know of a house without having seen it. She reiterates the legacy of Christian women who have previously inhabited the house. Hil makes use of the perspective of another student who describes her new residence as "a great location" near The Rock and Inn Pursuit, both of whose residents understand their signs to index their Christian faith. From Hil's perspective, the other student indexes herself as a member of "our groups" by orienting her future residence by the landmarks The Rock and Inn Pursuit. Hil thus highlights that the house signs index the Christian faith of residents by virtue of shared knowledge among "our groups," playing off the irony that the fellow student is a member of "our groups" but does not realize the indexical connection between Inn Pursuit and Hil's place of residence. Hil's lesson is that the discursive use of these particular names can clarify group boundaries. Kim, Lynn, and Hil then enact the interpretive habit by which a house name is a more convenient locator than an address. Kim overstates the case and is corrected by Lynn. Hil then sums up the interpretive habit with "It's just easier."

From the perspective of residents of houses who believe their signs to indicate their Christian faith, the excerpt presented above can be considered inward-looking. Among people who share the knowledge that such signs do indicate their residents' Christian faith, there is no interpretive problem.

But what of an outward-looking perspective? How do the residents of Inn Pursuit understand signs to mediate boundaries between groups—"ours" versus those of others? Whereas the residents of houses who understand their signs to involve a sexual element pick out particularly vulnerable onlookers, "kids," and downplay their own responsibility for the display of the sign, the residents of Inn Pursuit imagine their ideological others to be residents of houses in which transgressive practices go on (such as the already-mentioned use of marijuana). The next excerpt follows the residents' claim that they do indeed "party." In the excerpt, they characterize their own parties via the absence of what happens at some others.

CHAISE: some signs like are about **partying**, y'know overtly, like Boot 'N Ra::lly or . . . uh what else is there, High Life, u::m. Happy Hour

HIL: At Church and Almost High or something like that

CHAISE: At Church and Almost Hi::gh. do you think that your parties are a little bit different than the parties that go on in those houses or . . .

HIL: to some de . . . **yeah**, mostly definitely

KIM: yeah.

HIL: they tend to be tamer.

CHAISE: tamer

PEG: there ten . . . there doesn't really seem to be any illegal activities going on I would think, at our parties(4)

CHAISE: what sort of activities do you mean?

PEG: like getting high

ALL: #

PEG: not that **I**:: know.

KIM: and dri . . . like drinking under a::ge

Hil's offer of At Church and Almost High is interesting. One might argue that it is yet another sign that indexes partying, or one might argue that it achieves a degree of parallelism with the "High" of High Life offered by me. Unlike the ones I have just offered, Hil's example puns on the Christian ethos that the residents of Inn Pursuit understand their sign to index. When I ask just what differentiates parties at those houses from those that take place at Inn Pursuit, Hil offers "tamer" for her own. When Peg elaborates on the parties that do take place at Inn Pursuit, she does so negatively by describing what they exclude. She offers "illegal activities," and when I ask for specificity, she offers "getting high," followed by a caveat espousing ignorance. Kim follows with the underage consumption of alcohol. Sexual activity, the second element of the trio made explicit in Witty House Sign (Preferably with a Drug, Sex, and/or Alcohol Reference) and in countless characterizations of signs in interviews, is absent, but only momentarily.

An excerpt of the next moment in the interview shows that residents of Inn Pursuit decry any direct knowledge of such transgressive practices:

CHAISE: did you guys ever go to parties at those houses, or . . . (2)

HIL: other people's houses

KIM: yeah

LYNN: yeah(2)

CHAISE: but any of tho::se that have the signs about partying, like Boot 'N Rally.

HIL: **probably** none of the real fam::ous ones just 'cause I don't know anybody who lives in those

CHAISE: what are the famous ones

HIL: oh the ones you mentioned well I've never heard of Boot 'N Rally like, but I don't know. u::m, nothing that's really na::med for anything like that but.

How then, with the absence of experience, can the residents of Inn Pursuit maintain that ideological others exist, some of whom are in need of the house's Christian atmosphere? In the next excerpt, the residents seem to arrive at a solution. They do so by replacing experience at transgressive parties with house names and signs themselves.

> CHAISE: but when you say famous houses are there, d'you, do you think that there are some houses that have, y'know, infamous parties, or they're well known ⌈t' . . .
> HIL: ⌊**well** I wouldn't know necessarily about the **parties**.
> LYNN: just like the **names**
> HIL: just the names are funny I think, and when you drive by everybody like kinda **knows** where it is 'cause they've seen it around, but you don't necessarily know, **oh** at this house there's this certain kinda party or anything like that . . .
> CHAISE: right. what are those names, I mean . . . (2)
> KIM: oh. it's hard to remember 'cause, like you walk down the street and it's all about like, getting drunk or having sex pretty much like, all of the streets or all of the houses so it sort of runs together after awhile like I don't know of any infamous. houses . . .
> LYNN: like the one Morning Woo::d.⌈and like the picture on it
> PEG: ⌊**oh** yeah . . .
> HIL: I've never seen the picture.
> KIM: it definitely gives you an impression of what might go on in the house whether it's true or no::t that's what you think.

After several statements from the previous excerpt in which Hil claims not to know anyone in "famous houses" nor to have heard of Boot 'N Rally, in this excerpt she claims general ignorance of what happens in houses known for partying. A major shift ensues over the next several lines in which ambivalence about indexical connections between house sign and the kind of partying done inside the house disappears. Lynn initiates the shift by changing the focus to what is publicly accessible (rather than experienced within the house), houses' signs and the names displayed therein. Hil separates the house name, which is funny, from the activity that might happen inside. Kim shifts the focus to the names (and away from in-house activities). For the first time in the interview, a resident, Kim, characterizes the phenomenon as a whole in a manner similar to the ubiquitous claim that signs are about sex, drugs, and alcohol. In this case, Kim uses the activity of walking down the street to create a totalizing image of Oxford as a place bombarding one with messages and images—too numerous to remember—of "getting drunk and having sex." Whereas this served one of the residents of Morning Wood in his argument that kids have grown used to the signs, Kim seems to find in the ubiquity of house signs an environment that must be tolerated at best. Kim finally shifts the focus of sign interpretation from the intentions of residents who display the signs to the understandings of the people who view them. The burden of the interview's earlier problematic—that the residents of Inn Pursuit cannot attest to the indexical ties between names of houses and the activities of parties within such houses—is lifted. No longer is experience within the house necessary to draw conclusions about what happens within the house.

The replacement of experience with house names, however, opens up the possibility of indexical indeterminacy. In other words, the replacement of narratives of experience with the mention of house names opens up the possibility that a resident of Inn Pursuit can separate the residents of houses with transgressive names from transgressive activities. This potentially releases the residents being talked about from membership in a group to which the residents of Inn Pursuit oppose themselves. In an interpretive move reminiscent of the ways that residents of Octopussy and Hot Box appeal to indexical connections that reduce their own responsibility for the signs' display, a resident of Inn Pursuit appeals to the gender of the residents of Pop-N-Wood to argue against a construal of the house name as sexual.

> CHAISE: hm, why do you think people put up signs like that(2)
> KIM: hm. i guess to portray an ima::ge, that they think is cool, or, good ⌈or . . .
> TRISH: ⌊or they think it's fu::nny. i have some friends who named their house this year Pop-N-Wood(2) it's at the corner of Poplar and Woodruff, and. it wasn't necessarily any . . . 'cause it's a bunch of girls. so:: it doesn't necessarily carry any meaning but the two street names it was just something clever and creative that they thought was funny

The excerpt shows that the residents of Inn Pursuit do not always disavow knowledge of signs (and their houses' residents) that can be taken to index sex, drugs, and/or alcohol. Trish uses the familiar "funny" to replace Kim's more removed "cool" and "good." Trish goes on to explain that Pop-N-Wood is "clever" and "creative" because of its play with the names of the streets on which it is located. But, in noting that the residents of Pop-N-Wood are "a bunch of girls," Trish betrays the fact that she has imagined a meaning for the house name that might be deemed vulgar. Indeed, she seems to be arguing that the sign is not about sex because the genitals of the house's residents do not match those referenced by the house's sign. The claim that the residents of Pop-N-Wood are women, and thus uncoordinated with the name's potential to index an erection's (Wood) growth (Pop-N-), contradicts the interpretive practice argued for earlier by the residents of Inn Pursuit: that a house sign in and of itself indexes the residents' practices as embodying an ideological other, making such signs as Inn Pursuit indexical of practices particularly Christian.

Another example gives evidence that even residents who understand their signs to index their own Christian faith have trouble identifying the same index in other signs. They identify many, it is true, but miss the indexical connection between name and the Christianity of residents in another, and even get the name wrong. Jack begins by asking:

JACK: do you know of other . . . (2) well not nece, Christian but other religious . . . based . . . houses, signs, I know there's one that's like . . .
MARY: The Rock
JACK: the Christian, uh . . .
TARA: Cornerstone
MARY: yeah, that's Christian based
JACK: okay I didn't know that one was . . .
MARY: The Rock is . . . do they have a house sign up
TARA: yeah
ALL: [indecipherable]
JACK: is Inn, Inn Pursuit still up
ALL: yeah
KATE: yeah that one is. what's the other one, what's . . .
JACK: so you knew that one was . . . you knew that one was a Christian house
KATE: what's that
JACK: you knew that, uh, Inn Pursuit was [a Christian house
KATE: [uh-huh
TARA: what there was . . .

Jack initiates his line of questioning by broadening the category "Christian" to the more encompassing "religious." Even before he finishes his question, the residents of Crib of the Rib begin to offer examples. Mary offers The Rock and Tara offers Cornerstone. Mary offers "Christian based" as a descriptor for the signs, canceling Jack's broadened description. Indeed, Christianity was the only religion understood by house residents to be relevant to signs. Jack remarks that he hadn't known that Cornerstone is a sign understood by its residents to indicate their Christian faith. Jack himself interjects a house name to the list, Inn Pursuit. When the residents confirm that the sign is still up, Jack asks specifically whether the residents have knowledge that Inn Pursuit is a Christian sign. Kate confirms this.

Thus far in the interview with Crib of the Rib, there is parity between residents' knowledge and the connection between house names and residents' Christian faith. Jill, however, offers a sign name that disrupts this parity:

JILL: 12 Feet Inn

MARY: that's not . . .

TARA: is that Christian

MARY: there's six girls

JILL: I thought it was

TARA: really

JILL: and Living Water Closet(2)

JACK: Living Water ⌈Closet

TARA: ⌊that's not like . . .

JACK: I don't ⌈get that one

TARA: ⌊I thought it was just a bathroom . . . toilet

JILL: no . . . no that one's . . . Christian

TARA: Christian **people** live ⌈there but . . .

JILL: ⌊no it's a . . . I don't know how but it is a ba, a Christian-based name

TARA: it is

JILL: yeah(3)

JACK: I don't get that one

MARY: Living Water ⌈Closet

JACK: ⌊Living Water Closet

JILL: I don't either

ALL: #

Mary questions Jill's offer of 12 Feet Inn as belonging to a list of Christian houses. Tara too seems doubtful that the sign belongs on the list. Jill seems less sure when she states, "I thought it was." Jill then offers Living Water Closet, an incorrect rendering of The Living WC, which actually stands for The Living with Christ. The rendering leads to confusion as Jack and then Tara mention the lack of resonance between a bathroom and Christian faith. Jill asserts that it is Christian when Tara qualifies that Christian people reside in the house. Tara is separating the faith of the residents from the house name because she cannot see any resonance between the two. Jill recognizes this lack of resonance when she says, "I don't know how," and reiterates that it is a "Christian based name." Jack begins a sequence with "I don't get that one," prompting repetition of Living Water Closet. Jill, the person who has stood firm in her conviction that it is a "Christian based name" provides the release of laughter when she follows Jack's "I don't get that one" and the repetition of the name with "I don't either."

Jill then addresses Jack and refers to the very beginning of Jack's visit to Crib of the Rib when he and Jill spoke in the kitchen "at the table." This was before Jack began to record the interview, but it seems that their initial conversation involved the subject of Christian house signs and Jill's understanding that the residents of The Living WC are Christian.

> JILL: but I remember talking about you at the table or like . . .
> JACK: yeah 'cause you know the people in it
> JILL: yeah
> TARA: yeah we know the people
> JACK: so do you think that's . . . typical? like the, that the Christian houses know each other
> JILL: ⌈I think so
> TARA: ⌊yeah
> JACK: is that true, other stuff you guys do together. you like . . .
> KATE: like crusades and stuff like that
> JACK: yeah
> KATE: yeah(2)

Tara confirms that the residents of Crib of the Rib know the residents of The Living WC. When Jack asks whether residents of houses with Christian signs know each other, Jill offers, "I think so," at the same time that Tara offers, "Yeah." Perhaps Jill's response is more equivocal than Tara's because earlier

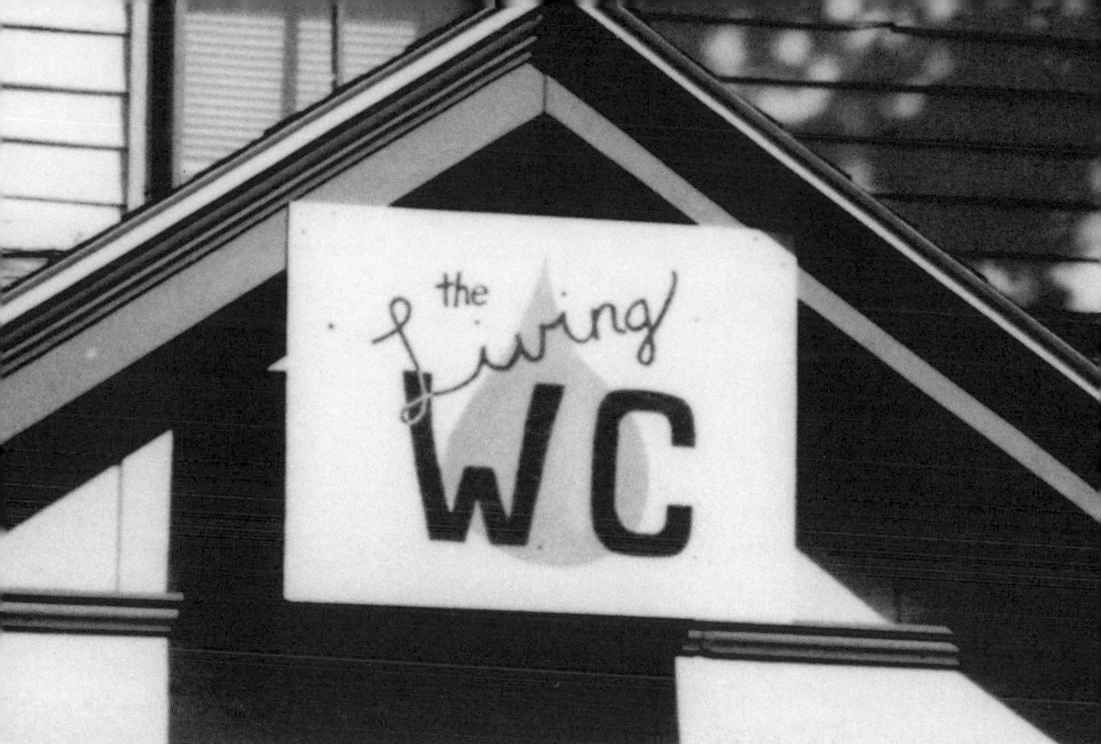

FIGURE 3.5. The Living WC

Jill offered 12 Feet Inn as a Christian sign, an example that no one readily confirmed. The relationship between a sign and its Christian residents seems less than perfect. And the confusing meaning of The Living Water Closet is never revisited in the interview. The residents of Crib of the Rib are not even aware that they have rendered "WC" in a way that differs from its understanding by the residents of The Living WC. Jack ends the excerpt when he asks about other activities that might join the residents of Crib of the Rib to residents of other houses with Christian names. Kate's answer is fascinating. She offers "crusades," the activity of gathering together to hear a preacher that ends with a call for attendants to accept Christ as one's personal savior. The relationship between self and group is undoubtedly different in participation in a crusade and participation in the display of house signs. In the former, the residents of Crib of the Rib no doubt assume that the event has brought their cohort of Christians together. An assumption about signs' ability to do the same stands on far shakier ground.

The ambivalence and indeterminacy involved in the group-indexing capabilities of signs, evidenced in the interview excerpts from Inn Pursuit and Crib of the Rib, demonstrate that signs in and of themselves are unreliable indexes of the very practices from which residents of Inn Pursuit and Crib of the Rib hope that their houses provide a refuge. When the interpretive practices of residents of houses who do not understand their house signs to index their Christian faith are considered, the group-indexing function salient to the residents of Inn Pursuit and residents of other houses with "Christian based names" disappears.

The Agency of Inn Pursuit Thwarted

Umberto Eco raises the question of the relationship between an interpreting subject and the interpretive practices that index membership in a community of practice when he writes, "The *possibilities* which the work's openness makes available always work within a given *field of relations*" (1989, 19). Further, he invokes the possibility that interpretive desires of authors might vary via a common linguistic phenomenon when he writes, "The invitation [to interpret] offers the performer the opportunity for an oriented insertion [making improvisation possible] into something which always remains the world intended by the author [wherein the improvisation might not be seen as such]" (1989, 19). Divisions within the house sign community of practice allow an investigation of the connections between Eco's two assertions. What happens to the desires of Inn Pursuit when their messages are interpreted in the larger house sign community? In the parlance of Eco, what is the relationship between "the world intended by the author" of signs like Inn Pursuit and "the field of relations" that shapes possibilities of interpretation in the community of practice? The answer is that the index of religion and the agency underpinning it—the reasons for which the women have chosen to live in the house and the reasons for which they display the sign—vanish. Whereas interviewed residents of named houses regularly found Che and The Dresden to be "dumb," "weird," or "gay," they did not necessarily make such judgments about houses' names that are meant by residents to reflect their Christian faith. But the fact that interpretive practices in the community of practice do not necessarily lead to negative judgments about names whose houses' residents understand to be Christian hardly renders such interpretations fulfilling of the authors' intentions. Indeed, most residents of other types of houses did not recognize the indexical connection between house name and the Christian faith of the house's residents. Yet they recognized something in the house name, to be sure. It was precisely such interpretive possibilities that thwarted the agency—the provision of an invitation for refuge—envisioned by residents of Christian houses.

In the interview segment below, Ben (of Morning Wood) responds to a remark made by Jay, the student interviewer, about the category of houses that are religious.

BEN: which one's **religious.**
CHUCK: yeah
AL: At Church and Almost High.
BEN: no, that's more, that's ⌈**drugs**
CHUCK: ⌊that's not ⌈**religious**
ALL: ⌊#
DAN: no no no, that's sorta::'s against, like.
CHAISE: which ones
JAY: the::re's one called The Rock, or something like that, and ⌈uh Inn Pursuit
CHUCK: ⌊hm. is that a wrestler
JAY: ⌈**no, n::o**, it's a biblical reference
ALL: ⌊#
CHUCK: OK, alright alright, I understand that

It is impossible to know whether Al was trying to be funny by offering At Church and Almost High, a house sign that utilizes the names of the streets closest to the house. In other words, one cannot know from the transcript whether Al was aware of his example's playfulness vis-à-vis notions of "religious." He does not speak again in the segment, whether to take credit for the ensuing laughter or to acknowledge recognition that his example misses the mark (as Chuck does). Indeed, after Al's mention of At Church and Almost High, the interviewers introduce new examples of house names. But even after Ben, Chuck, and Dan participate in the clarification that At Church and Almost High has to do with drugs and not religion, Chuck interjects "a wrestler" as a possibility for The Rock. When Jay, the student interviewer, corrects him, all laugh uproariously. Jay does sound a bit exasperated as he explains this, and his tone might contribute to the ensuing laughter.

It does not seem that active play with Christian house names and their other possible meanings is something that is routine at Morning Wood. Thus I do not wish to argue that the residents of Morning Wood purposefully in-

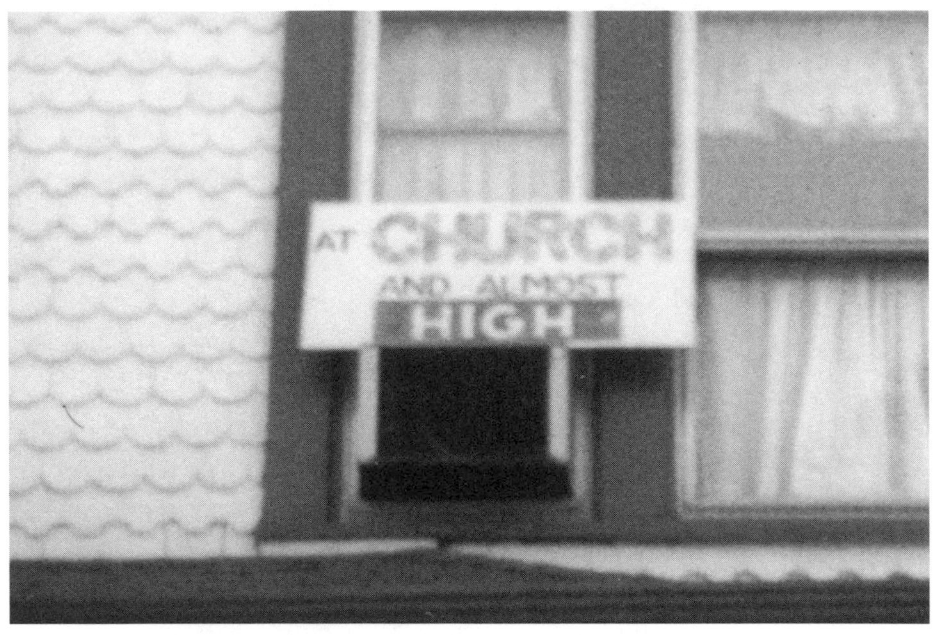

FIGURE 3.6. At Church and Almost High

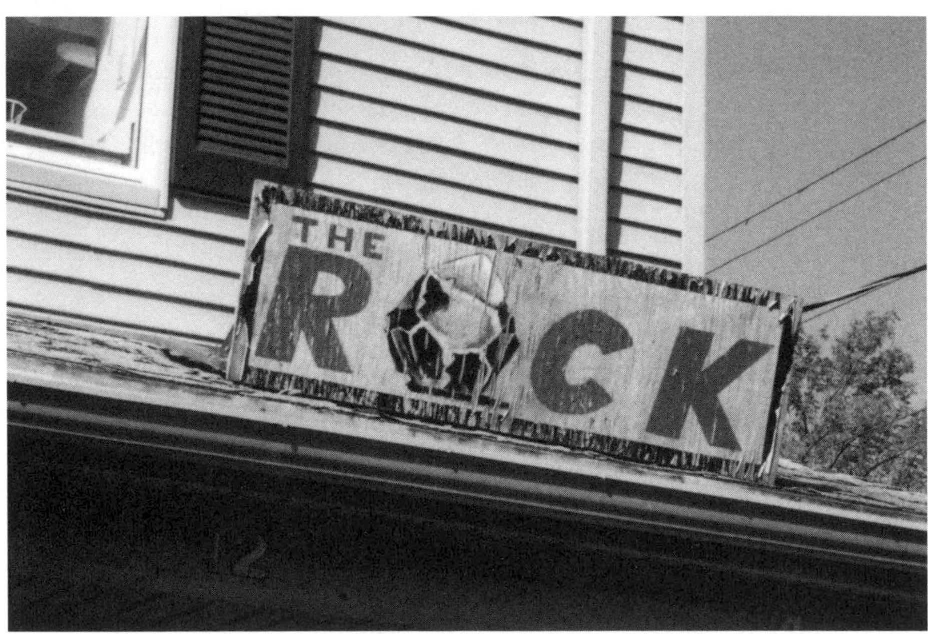

FIGURE 3.7. The Rock

voke house names that involve drugs or mass entertainment to create a humorous juxtaposition with a religious sphere of meaning. Rather, what seems to be happening is that the residents of Morning Wood are enacting what they earlier described to be their motive for displaying their sign: "to be funny." To be funny, in turn, sits comfortably under the umbrella of the explicitly metapragmatic and universal "to be clever." In short, that there are houses that are intended to be religious comes as a surprise to the residents of Morning Wood. They interject examples, guess at the possible referents of others, and then laugh about the unfolding incompatibility of these with the category of religion.

This is a practice that is hardly confined to our interview with the residents of Morning Wood. The Rock is a house like Inn Pursuit in that its residents understand their sign to indicate their Christian faith. Yet only in interviews with residents who understand their signs to indicate their Christian faith was there recognition that The Rock was related to Christianity. Residents of other kinds of houses consistently thought The Rock to be clever but had divergent rationales. Some interviewees—all of them male—mentioned, like Chuck of Morning Wood, that The Rock is Dwayne Johnson, a professional wrestler of unusual bravado. Several of these interviewees included that The Rock had been a college football star before taking up a career on television. One interviewee explained that The Rock has a signature facial expression and proceeded to open one eye wide while squinting with the other.

Yet other interviewees—both male and female—explained that The Rock fits into a larger category of signs involving drugs. Those mentioned across interviews include Rolling Stoned and At Church and Almost High. They also include two signs involving the animated television show *Scooby-Doo:* Scooby and Scrappy. Interviewees explained that "Scooby Snacks" are good to eat with marijuana-induced "munchies," and one interviewee explained that Shaggy, one of the main characters of the show, "was a model pothead." However, some interviewees pointed out that whereas most signs involving drugs are about weed, dope, or getting high, The Rock is not. They explained that The Rock is not indicative of the kind of drugs recreationally used by students in Oxford. Indeed, any interviewee making the argument that The Rock is about drugs was explicit about the kind of drug involved: crack cocaine. In most instances in which students discussed signs that they believed involved drugs, "drugs" sufficed without further specification. Some interviewees who argued for the connection with drugs mentioned the object depicted on the sign and serving as the "o" of "The Rock." In one case, the student explained, “It matches the substance it shows.” And, in another case, a student explained, “It’s exactly what it says, rock,” employing the term for its colloquial ability to mean crack cocaine.

Not all—or even most—house names understood by the houses’ residents to indicate their Christian faith drew such comments during interviews. Jim, the student interviewing the residents of Welcome Back, forestalls the possibility of reflections on signs such as the one that takes The Rock to index drug use rather than Christian faith. Indeed, he mentions faith before any particular house name:

> JIM: what do you think about, uh, religiously charged house signs. such as, uh, Crib of the Rib. o::r The Living Water Closet(4)
> STAN: not much to tell you the truth, I don’t care. I’m . . . I’m Jewish(2) and(3) I think some house signs just go over my head
> JIM: The Crib of the Rib, they have a little thing(3) Adam lost [his rib
> STAN: [his rib. Eve was created from his rib. see I **knew** that but I would never have thought that was an **un**creative sign

Stan’s reply is a typical one given by house residents who are questioned about whether signs might actually reflect some identity-marked attribute of residents: “I don’t care.” This is in keeping with the idea that signs should not be taken too seriously. Initially, however, he interjects religious difference as a possible reason for his inability to understand some signs. When Jim, seemingly taking Stan’s previous utterance as a request for explanation, begins to explain the religious significance of Adam and his rib, Stan claims to already know it. The connection is significant in Judaism, after all. His last utterance is interesting. He implies that he finds the sign creative apart from its religious underpinnings.

In contrast, The Living WC emerged in many interviews as an example of a “dumb” sign. Some interviewees ventured a guess that “WC” must stand for “water closet,” but this possibility was also described as dumb. Jim makes this mistake when he refers to The Living Water Closet rather than The Living with Christ. Jill’s rendering of the sign as Living Water Closet is even more surprising given that she lives in Crib of the Rib, a house whose residents understand their sign to reflect their Christian faith. In one interview, a student compared The Living WC to The Dresden, saying that both must be a private joke. Crib of the Rib surfaced in an interview as being about barbecue, which the resident explained was too tied to the preferences of the house residents who erected the sign. And finally, Green House was taken to be dumb for its inferred relationship to the residents' love for plants. Another student interjected that biology majors must live in the house. In another interview, drugs surfaced as an explanation. The implication was that the notion of a greenhouse raises the possibility of marijuana being grown inside. Whether eliciting ridicule or prompting the excitement of explanation and comparison characteristic of signs judged to be clever, the potential for signs to indicate Christian faith was absent in interviews with all but a handful of students. And those students were already in the know (and of that faith).

One's interpretation of visual language implicates one in the complexities of the boundaries between groups, which, in turn, shapes one's ability to participate. Scholars who study the social life of language must not take for granted that indexical relationships between linguistic forms and groups are achievements already accomplished. Any speaker of English, for example, might see in a house sign an indexical tie to historical figures, events, and practices or might see across signs a common indexical tie to a street, the number of residents living in a house, or commercial practices of lodging. But foregrounding such features as the most important indexical relations will itself index the interpreter as an outsider to the house sign community of practice. For a member, the signs' abilities to show that a particular sign's creators are clever or dumb, to provide a locator for a house that is much easier than an address, and to indicate the practices of engaging in sex and consuming drugs and alcohol, captured in the word "party," are paramount. Those who foreground other sorts of indexical relationships "don't get" the signs because they "take them too seriously." In the particular world of signs, one might put it thus: in order to be taken seriously, one must not take the signs too seriously.

But this insight foregrounds only one level of complexity in the ways that practitioners of folklore indicate differences between themselves and others. If taken to be sufficient, this insight can actually hide different ways of reading signs, different viewers, and different consequences of display. Scholars must also be aware that once a set of interpretive practices can be identified with a group, issues of agency underpinned by responsibility can reveal yet subtler boundaries. On the one hand, the residents who understand their signs to involve sexuality engage especially complex constructions of self (college kids), places (a nursery school, town, residential area, and other campuses), and others (kids, townies, and the user of the phrase "to push boundaries") in order to obviate their responsibility for the sign's display. On the other hand, residents who understand their signs to index their Christian faith do not decry their responsibility for the sign's display. They look outward, to other houses, and find that the majority indicate residents' need for "fellowship."

Each of these groups can be defined, in part, by its central problematic regarding agency. The residents of Morning Wood give evidence that they sense that someone might be offended or even harmed by their sign at the same time that they claim to have a particularly charged sign by "taking it over the edge." They mediate the contradiction by arguing that "kids" do not have access to their sign and by lampooning someone who needs to ask for an explanation of what the sign means. In short, they reject engagement with Bakhtin's other. The residents of Inn Pursuit replace experience with transgressive practices with transgressive house names in order to distinguish themselves from people who attend "infamous parties," adding salience to an offer of refuge. Their central problematic lies in the ways that residents of Inn Pursuit can themselves recognize indexical ties between other signs and practices that obviate the offense or harm done by those signs. In other words, the strategies through which they identify Bakhtin's other leak. Unlike in the case of Morning Wood, neither the residents of Inn Pursuit nor the residents of other houses with Christian signs engaged in a set of strategies to resolve the problem.

The kind of interpretive indeterminacy illuminated by the argument that Pop-N-Wood "doesn't necessarily carry any meaning" because its residents are girls is exacerbated when signs understood by their houses' residents to offer Christian fellowship are viewed by residents of other kinds of named houses. Thus a type of boundary can be crossed whereby the agency that a group hopes that its sign embodies is thwarted. This boundary encapsulates the ways that the house sign community of practice "grant[s] some individuals or groups the right to interpret while depriving others of the right to reclaim their original intentions" (Duranti 2001, 130). Indeed, the boundary is selective with regard to interpretive salience and agency. When signs considered by the people who display them to offer Christian refuge pass over the boundary, the offer is no longer salient. Indeed, residents of many houses connect signs meant by those who display them to indicate Christianity with the very transgressive practices that Christian residents see as their other. The agency embodied in the ability of Morning Wood to be considered "over the edge," however, is preserved when presented to the residents of Inn Pursuit.

The boundary between the two types of houses is selective in that the agency embodied by only one survives the boundary's crossing. Although an understanding of the ways that the practice of some form of folklore mediates agency must rest in part on the interpretive desires and practices of practitioners, such desires and practices do not necessarily reflect the risks involved in participation.

CHAPTER FOUR

Ghetto Fabulous and Plantation: Racial Difference in a Space of Fun

There is not, in everyday life, a direct correlation between place and appropriate behavior.

—TIM CRESSWELL, *In Place/Out of Place*

Like many towns and cities in which institutions of higher education exist, Oxford has a ghetto. This is where most of the named houses considered in this chapter are located, and "Ghetto" is common in names. College Prowler, a series of guidebooks that focus on student life, first mentions the Ghetto in the chapter entitled "Nightlife" under the heading "Local Traditions."[1] It appears in the context of a description of GhettoFest: "This is a gigantic block party held every spring past the north side of campus. It is located in what students refer to as Oxford's ghetto. It's really not a ghetto. It's just where the cheaper, more run down student housing is located off campus" (Garrett and Shultz 2005, 76). The second mention appears in a chapter named "The Inside Scoop" under the heading "Miami University Slang," where the book defines the term "Ghetto": "neighborhood immediately to the north of campus. The houses are typically more run down here. Also the site of Miami's popular annual GhettoFest" (Garrett and Shultz 2005, 115).

The Ghetto, the guidebook reveals, is a place constructed by geography, but also by an activity, a party. It is a relatively small residential area abutting the Mile Square's northern boundary.[2] The Ghetto is inhabited almost entirely by students. Students and faculty told me that the Ghetto is not a "real ghetto" because the area does not exhibit violence. Nearly everyone who mentioned the Ghetto also mentioned GhettoFest. One student described it to me in class as "the party of all parties." And just as a realtor told me not to live in the Mile Square because of the omnipresence of students, the very first colleague I met on campus told me not to rent in the Ghetto unless I enjoyed having trash blown or thrown into my yard and hearing loud parties. He launched into a description of the GhettoFest complete with an empty beer keg tied between trees. Participants pull the rope, he explained, giving the rider something like the experience of riding a bull. Finally, everyone said the quality of housing in the Ghetto was shabbier than elsewhere in Oxford and the rents were cheaper.[3]

On the other hand, the College Prowler's descriptions of the Ghetto are selective. The publication fails to mention that the Ghetto was once the area of Oxford where most African Americans lived. A man whose interview was published in a book of stories collected from African Americans by an eighth-grade class in Oxford refers to the area's past:

> We're able to go to different programs and different activities that we weren't allowed to go to as children. The town used to be kind of divided as far as the races go. We had the Afro-American people living on the north end of town from like Vine Street on north. But now we're able to move around to different places in the subdivisions and so forth. (Pettitt 2007, 49–50)

While African Americans still inhabit Oxford's Ghetto, few students or faculty—like the College Prowler—seem to be aware of their presence or past predominance there.

Does the increasingly unbounded movement and residence of African Americans in town make issues of race irrelevant to the house signs found in the Ghetto or to what students claim those signs reflect? It is true that students do not see race as salient to their display of house signs, but rather describe life in the Ghetto by combining the fun indexed by house signs generally with a spatially delimited lack of care indexed by disorderly behavior, nonstandard practices, and the presence of trash. The ways in which students describe the Ghetto thus give evidence that it has become a place where dispositions indexed by house signs can be realized to their fullest. Parties that occur there, as well as the area's ambience, provide a space in which students are unfettered. Students also explain that partying exists because the area is different from "real ghettos" elsewhere. Elements of those real ghettos, students claim, come to GhettoFest, the yearly party about which the College Prowler writes.

Perhaps the claim by residents of the Ghetto that the area's significance rests on partying and has little to do with race simply demonstrates the fact that the term "ghetto" has had different meanings in different times and places and that its most recent meanings are indeed seemingly free of any racial distinction. Anthropologist Carol Delaney, for example, notes:

> *Ghetto* used to refer to sections in European cities set aside for Jews; it has become generalized to refer to an area in cities where poor people or minorities live. The *barrios* in Brazil and the *gecekondu* in Turkey are similar phenomena. But there are ghettos at the opposite extreme. I live in what is called "the faculty ghetto" at Stanford because it is a place on the campus where *only* faculty can live. It used to be a facetious and somewhat derogatory name because of all the gorgeous homes there. Now, because of the enormous housing costs in the surrounding Silicon Valley, it is about the only place where faculty can afford to live. The recent development of "gated communities" is, perhaps, a better example. These are "ghettos" of the rich; they keep out "unwanted elements" and keep in "desirable" people like themselves. Some of these communities make further distinctions when they are designed expressly for singles or for retired people. (2004, 43)

A racial distinction underpins the imagination of partying in the Ghetto because the "real ghetto" that serves as the Ghetto's distant opposite emerges as a profoundly racial place when invoked by students who claim to have experience there. As long as the real ghetto remains unmentioned (beyond the assertion that it is absent locally), the celebratory dynamic of talk about the Ghetto can commence. In those rare moments of interviews when a resident gave evidence of experience of the real ghetto, however, racial difference emerged and quashed the celebratory dynamic beyond repair. When students did attest to having experience of the real ghetto, housemates distanced themselves from the invocation.

The house Plantation provides a contrasting case in that residents confront the racist potential of the house name directly, albeit crudely and ambivalently. This chapter argues that because Plantation is located outside of the Ghetto, its residents do not have access to the celebration of disorder, trash, and nonstandard practices heard in interviews conducted with residents of the Ghetto. Race is relevant to the maintenance of the fun to be had in an extreme form in the Ghetto. Indeed, race's exclusion is necessary for the perpetuation of fun. Race is largely absent from residents' reflections on the Ghetto, but that hardly makes its absence irrelevant. Racial distinctions thus

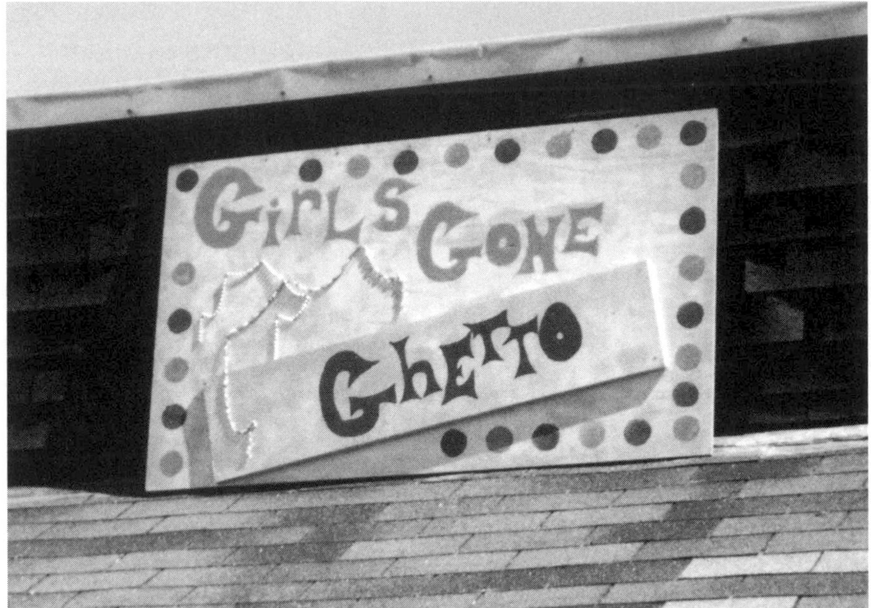

FIGURE 4.1. Girls Gone Ghetto

underpin the enhancement of fun that the Ghetto provides, but its mere mention destroys that fun.

"This Was Like Their Bar"

The residents of Girls Gone Ghetto were the only people we interviewed who were aware that the Ghetto was once the black section of town. The ways that they describe the area's past and its transition help to explain the general absence of an awareness of the significance of race to the area. Jack, the student conducting the interview, asks the residents whether they had other ideas for a name for their house.

> BRITT: the Old Town Tap because our house used to be a bar
> JACK: oh really
> BRITT: yeah
> MISSY: that we've learned, from other people, and it was called the Old Town Tap, like we actually had a few visitors who came by to see it because it used to be a bar
> JACK: really like how long ago
> MISSY: like, ooh

ALI: thirty years ago or something
MISSY: thirty-plus years ⌈ago
BRITT: ⌊seventies
JACK: oh
MISSY: yeah. yep, it was called the Old Town Tap so, late, like this year we thought about changing the name, to that but we decided to stick with Girls Gone Ghetto 'cause it's more fun

After Britt answers Jack's questions, Missy identifies the source of house residents' knowledge of the house's history, but only vaguely. Before she is able to do that, however, Jack asks for the residents to identify how long ago the house was a bar. The series of answers that follow date to the emergence of the house sign phenomenon and provide one of the earliest temporal frames for discussing house signs in our interviews. A much older, though isolated, frame emerges in the interview with the residents of Plantation. Most historical frames were introduced in interviews to account for the emergence of the band, film, or television show from which the house name was taken. Octopussy, 4 Non-Blondes, and Pee-wee's Playhouse are all examples.

The historical frame introduced in the interview with Girls Gone Ghetto will allow for the introduction of racial difference as a feature of life in Oxford. In the final line of the excerpt above, Missy moves action closer to the present with "so, late, like this year." She proceeds to foreshadow one of the ways in which students' characterizations of the Ghetto inform the reasons for which they find their residence there important. She uses a word that we would hear regularly in interviews with residents of houses in the Ghetto: "fun." Before exploring this theme, however, the residents offer a description of the area's demographic change. Jack facilitates revisiting the historical frame in which residents' descriptions of the house's and Ghetto's past emerge. Rather than responding to Missy's most recent characterization of Girls Gone Ghetto as "more fun," Jack offers an explicit guess as to whom Missy might have earlier been referring with "a few visitors who came by":

JACK: so like, alumni came back and were like looking for the bar
BRITT: yeah, like, some random guy just got ⌈out of his car, "can we see the house"
JACK: ⌊#
BRITT: he played in a band here, like when he was young
JACK: oh, ⌈so was there any . . .
MISSY: ⌊**supposedly** James Brown played here when it was a black bar
JACK: really

BRITT: yeah, that's true
JACK: so it, it was an African American, it was a black bar
BRITT: yeah
ALI: ⌈yes
BRITT: ⌊yeah(2) 'cause the Ghetto used to be all, like, segregated
JACK: so ⌈this was, the, like the African American, ⌈side of town
BRITT: ⌊the Ghetto was like . . . ⌊community
MISSY: ⌈yeah
BRITT: ⌊and then, yeah, and this was like their bar . . . and James Brown played here(4)
MISSY: you got all the history
ALI: yeah. we got the info

Britt introduces a band member who performed in the bar that is now Girls Gone Ghetto. Once Britt mentions that bands played in the bar, Missy trumps the fame of Britt's "random guy" with James Brown. Missy's use of "supposedly" emphasizes James Brown's fame and the improbability of his having played in the bar, but she follows the introduction of James Brown by pushing the temporal frame further back with "when it was a black bar." For the first time, someone names the racial identity of the area's past: "black." Britt elaborates that the Ghetto used to be a locus of an identity because it was "segregated." Britt uses the possessive "their," creating an indexical tie between James Brown's appearance and the racially inflected "community."

When Jack probes further, Britt provides the residents with the means to describe the Ghetto's change in racial makeup.

JACK: so what else do you know about the history ⌈of the area, or the . . .
MISSY: ⌊um . . .
BRITT: of the house
JACK: of the house or the area, yeah
BRITT: um . . .
MISSY: IT got switched to like a . . . (3) hippie type where like the Doo::rs, they played like that kind of music in the:: sixties, er, the early seventies . . . y'know, um . . . we know, that, in nineteen eighty:: . . . two
BRITT: yeah it ⌈was the year I was born
MISSY: ⌊someone was living here for sure
BRITT: it was a [fraternity name] annex house because, during

> homecoming weekend like, a guy and his wife actually came back and they wanted to see my bedroom which was kind of scary 'cause it made me realize what probably went on in my bedroom twenty years ago

Jack follows Missy's and Ali's claims of knowing about the past by asking what else house residents might know. He introduces a relatively broad means of ascertaining a relevant past by referring to "the area." Britt might have taken Jack's unfinished presentation of an alternative reference as an invitation to guess that it was to be "the house." Whatever the case, Jack repeats Britt's offer of "the house," but also repeats his initial offer of "the area." What is certain is that Britt and Missy use the house as a locus for understanding transformation, and want to explain transformation through the names of performers and bands associated with the former bar. Missy thus follows Britt's reference to "the house," talking about "it" as a bar.

Missy's remark that "it got switched to like a hippie type" is revealing of the ways in which the residents of Girls Gone Ghetto address the significance of race in two respects. First, Missy contributes to the structure of differences that mark the transition from one state of affairs to another in a way that allows the discussion to be framed by the bar's musical performers rather than by the larger neighborhood's racial demographics. Thus James Brown and "black" become the Doors and "hippie." Missy's mention of the Doors is especially interesting because she does not claim that they actually played in the bar. Rather, it seems to follow James Brown in being a representative group for a style, "hippie." "Hippie," unlike "black," does not make racial distinctions. Missy does not, for example, contrast James Brown and "black" with the Doors and "white." Indeed, the residents forego a description of the area's increasingly white student composition.

Second, Missy describes the transition of the type of performers at the bar with the statement "it got switched." She describes the transition without agent. Not only does she invoke and then safely dismiss the issue of race, but she ignores the forces or decisions involved in changing the bar and its performers. Missy contrasts the style of the Doors in the 1960s and 1970s with 1982, using the more particular date to index a time when the residents of Girls Gone Ghetto are sure that the house was used as a residence and not a bar. The significance of race has long faded by the time Britt mentions that the year corresponds with her birth and then narrates a story of a couple and their unsettling interest in her bedroom. The residents of Girls Gone Ghetto never again revisit descriptions of the race-inflected transition of the Ghetto in the interview.

The Ghetto as a Moral Geography

The residents of Girls Gone Ghetto were exceptional in that they were aware that the Ghetto was once predominantly black, but they came to resemble other residents of named houses in the Ghetto once the subject of race was left behind. Indeed, they came to resemble all residents living in named houses in Oxford, in that they believed their house names to have specified uses and proper interpretations. In keeping with the idea that a house name is easier to remember than an address, Jess, a resident of Ghetto Fabulous, reported, "It's just kind of like our house number, instead of saying our address, 501, we say Ghetto Fabulous."

Much more elaborate were explanations in keeping with the idea that house signs should be "clever" and "just for fun," be easy to understand by an onlooker, and not be "taken too seriously." The residents of Girls Gone Ghetto, for example, explained that they wanted to use the word "ghetto" and the name Girls Gone Wild, and found a clever possibility in the use of both:

> BRITT: anyways, um, we were just trying to, come up with a clever name that had "ghetto" involved in it since we were living in the neighborhood of the Ghetto, and then, it's kind of a play off like, the "Girls Gone Wild," like, "Girls Gone Ghetto," like the alliteration, like it just, kind've flows
> JACK: uh huh. and, was Girls Gone Ghetto, er Girls Gone Wild already . . . taken, at that point
> MISSY: yeah, but we just wanted one that had "ghetto" in it
> JACK: okay
> MISSY: I didn't even know about the Girls Gone Wild until, we had already thought about this one. We just, those advertisements were on TV all last year, so it was very . . .
> BRITT: prolific, yeah

Britt noted that Girls Gone Ghetto is a play on Girls Gone Wild and had the added benefit of increased alliteration. Jack asked about Girls Gone Wild, knowing that there was a house sign of that name. Missy claimed not to know about the particular sign, but rather the television commercials for a set of soft-core pornographic videos of the same name. This seemed to be in

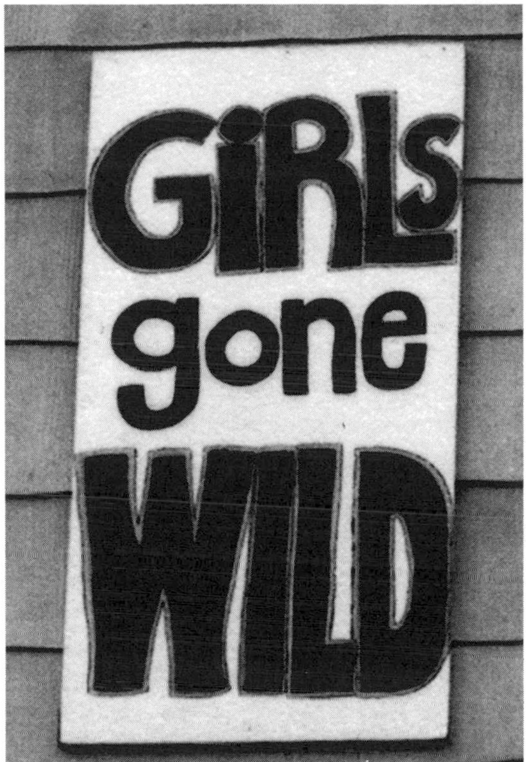

FIGURE 4.2. Girls Gone Wild

keeping with the idea that in order for a house's name to be seen as clever, it must not be a private joke among residents. And in keeping with the idea that one should not take house signs too seriously, Britt explained that the seemingly unrelated elements of residence in the Ghetto and an advertisement for a video were brought together because "it just kind of flows." Britt presented the idea that alliteration can be taken as a particularly salient focus for understanding the sign, an alliteration that depends on a widely known television commercial.

"Clever" and "fun" often emerged together in interviews with residents of named houses whether living in the Ghetto or not. When asked by Jack, "What do you think about the other signs around?" Polly, a resident of Ghetto Fabulous, responded, "Some of them are really clever." The residents noted that the name provided the means to make the production of the sign "fun" and the product "cool."

BETTY: and we had a lot of ideas, and we went over and over and we just decided on Ghetto Fabulous because we thought of a cool way to make it look like ⌈on the sign, the actual sign

JACK: ⌊the actual ⌈text of the sign

POLLY: ⌊like the actual sign

BETTY: like we thought that would be the funnest one, er, the most fun one to . . . paint and . . . ⌈create . . .

JACK: ⌊why don't you describe the sign a little bit

POLLY: well it's like block letters, with like blues and greens and some yellow, with black outline for the "ghetto" and then the "fabulous" part we took red a::nd silver sequins and we outlined it and then filled in the sequins for the "fabulous"

JACK: mm-hmm

POLLY: so we thought that would be cool-looking

BETTY: like sort of, the "ghetto" was kind of, um like, what do you call it, graffiti kind of, made it look like and the "fabulous" was pretty and . . .

POLLY: shiny and . . .

JESS: fancy

JACK: fabulous

POLLY: like kind of cursive writing too

In this excerpt, the residents focused on design elements themselves, explaining that the use of the word "ghetto" made for a sign would be "the most fun one to paint." Other possibilities mentioned were Girls in the Hood and Cornhole. The women explained that the former was inspired by their habit of wearing hooded sweatshirts and the latter by their enjoyment of a yard game of the same name. While one might argue that these two ideas for the house's name point to rather specific practices that involve the house's residents and thus might be considered a private joke, "hood" is a well-known word for neighborhood, especially, but not necessarily one with marked economic or racial attributes, and cornhole is played by many people we interviewed and known about by many more. While Girls Gone Ghetto pointed to their name's alliteration, the residents of Ghetto Fabulous located the potential for fun in constructing a cool sign in colors, stylistic elements, and the use of glitter. The residents noted the juxtaposition of the graffiti quality of the word ghetto rendered in block letters and black outline and the pretty quality of the word "fabulous" rendered in cursive writing and outlined in red and silver sequins.

Students' understandings of the significance of their residence in the Ghetto thus give evidence that the Ghetto is a location in a moral geography. A few scholars have developed a way of approaching constructions of space and location as they emerge in moments of spoken interaction. They pay particularly careful attention to the dynamics of interaction in a setting at hand, but also consider the ways in which territories and identities are invoked, recreated, and sometimes shaped within and between specific moments of discourse. Keith Basso, for example, demonstrates some of the ways in which "Apache constructions of place reach deeply into other cultural spheres, including conceptions of wisdom, notions of morality, politeness and tact in forms of spoken discourse, and certain conventional ways of imagining and interpreting the Apache tribal past" (1996, xv).

Jane Hill (1995) coined the phrase "moral geography" to explain the ways in which Don Gabriel, a dying man said to be the last speaker of Mexicano in a small town near Puebla, Mexico, contrasts a world of peasant communitarian values with a world of business and profit. It is from the former to the latter, Hill demonstrates, that Don Gabriel travels as he narrates his son's murder and his own quest to find and bury the body.

Gabriella Modan uses Hill's notion of moral geography to understand some of the discursive dynamics through which different people create various ways of understanding Mount Pleasant, a neighborhood in Washington, D.C., as a place. People invoke an array of oppositions including city vs. suburb, filth vs. cleanliness, solidarity vs. individualism, public vs. private, cooperative membership vs. private ownership, and masculine vs. feminine to construct themselves and others as definable, in part, by their emergent relationship to Mount Pleasant. Although Modan points out that the Washington, D.C., suburbs are more ethnically diverse than the city itself, in Mount Pleasant and elsewhere, filth, fear, and aggressive masculinity become highly relevant (but not inevitable) in identity constructions and performances. Modan argues that various vectors of identity can be brought to bear and aligned in specific moments of interaction: "Whiteness can be used to index fear, fear can be used to index gender, wealth can be used to index order, and any of these can be—and are—used by community members to index a suburban identity" (2007, 107). Modan explains generally, "A moral geography is an interweaving of a moral framework with a geographical territory. Through the use of various discourse strategies and themes, community members create alignments and oppositions among people and places" (2007, 90). Thus social and psychological dispositions as unrelated as fear, wealth, and order can be invoked to make territorial differences salient.

In many ways, the residents of Crib of the Rib live on the periphery of the Ghetto. They were the only residents who foregrounded the presence of violent crime there.

JACK: so what do you, what do you understand, like, the Ghetto to be(3)
TARA: shady . . .
GIRLS: #
MARY: well, we hear like, gunshots and stuff every once in a while
JACK: really #
TARA: ⌈we've, we've heard gunshots, yeah, #, we're paranoid
KATE: ⌊there's been a burglary, behind our house
GIRLS: #
JILL: and like, we had like, there was like an alarm system [indecipherable] across the street one day, and . . .
KATE: a burglary right there
JILL: oh yeah, police were next door because they thought the kid next door was the one who, I don't know
TARA: stole an air conditioner
KATE: [indecipherable] all like the first week of school sort of like a . . .
ALL: #
JILL: it **is** the ghetto

Jack expresses surprise when Mary mentions gunshots as an example illustrating Tara's descriptor "shady." Tara's use of "paranoid" is interesting in that it seems to be in response to Jack's surprise.

When Jack asks whether the house residents believe that such activities are more characteristic of the Ghetto than elsewhere, they initially respond affirmatively, noting the presence of traffic and the Ghetto's remoteness with Kate's "back here":

JACK: so do you think . . . those type of things would occur more in the Ghetto than the other places of the, of Oxford(4)
KATE: I think just because like, well and also, like there's not a lot of cars driving by back here and, I mean it would be easier to

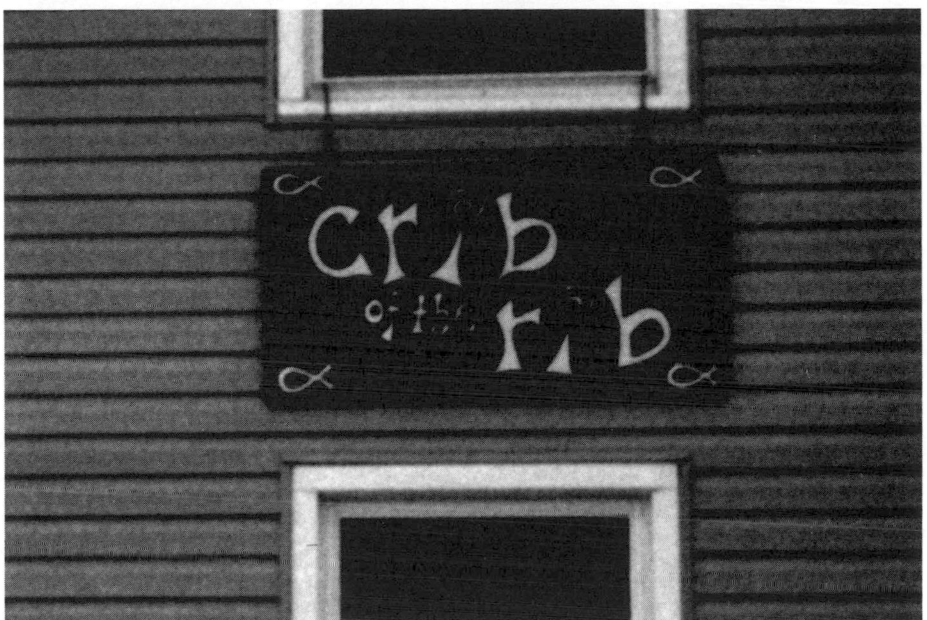

FIGURE 4.3. Crib of the Rib

> break in somewhere back here than, you know, like ⌈on Spring Street or something
>
> MARY: ⌊maybe like a mental thing too like since we're in the Ghetto we feel . . . things happen more, you know
>
> KATE: they might not
>
> ALL: #

With "mental thing," Mary offers the possibility that residents' perception of the incidence of crime might be distorted by residence in the Ghetto.

Immediately after mentioning the possibility that living in the Ghetto might predispose residents to exaggerate the incidence of crime, Jill and Tara explain that the house is on the periphery of the Ghetto:

> JILL: I kind of feel like we're in a different part of the Ghetto though
>
> GIRLS: yeah
>
> TARA: we're on the outer skirts [*sic*]
>
> JILL: yeah this street and over is long, yeah
>
> TARA: we're not the main Ghetto

FIGURE 4.4. Too Poplar for the Ghetto

GIRLS: #
JACK: so is the heart down . . . this way west
JILL: yeah

Whether one would find a higher or lower incidence of criminal activity in more central areas of the Ghetto the house residents never address. But they make certain that they feel that they are spatially peripheral.

The residents of Crib of the Rib are like the residents of Inn Pursuit, because they consider their sign to offer an invitation to those needing Christian "fellowship." But this fact does not explain their peripheral location in the Ghetto. The residents of another house, Too Poplar for the Ghetto, do not see a connection between their house sign and Christian faith. "Poplar," of course, is a pun on "popular," and Poplar Street forms the outer boundary of the Ghetto.

When statements of residents living in more central parts of the Ghetto are considered, the moral stance of the residents of Crib of the Rib emerges as peripheral. Rather than emphasize violent crime (or their spatial disposition), residents in the central part claim that they can achieve some of the major attributes indexed by all house signs, but in the extreme. In contrast to the residents of Crib of the Rib, the residents of Ghetto Fabulous consider themselves to live in the central part of the Ghetto. Betty introduces the ubiquitous notion that house names should be both clever and readily accessible. When Jack offers an example of a house name with the word "ghetto" in it, the house residents and he embark on a discussion that includes the distinction between peripheral and central places in the Ghetto, the notion that the center of the Ghetto is a dead end at the very edge of town, and that linguistic play with the distinction between peripheral and central is widely understood.

> BETTY: I like the little clever sayings that like mean something that everyone can get, that was the hard part, we wanted to do something like that but we didn't really come up with anything
>
> JACK: so the Not Quite Ghetto sign, do you remember where that one was
>
> BETTY: it's right on Sycamore, like, up here, take a right and it's a couple houses down
>
> JACK: so is it in a place you would consider, like, on the edge of the ghetto
>
> BETTY: yeah, I think it was very appropriate #, 'cause they're, you know they're not **quite** in the Ghetto. but they're close
>
> JACK: so you think the Ghetto has pretty definite sort of boundaries
>
> POLLY: yeah
>
> JESS: mm-hmm
>
> JACK: yeah
>
> POLLY: I think, like, this is pretty much like the heart of it, right here
>
> JACK: and how, how do you determine, like, what cues are there that make those boundaries evident?
>
> POLLY: I think . . . I don't know
>
> BETTY: like the dead end down here, and then when you get to Sycamore pretty much that's the end, and then like, when you go straight this way, where it dead-ends, well where it starts to curve up again and then this way where it dead-ends

Betty's final description emphasizes the Ghetto's overall peripheral disposition to Oxford: Sycamore Street, a street linking many others in town, emerges as a named location, whereas the Ghetto proper is described as a series of nameless dead-end streets.

While all residents of named houses in Oxford advise that house signs not be taken too seriously, residents of the Ghetto attribute specific qualities of life to the area. Indeed, they see the area as spatially distinct and morally specific. Unusual housing and behavior coexists with a friendly and laid-back atmosphere. When Jack asks, "So how do you understand what the Ghetto is, like what that means?" Betty answers, "GhettoFest." This was one of the most quickly offered and typical responses to such a request. Jess concurs, "Yeah, that has a big thing to do with it." After these two utterances, however, the residents begin to describe the housing stock in the area:

> JESS: just kind of, there are also just, like, random houses down here too, I think . . .
> POLLY: like maybe ⌈old, older
> JESS: ⌊on more of campus they're kind of just like, you know you could see maybe like a family living there and I think down here it's like, very **awkward** houses, you know, and they're all ⌈facing different wa::ys and, like, ours is like one big house, they're all separated, you know what I mean, they're just kind of . . .
> POLLY: ⌊like even this one right here, like all three attached # . . . Random House
> JESS: they're ghetto #

The residents mention the haphazard living quarters that do not conform to their idea of a single-family house as well as the houses' age. Jess modifies the deictic "here" with "down," emphasizing the area's peripheral location with respect to campus and the Mile Square. Many of the structures on campus and within the Mile Square are older than the houses in the Ghetto. Polly offers the descriptor "older," whereupon Jess stresses the awkward quality of the houses' arrangement. Polly orients her own perspective on the Ghetto to Jess's description, leaving off her own previous description stressing the age of the houses. She offers her own and adjacent houses as examples of Jess's description of "awkward." Thus Polly mentions Random House, a house joined to her own.

Practices also participate in constituting the moral geography of the Ghetto. The residents of "Ghetto Fabulous" describe the method they used to fill their pool during the summer to demonstrate a usage of their house name and, by extension, illustrate a quality of the Ghetto:

> JACK: so what would, what would qualify as something being ghetto fabulous
> ALL: #
> BETTY: I got one, like, um, we don't have a hose, attached anywhere, so [indecipherable], we had a big pool this summer, to fill it up,

we had to duct tape it to our sink and turn on the water, and we also had buckets like from the shower and the kitchen sink, bathroom sink, and we had . . .
JESS: **that** is ghetto fabulous
BETTY: **that** was ghetto fabulous
POLLY: just like something that's funny . . .
BETTY: unconventional . . .

With the descriptors "funny" and "unconventional," one can see that a cluster of qualities is beginning to emerge in students' reflections on house signs such that one can discern the existence of a moral geography. Qualities that are believed to be important in appreciation of house signs generally turn out to be aspects of life itself in the Ghetto. Just as house signs are supposed to be funny, qualities of life in the Ghetto are humorous for their nonstandard qualities, from the haphazard arrangement of houses to the way in which residents filled a swimming pool. And just as one "shouldn't take house signs too seriously," life in the Ghetto is "laid-back." Missy of Girls Gone Ghetto explains:

> yeah I like it better, cause it's **a::ll** students around, and like, I don't know you always see like guys playing football in the street and like . . . you don't really get much traffic down here except for people who **live** in the ghetto, you know what I mean, so it's just kind of a laid-back atmosphere.

Polly of Ghetto Fabulous describes what the neighbors told the current residents when they were contemplating renting the house:

> before we moved in they told us, like we were looking at houses, you know, around here and they said that, it was like a different atmosphere down here it wasn't like, typical Miami they said people are a lot more friendly, laid-back and, y'know everyone, talks to their neighbors and gets along, they said it's, they like, loved it down here 'cause it was, they felt like it was kind of like a different, more laid-back atmosphere

Not all of the Ghetto's attributes are positive. A frequently mentioned aspect of the Ghetto was the presence of trash as an insurmountable nuisance.

AMY: it's like, we kno::w that our area of town is, trashier or like, crappier than . . .

BRITT: it's not taken care of as well like . . .
AMY: there's trash **everywhere** if you noticed outside and it just stays . . .
BRITT: yeah
AMY: but . . .
JACK: you think that's . . . the, the students, living down here or do you think the, the landlords also, ⌈contribute . . .
BRITT: |little of column A, little of column B
AMY: ⌊little of column A, little of column B
ALL: #
AMY: like, if you look out in the woods, there's **so** much trash, a::nd **I** don't like to live in trash, **but** I also didn't want to go and pick it up and then have more trash there the next day, so it was such a big project that we just kinda . . . left it, so . . .
BRITT: and like, I know like at the beginning of the year it was because there's a lot of, there's all the wooded areas right here so there were a lot of raccoo::ns and things, which . . .
AMY: cats . . .
BRITT: most of them have been tra, like the raccoons and most of them have been trapped and taken out by like the police, like, it's, for garbage day, like, put all the garbage out, like, you'd wake up in the morning, it's everywhere, and then the garbage man's like "I'm not, taking, like, bags that have been ripped up" so then they'd just sit there and then it'd get even worse and then you'd have to go . . .
AMY: yeah, so, trash is a big problem
ALI: #
BRITT: yeah, and broken glass
AMY: yes
BRITT: like I don't know why, like, I don't know if you, noticed like, even walking to our house, like, which we don't drink anything out of bottles but there's always like broken bottles in the street, like forties, empty forties like, laying around and stuff like that

"Trashy" as adjective becomes "trash" as noun as Amy shifts from describing the neighborhood to noting the presence of trash. Jack introduces two possible culprits, students and landlords. Britt and Amy assign culpability to both.[4] Amy emphasizes the peripheral location of the Ghetto by noting that the trash can be found in the adjacent woods. Whether the residents actually cleaned the area or simply assumed that the trash would return is unclear. Britt introduces the idea that animals are primarily responsible for the trash. This retroactively explains Amy's introduction of the woods and their connection with trash. With Britt's introduction of broken glass, however, raccoons and cats fade and humans appear as culprits. Britt remarks that the interviewers might have noticed during their approach to the house that bottles lie about. She is no longer talking about raccoons in the woods tearing into residents' trash, but rather people littering. Her mention of "forties," a name for malt liquor that comes in forty-ounce bottles, makes apparent that she is talking about the results of partying. Though the residents do not like (or contribute to, in this particular case) the results of partying, the fact that their discussion of trash's omnipresence in the Ghetto concludes with the presence of alcohol provides a link to what residents find especially important about living there, GhettoFest.

In a single excerpt, the women of Girls Gone Ghetto bring together the various elements mentioned in the multiple excerpts above that constitute a moral geography for the Ghetto. They include cheap, unorthodox, shabby housing, a laid back atmosphere, and the pervasiveness of partying:

> AMY: we understand it to be the crappiest looking houses on campus
> MISSY: white trash everywhere
> AMY: like, all the houses look kinda, they're just **odd**-looking houses like . . . like, who designed this house were they, smoking some sort of drug, I guess
> JACK: #
> AMY: like and uh, it's really cheap living
> BRITT: and I think it's stereotyped as like a very laid-back atmosphere, like . . . like . . .
> MISSY: parties

Missy's mention of white trash is isolated, never repeated or explained in the interview and never attributed to the Ghetto by residents of other houses in the Ghetto. Many of the people in the same interview had mentioned the presence of trash in the Ghetto and the trashy appearance of the neighborhood. Thus one can only speculate that Missy's use of a racial epithet might be in keeping with a well-documented class-inflected racialization of white people (Hartigan 2005). Such a usage would certainly rise to the task of jokingly denigrating the area's physical presence, but perhaps not its collegiate residents. Just such a white racialized other will figure prominently in a narrative presented later in the chapter, but the denigration of the narrated person will be unambiguous. For the residents of the Ghetto, the ability to party in a carefree, friendly environment coincides with the residence of students in unorthodox, cheap, and shabby housing.

Before describing GhettoFest, it is important to note a consistent assertion across interviews: that Oxford's Ghetto is not a "real ghetto." This assertion makes the residents of Oxford's Ghetto atypical with respect to people discussed by Hill and Modan. Hill and Modan are careful to show that moral geographies are underpinned by a great deal of stereotyping with which people narrate specific events. Such stereotypes draw on and create social distinctions in space. Residents of named houses in the Ghetto are no different, except that they understand the area in which they live to be a less real, even fake, version of an area elsewhere. The real ghetto, importantly, is unavailable locally. Betty of Ghetto Fabulous notes, "I think it's almost a joke #, it's like, the Ghetto, haha."

> POLLY: yeah it's like a joke like, like this is **so bad** you know, I know, actually I know my parents were always like yeah the Ghetto like, they were talking about, remember our parents were talking about this weekend like they, they call this the Ghetto you know, try going like, in Chicago to the real ghetto you know like, it was like a joke you know, just . . .
> BETTY: we knew that, we're not like ooh we live in the Ghetto,
> [watch out, lock your doors
> POLLY: [we don't think that this is like a dangerous part of town

Affirming the distance of Oxford's Ghetto from the residents' (and their parents') understanding of a real ghetto is the residents' assertion that the very identification of the area in which they live with the word "ghetto" constitutes a joke. When Betty and Polly reflect on the Ghetto's name, they simply emphasize its humorous lack of resonance with reality, but when Polly quotes her parents, she seems to indicate something besides the potential for humor. Thus Betty responds somewhat defensively in that she emphasizes the residents' knowledge that Oxford's Ghetto is not dangerous. Betty states that the residents do not typically assert, "We live in the Ghetto," with the accompanying warning, "Watch out! Lock your doors." Polly desists from a hypothetical quote and states that the residents do not find this part of town to be dangerous. By this point, using the name Ghetto to refer to their present location seems unlikely, as the emphasis is on the lack of burglary and danger that exists in Chicago and other places outside of Oxford.

Britt of Girls Gone Ghetto recounts her initial surprise at hearing of the Ghetto in Oxford:

> I remember like when I was a freshman and people say like going to the Ghetto I'm like, Oxford doesn't have a ghetto like what are you talking, you know, 'cause it's, I don't . . . just picture a group of houses like, a block, like a neighborhood I, I just picture them like, **projects**

She explains that before she learned that Oxford's Ghetto was indeed "just a group of houses," a block, and a neighborhood, she was more inclined to think that housing projects should be an appropriate referent for ghetto. With her explanations, Britt intimates that she could not imagine the existence of projects in Oxford. Once again, residents of the Ghetto demonstrate their understanding that the authentic ghetto is elsewhere.

Later, when Jack says, "Miami's Ghetto isn't, like, a ghetto you think of, y'know like, in a big city," they describe what they understand a real ghetto to include as well as a reason for which such elements are not found locally:

> ALI: there's no gunshots, ever
> BRITT: no
> AMY: there's . . . no:: higher crime that we know of, there's no, like . . . everyone here is like, in college, it's not . . . there's not any local people I know of who live anywhere near here . . .
> [sounds of agreement]
> MISSY: which is, which is actually like, I don't know, I like it
> BRITT: it's kinda cool

While residents of houses with sexualized names like Morning Wood downplay responsibility for the display of their signs when they argue that only other college students have visual access, residents of named houses in the Ghetto celebrate the absence of locals in the neighborhood more generally. Rather than limiting the damaging effects of their signs, or boasting of the same, residents note a relatively free use of space—apart from the effects of their sign on an onlooker. Britt sums up the exclusive residence of students in the Ghetto as "cool."

GhettoFest: Aspects of the "Real" Ghetto Come to the Ghetto

One reason that GhettoFest is such an important dimension to the moral geography of the Ghetto and to residents of named houses more broadly is that house signs are supposed to indicate the frequent partying that goes on inside. At GhettoFest, partying is not confined to a single house but takes place in many simultaneously and even spills onto yards, sidewalks, and streets. People are able to identify a party situated in an entire neighborhood, the Ghetto, and not just a single house via its name. One might say that the association of houses and their names with a party goes public in the case of GhettoFest. Jess of Ghetto Fabulous uses the example of teachers with whom she works to attest to the pervasiveness of knowledge about GhettoFest:

> well actually, I am, student teaching right now, and I have some colleagues, co-workers that live in Oxford, and they were all asking me "where do you live, where do you live" and I was like "o::h north campu::s" and I'm like trying to explain it to them, they're, you know, fifty years old, and I said, um, "well I, I live in the Ghetto," and they're like, "o::h okay," you know what I mean, so, I mean they've lived in Oxford all their lives, so I think they definitely know where the Ghetto is, they're like "isn't that where that big party is" #, so . . . [5]

Even teachers—who would never be found at GhettoFest—know of "that big party."

The assertion by residents (and their reports of the assertions of their parents) that the real ghetto is to be found elsewhere, in cities where there are housing projects and crime, helps to explain why, in interviews, GhettoFest is especially important. It facilitates the establishment of the Ghetto as the place for a communal party at the same time as a time and place for entry of elements deemed missing. The residents of Girls Gone Ghetto emphasize the first and then the second of these characteristics of GhettoFest. Just after discussing the history of their house using its former life as a bar as a starting point and as a means of describing the neighborhood's changing racially inflected demography, the residents argue that GhettoFest itself emerged from the bar:

> JACK: so do you know anything, like around the immediate area that was as old, that was around back then or . . .
> AMY: there, I've heard rumo::rs, that like . . . I don't know anything about the area really but, I've heard rumors that GhettoFest, it

was like started kind of because of our house, like, it had something like the beginning of GhettoFest had something to do with the bar that was here, so . . . (4)

The residents proceed to describe GhettoFest when Jack prods:

JACK: so . . . I've heard of GhettoFest but I haven't **seen** GhettoFest, so explain GhettoFest a ⌈little bit
AMY: ⌊okay, picture, all of Miami, in the Ghetto, in the Ghetto, trying to get, to a keg
ALL: #
AMY: and there's ba::nds everywhere, like, um . . .
BRITT: mud wrestling
MISSY: mud wrestling . . . beer bonging on roofs . . .
BRITT: it usually starts at like eleven [AM] . . . it's always the weekend before the last weekend of classes, so in April
JACK: okay
BRITT: and what it, it like starts at ten like, every house gets at, like at least ten kegs I'd say like it's, pretty crazy, and um, like I know last year they'd like, string up kegs and it was like riding a bull like they'd shake the ropes like an empty keg people riding it, and just like people in the street and . . .

Amy begins hyperbolically with her utterance, "all of Miami," stressing the GhettoFest's draw of students from outside the neighborhood who are "trying to get to a keg," stressing the limited resources given the number of participants. Another hyperbole follows with Amy's assertion that "there's bands everywhere." Britt mentions mud wrestling, and Missy repeats this before adding "beer bonging on roofs." Both of these activities are highly public and are not common at parties held at named houses outside of the temporal and spatial boundaries of GhettoFest. Britt describes GhettoFest by noting its scheduling. She demonstrates that the academic calendar governs the party's schedule. Britt finishes her description by altering her own claim slightly, claiming a ten-to-one ratio of kegs of beer to houses, and emphasizing one way in which the GhettoFest is noteworthy by virtue of its public spectacle.

Missy, Ali, and Britt provide a finale to the concerted description of GhettoFest. It is in these lines that the residents illustrate one of the most charged aspects of GhettoFest that differentiates it from parties held in single named houses.

MISSY: lots of cops
ALI: lots of cops
BRITT: yeah, they just pretty much line the streets and wait for someone to walk out on the sidewalk holding a drink or like what, you know what I mean
JACK: yeah

A number of published documents use the name GhettoFest in such a way as to give evidence that the presence of police and the possibility of arrest or having one's party declared a "nuisance party" and shut down are some of the most important aspects of GhettoFest that differentiate it from other parties. The investigative unit of the Ohio Department of Public Safety, for example, uses the name "GhettoFest" in lieu of the name of a tavern to report arrests made at three residences and several public locations on April 12, 2003. The offenses include underage possession, underage consumption, possession of an open container of beer or intoxicating liquor in a public place, and resisting arrest coupled with one of the aforementioned. Attesting to the extent of police presence, Kaila Gregory reported in the *Miami Student:*

> At GhettoFest 2002, OPD [Oxford Police Department] officers and officials from other law enforcement agencies made more than 200 arrests. That year two party-goers were stabbed by an out-of-town male during a confrontation regarding a stolen cell phone. (2004)

As far as I know, that kind of violence is uncommon at GhettoFest, yet very worthy of conversation and reporting. A much more relevant fear was the ability of the police to arrest one for underage drinking or possession of an open container in a public place. Similar events unfolded the two years that I attended GhettoFest. Police officers walked or rode on a horse or in a car down the street after the keg ride concluded the communal event. People headed into front yards until the police passed, at which time most would reoccupy the sidewalk or street. People at the head of the block would scream warnings down the street as the police approached for another sweep. This pattern went on for several hours.

The notion that the Ghetto is special because residents may occupy the street in the absence of traffic is problematized during GhettoFest. The distinction between the front yard and the sidewalk becomes a boundary to be transgressed, as the police can arrest anyone with the accoutrements of partying found on the sidewalk or the street. Alexandra Barlow reported a police officer's understanding of the distinction in the *Miami Student:* "'People can drink on their property,' Lewis said. 'From the sidewalk to the curb is public property, from the sidewalk to the residence is private property'" (2006). In another report in the same paper, Brett Roller and Anna Michael present the sympathetic perspective of Oxford's police chief: "Schwein said that with a party made up of thirty to thirty-five houses, it is very easy for someone to walk from party to party with an open container of alcohol and not think about the consequences, especially when that person has already had several drinks" (2003). Indeed, the fact that GhettoFest brings liquor past the front yard, subjecting the possessor to arrest, is of concern to participants and police alike. The police chief does not remark, however, on the risk evoked by inhabiting the sidewalk and street that lends GhettoFest much of its excitement.

Consideration of what names are used by which people for the huge party indicate that students and some other residents and elected officials used "GhettoFest," but students never used the name "North End Party." "North End" refers to the same area that "Ghetto" does. One cannot be certain of what was said at Oxford City Council meetings. For example, the secretary recorded the minutes such that complete sentences represent the gist of the utterances of single townspeople and elected officials (as in the representation of Police Chief Schwein's utterances above). But minutes of the meeting of April 15, 2003, show that townspeople use both names for the party.[6] First, the secretary reports, "Mr. Jones thanked Chief Schwein for the ride last Saturday and noted the GhettoFest was well attended, well behaved and everything worked extremely well" (City of Oxford, 2003). The secretary reports the next mention of the huge party, "Mr. Smith congratulated the police department, staff, and students for their cooperation resulting in a successful North End Party this year." Finally, the secretary reports, "Mayor Bogard echoed the compliments to the Police Department and students of the North End Party." The use of both "GhettoFest" and "North End Party" likely happened at the City Council meeting, as it is unlikely that the secretary is solely responsible for the appearance of both names.

What is certain is that students never used "North End Party" to refer to GhettoFest or the "North End" to refer to the Ghetto. Additionally, students never used "North End Party" in large banners announcing GhettoFest, nor was there a house sign that used the name "North End" in its linguistic play. Students sometimes used "North Campus," but this includes a much larger area than the Ghetto. Since students exclusively used "GhettoFest" and townspeople and elected officials used both "GhettoFest" and "North End Party," use of the latter might be seen as a means of avoiding the use of the former.

The statement of Oxford Police Department Lieutenant Holzworth, reported by the *Miami Student,* lends weight to the possibility: "Holzworth suggested that the name GhettoFest could attract many unwanted guests, and he suggested promoting the party under the name the North End Party" (City of Oxford, 2003). In sum, GhettoFest facilitates several kinds of transgressions. Police patrol what is otherwise claimed as student territory, and one cannot be certain that revelers are students.

The "Real" Ghetto Makes Fun Disappear

What of race? Thus far in the discussion of the Ghetto and GhettoFest, the residents of just one house have been aware of the Ghetto's racialized past, but have excluded the significance of race to the present. What makes race irrelevant to Oxford's Ghetto in an overt manner is the fact that the real ghetto exists elsewhere. Students explain that real ghettos exist in big cities where serious crimes occur. Some remark that the existence of projects are indicative of a real ghetto. The involvement of the police and the possibility of arrest during GhettoFest lend the Ghetto some of the properties of the real ghetto, but these possibilities do not involve racial distinctions overtly. Throughout their reflections cited above, residents of the Ghetto, townspeople, police, and writers for the College Prowler alike never invoke racial distinctions.

An excerpt from an interview with the residents of Girls Gone Ghetto demonstrates what happens when someone gives evidence of experience with the "real" ghetto, or at least with a person whose manner is understood to be representative of it. The place and person emerge as racially distinct. When the interviewee describes a resident of the real ghetto, her housemates express disapproval and distance themselves from her descriptions. Talk shifts from a celebratory disposition toward Oxford's (fake) Ghetto to a negative disposition toward the particular house resident's descriptions. Indeed, talk shifts from a focus on the celebration of life in the Ghetto to a focus on the condemnation of the particular house resident who has described the real ghetto. By showing that the real ghetto is a profoundly racialized space whose residents must not be invoked, much less described, this chapter argues that race underpins the moral geography of Oxford's Ghetto because it must be absent locally.

Jack begins by asking about Ghetto Fabulous and whether its residents ever heard people use that name as a term. Jack and the residents embark on an exegesis of the name.

AMY: yes
GIRLS: #
JACK: is that kinda popular
[sounds of agreement]
ALI: no **I've** heard ghetto fabulous
JACK: so what do you . . . ⌈understand that to mean
BRITT: ⌊I don't even know what that means
AMY: well I, I picture it as someone who has the bling-bling o::n like, gold chai::ns, who's like, the viso::r upside-do::wn, the ⌈baggy pa::nts . . .
ALI: ⌊like **rich** ghetto people
AMY: see I just picture it as like ECM [East Coast Mafia?] and their, I don't know like, suped-out car with the ghetto blaster #, that's what I think of when I think ghetto fabulous, it's like . . . extravagant, # like, rapper kind of, is what I think of

In these initial utterances, Ali, Britt, and Amy establish their dispositions to the term that will develop further in ensuing discussion.[7] Ali claims to have heard the term as her housemates wonder aloud whether they have heard it and what it might mean. When Jack asks for a description, Britt claims ignorance. Amy offers a kind of person as a referent for the term, identifiable by the juxtaposition of expensive jewelry, "bling-bling," and a particular style that itself manipulates the mundane, "visor upside-down" and "baggy pants."

While GhettoFest invokes violence as an attribute of the ghetto and facilitates its incorporation in the Ghetto, "Ghetto Fabulous" invokes the ostentatious display of wealth. Ali sums up Amy's description by emphasizing "rich" alongside "ghetto," and Amy elaborates again, this time extending clothes to a car's sound system ("ghetto blaster"). Her use of "ECM" is confusing in that it is an acronym of indeterminate meaning. Our class first imagined that "EC" might stand for "East Coast," a variety of rap music different from western or southern varieties by virtue of associated individuals and groups, and we imagined that "M" might stand for "Mafia," a persona akin to the gangster or boss of an earlier age of organized crime. A very few rap artists do use "mafia" as part of their names, sometimes as an acronym for a longer name, but Amy does not seem to be familiar with any of these.[8] She includes the descriptor "extravagant" and returns to a person as a referent with her descriptor "rapper." I have been unable to find anyone aware of "ECM" as a salient acronym in the world of hip-hop fandom.

The residents continue to discuss the house name:

JACK: so where have you heard that term
MISSY: where **would** you hear that
JACK: do you hear ⌈students using that term, or . . .
BRITT: ⌊I know, I don't hear that term
MISSY: yeah, I ⌈know, not . . .
BRITT: ⌊ever
ROB: BET [Black Entertainment Television]
BRITT: ⌈I knew of it, ⌈I knew it once
MISSY: ⌊BET
ALI: ⌊I'd say more in high school I heard of it than here
AMY: at my summer job we would say that customer is ghetto fabulous, #
JACK: so what, like describe that customer, would . . .
AMY: they, well, one time, she was, this woman was wearing, a T-shirt, okay she looked . . . very . . . ignorant, like, trashy, kind of . . .
ALI: you look ignorant #
AMY: no she just, she, spoke, she, spoke incorrectly, sh, uh . . .
MISSY: the views of number twelve do not reflect the views of the house, proceed
ALL: #
AMY: okay, she looked ignorant, I'm sorry but you can look stupid, anyway . . . so . . . we, we were like, that woman is ghetto fabulous she's like, it's just the way she was ordering too, just, her mannerisms, and she actually had a T-shirt on that said "fabulous" on it in glitter, glittery, bright paint, and it was like a tight navy T-shirt #, it fit the, didn't leave a tip . . .
ALL: #

Several features of ensuing lines give evidence that Amy and the other residents understand the mention of failing to tip as indexing racial distinctions and understand such an invocation as highly inappropriate.

AMY: X, X that part off
BRITT: disclaimer: the views of number twelve . . .
AMY: number twelve is not a racist . . . number twelve has had some

experience with low-class blacks which, I'm not o, generalizing, but, trashy . . . people

ALL: #

BRITT: number . . . nine has not had **any** experience with, with . . . **any** black people

ALI: oh my god

AMY: can I, can I, back myself out of that hole okay

JACK: sure

AMY: I work at a restaurant that attracts people, that's close enough to the ghettos of Cleveland to attract that kind of clientele, and it has nothing to do with color, but a lot of the people who live there **are** black, and when they come to the restaurant, they don't know how to act, they don't tip you, they're rude, and that's what and like, if they have, the blingage on . . .

ALL: #

AMY: we would call that person ghetto fabulous and it, it, it really has nothing to do with culture it was just, like, that group population

Amy intimates that she has said something that she would not want others to hear when she commands, "X, X that part off."[9] Britt repeats Missy's earlier statement, "the views of number twelve," after announcing "disclaimer." Britt's humorous utterance trails off as Amy defends herself at the same time that she makes the significance of race explicit. She follows the humorous key of her housemates and refers to herself as "number twelve" in order to deny being a "racist." She struggles with this, however, and switches to "I" amidst many pauses and qualifications. Amy's claim not to generalize follows her qualification of having had "some experience." Those with whom she has had experiences are specified as "low-class blacks" and then "trashy." Race emerges as part of what constitutes ghetto fabulous, but race qualified by a class position. This qualification, Amy seems to be arguing, makes her assertions less noxious.

Whatever particular maneuvering Amy engages in during the interview, she invokes the spatial boundaries and dispositions and their evaluative nuances consonant with the moral geography developed by residents of named houses in the Ghetto earlier in the chapter. This time, Amy's job elsewhere, away from the college town, provides experience of the real ghetto unavailable in Oxford. Amy's description of a person in the real ghetto is met with a very different reaction than discourse on Oxford's Ghetto. GhettoFest facilitates the invasion of Oxford's Ghetto by crime and police surveillance. These are the elements said to differentiate Oxford's Ghetto from real ghettos elsewhere. The discursive interaction focusing on this invasion is celebratory just as the explicit mention of race is absent. Amy links the name Ghetto Fabulous with race, claiming familiarity with the real ghetto. Her descriptions quickly become oriented toward moral acceptance, however, and Amy's best hope is to avoid being called a racist. As soon as race is invoked explicitly, the celebratory potential of Oxford's Ghetto vanishes, and the concern with the individual as a racist replaces it.

Plantation and the Overt Relevance of Race

Plantation was the one house in the research project in which residents invoked race as a meaningful frame of interpretation for the house's name. Plantation is located far from the Ghetto, and neither the residents nor anyone else we interviewed saw any relationship between the house and the Ghetto. Indeed, such an assertion would come as a surprise, since residents of houses located in the Ghetto did not see the relevance of race to their signs and noted consistently that the real ghetto is elsewhere. Whereas Amy of Ghetto Fabulous alters the relationship between space and the special enjoyment of life in Oxford's Ghetto with the invocation of her experience with the real ghetto (and race), the residents of Plantation invoke race from the very beginning.

RITA: um(2) anyone . . . do you guys, why do you think they came up with the name Plantation for the house(2)
RYAN: it kinda, it kinda **looks** like a plantation ⌈house
ALEX: ⌊it's a big white house with a huge yard out there and it's perfect for growing cotton or something
RITA: ⌈oh my god
FAYE: ⌊oh my god
RYAN: #
ROB: **it is** #
ALL: ⌈#
COLIN: ⌊not really, I ⌈saw . . .
ALEX: ⌊we were actually #, ⌈we were gonna live with a black dude named Johnny Doe before he got kicked out of school, you know
ROB: ⌊#

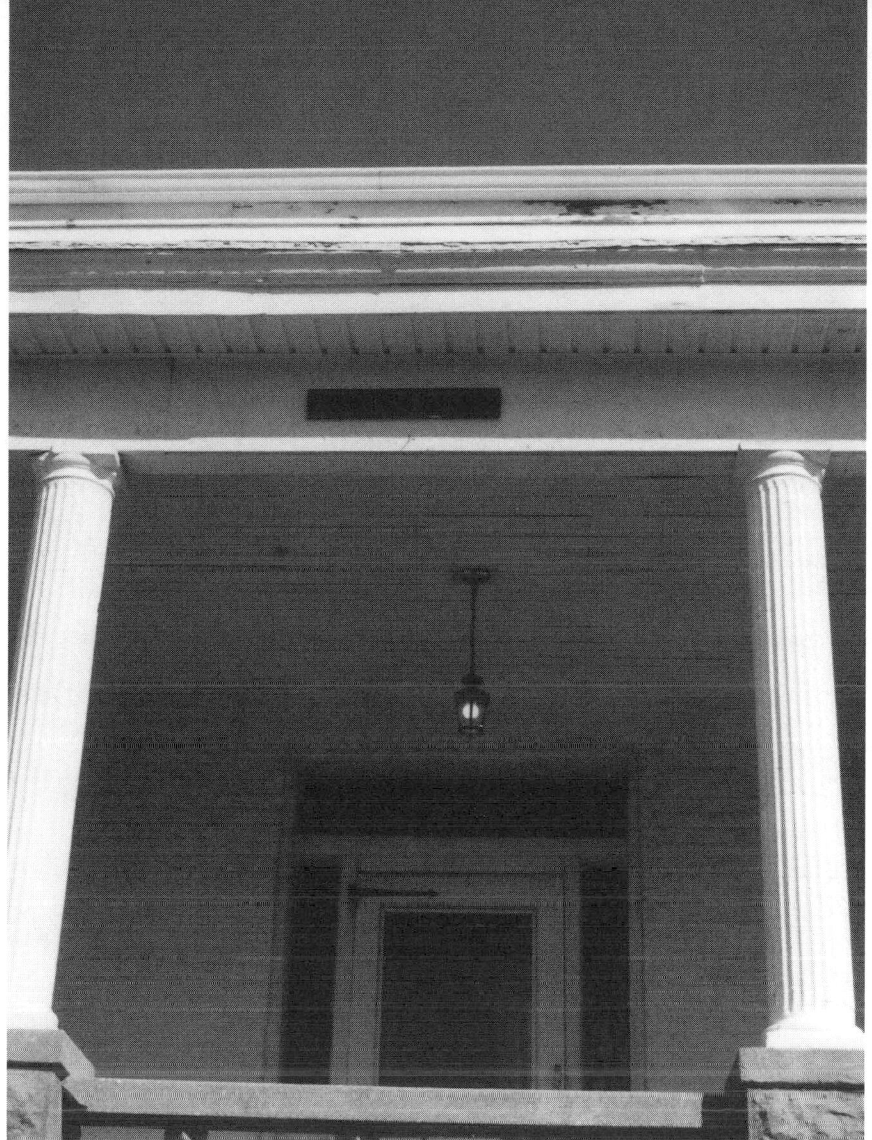

FIGURE 4.5. Plantation (house)

FAYE: yeah

ALEX: actually did you know this place was haunted

FAYE: **no**, never heard this

ALEX: well . . . it's speculation that it's haunted, it's not, not really haunted, like they've left us alone ever since the [spring] semester started

Rita, one of the student interviewers, begins by asking the residents about the house name's origins. She assumes that the current residents have not named

FIGURE 4.6. Plantation (house sign)

the house because the sign is so old and weathered. Ryan, a house resident, notes that the house physically resembles a plantation house. Alex also begins by describing the house's resemblance to a plantation house, but when he describes the yard, he characterizes its use as "perfect for growing cotton." Rita and Faye, another student interviewer, are shocked by the comment and express dismay. They recognize the association of a plantation and the activity of growing cotton as indexical of slavery. Ryan initiates laughter when Rob reasserts Alex's characterization. Alex then joins in the laughter. When Rita and Faye remain silent and do not laugh, Colin offers a retraction. Alex then claims the relevance of race rather explicitly, seemingly in order to obviate racism on the part of the house residents. One of the residents was to be a "black dude." Rob laughs, and Faye utters "yeah" ironically. Alex, perhaps sensing the negative way in which Rita and Faye have responded to the conversation thus far, initiates a topic shift.

During the next year of the project, Sam visits Plantation to conduct one of his interviews. He begins the interview less neutrally than Rita did the year before:

> SAM: could you understand anyone having issues with your house name(2)

> TIM: I mean not really, you can't take it literally. I mean it's just a house that looks like a plantation. I mean it's not like we're named sla::ve shi::p or anything.

Sam begins his interview by placing the residents in a problematic position. He intimates that the house sign could indeed evoke "issues" in the people who see it. Whereas in the interview from the previous year Alex offers an offensive image to describe the house, Tim explains that the house name could be far more explicit. The alternative that he suggests, "slave ship," however, corresponds with Alex's offer of "growing cotton," because both index a past of maximal inequality underpinned by slavery.

In a sense, the interviews with Plantation are typical when they are understood in the context of the three ways in which residents of named houses reflect on house signs. If someone is offended by Plantation, she or he has taken house signs too seriously. This notion seems to be at the heart of why Alex interjects his heinous characterization of the house. When Rita and Faye do not join in the nervous laughter, Alex claims the (unrealized) presence of a black person as proof that he is not racist. Tim takes a different approach more in keeping with—but not identical to—that of residents of houses who sense that their name or sign might cause offense. He names another. While residents of houses with sexually charged signs name another actual house, Tim makes one up. His coinage, he argues, extends beyond a mere description of the house. His answer, however, gives evidence that he understands that the "issues" someone might have with the house have to do with race.

When considered in the context of this chapter, however, the interview with Plantation takes on a significance that cannot be explained by bringing to bear the three typical ways in which residents of named houses reflect on house signs. Unfettered by an overt connection to race, life in Oxford's Ghetto offers an enhanced playful quality embodied by house signs generally. In the interviews with Plantation, race emerges quickly as a possibility in the house name's interpretation. The residents attempt to put the onus of understanding the house in such a way on the viewer, but they initiate the offensive images that a racially based interpretation might produce. Also notable about interviews with the residents of Plantation is that they fail to engage in the celebratory reflections typical of residents of other named houses. The relevance of race engages the residents of Plantation in a way that it does not engage most of the residents of houses in Oxford's Ghetto. And just as Amy's invocation of race brings to a halt the celebratory possibility of Oxford's Ghetto, the possibility of the relevance of race to the interpretation of Plantation prevents the residents from drawing on the celebratory possibilities of house signs.

There was one moment—defined by a narrative—in which one of the residents of Plantation does engage in celebratory discourse about house signs. Alex narrates the theft of a house sign by him and his friend. Even in this rare moment of celebration, however, the residents of Plantation differ from residents of the Ghetto in their stance toward house signs. The focus is not on the atmosphere of partying that their house sign and house location foster, but is rather on another sign, the object of their desire. The narration follows the mention of the other sign, Gary Coleman Fan Club.[10]

FAYE: what are some of your all-time favorite names, in Oxford, that
you've seen(2) ⌈house names
RYAN: ⌊Gary Coleman Fan Club
ALEX: I stole that sign actually ⌈and somehow they got it back
RYAN: ⌊that's a great one
RITA: ⌈you stole **that** sign
FAYE: ⌊you stole **that** sign
ALEX: put that on the record, I stole your damn sign, it's **number**
four, ⌈**bitch**
ALL: ⌊#
RITA: do you know them
ALEX: ⌈no I don't
FAYE: ⌊how'd they get it back
ALEX: I don't know, ⌈it was in the basement of our house
RYAN: ⌊did, didn't they have like a, didn't they have
like a . . .
ALEX: **there was an alarm on their** ⌈**sign**
RYAN: ⌊alarm on it, yeah
ALEX: I was up on the roof at like four in the morning last day of the
last semester
RITA: **why**
ROB: yeah listen this is a good story
ALL: #

Faye's question about the residents' favorite house signs prompts an immediate answer from Ryan. His answer actually overlaps with the end of her question. That the sign is well known to the residents of Plantation is made evident when Alex explains that he stole it. Alex proceeds to address the residents of Gary Coleman Fan Club directly, playing with the different frames of the interview and the address of residents of another house. He commands Faye and Rita with "put that on the record," he addresses residents of Gary Coleman Fan Club with "I stole your damn sign," and he refers to himself as "number 4," in the parlance of the interview that lends anonymity. Rita seems to want to know how it was that the particular house sign was targeted and how the residents of Gary Coleman Fan Club managed to get the sign back without knowing who stole it. Ryan then indexes a detail of the event that will prompt Alex's extended narrative in the next excerpt. First, Alex provides the detail, Ryan confirms it, and Alex sets the physical scene in terms of location and time. When Rita asks why, Rob makes explicit that a concerted narrative is about to be told. Everyone laughs in anticipation.

Rathe than focusing on himself in the narrative, however, Alex introduces another character, a friend with whom he steals the sign. Indeed, he credits his friend with the idea.

ALEX: #, my **buddy,** was going to Europe, and, he's like, he's, and he's, gets drunk, he gets real emotional he's like, he's, talks real fast he's from Kentucky he's like, "all, all a::h, all a::h wanna do, is steal a, steal a::, Gary Coleman sa::hn tonight." I'm like "sh, Paul I'm your man we can do this y'know," so, we wait till, everyth . . . all the bars are closed and, y'know people are gone because it's the last day of the semester and it's like that Friday night so nobody's really around, so we go up there, fi . . . we got erection [*sic*], I'm, unscrewing it, I keep hitting the deck and I think cops are coming and stuff, so I unscrew the top right one, and then I unscrew the bottom one there's three of them, two in the corners and one in the middle of the bottom, I unscrew the bottom one, and it swings down, breaks an alarm, three **loud-ass** beeps like **bee::p bee::p bee::p** like that. so then uh, so then I, I hop off the roof and like, scrape myself up get all dirty and stuff and take off running across the street, we're both in his jeep kick the seats back and we're just laying there like all right. we're gonna wait fifteen minutes, no one shows up we're ⌈going back up there

RITA: ⌊you didn't have the sign though the sign was ⌈just hanging there

ALEX: ⌊no, the sign was just dangling like that, so we go back across the street I hop back up there, and I'm unscrewing it and this thing won't s-unscrew

I'm like "fuck this" so I just take the sign and rip it off, and uh, hand it down to him, throw it in the back and took off. and then we had it in the basement of the [fraternity name] house and then ⌈ somehow they got it back

RITA: ⌊so why that sign though like of a::ll ⌈the signs in Oxford

ALEX: ⌊I, 'cause that sign, is just the artistry it's just

RITA: #

ALEX: it's **Gary Coleman**

RYAN: it's Gary Coleman

ROB: #

ALEX: it's probably one of the best signs on campus

FAYE: have you watched his shows throughout your life

ALEX: I'm not really ⌈familiar with Gary Coleman he's just, he's like ⌈**forty-five** and he's a tiny black man

FAYE: ⌊I guess what . . . ⌊*Diff'rent Strokes*

RYAN: what you talkin' 'bout Willis [imitating Gary Coleman]

FAYE: ⌈kinda like *Webster*, ⌈same type

ALEX: ⌊it's intriguing, ⌊yeah

RITA: and they somehow got the sign after ⌈that . . .

ALEX: ⌊you guys live there don't you

RITA: # no do you know who **does** live there

ALEX: no. do ⌈you

FAYE: ⌊no, we don't

Two features of Alex's narrative and the ensuing talk are relevant to this discussion of the racial dynamics of house signs. First is Alex's representation of his friend. Initially, Alex describes his friend from Alex's perspective, noting that he talks fast, is emotional, and is from Kentucky. Alex then switches stance to represent his friend's words with a "voice"—in Bakhtin's rubric reviewed in the previous chapter—separate from his own. While doing so, Alex lengthens vowels in a way that is stereotypical of people from Kentucky. One might argue that Alex performs a certain kind of whiteness: one that is not made explicit beyond the emotional and regional descriptors he uses, but one that is certainly different from his own. He also attributes the desire to steal the sign to his friend.

That Alex's performance of his friend depends on racial difference becomes more apparent because the particular sign that is the target of the theft is racially marked, too. When Rita asks why Alex would want to steal the sign with Gary Coleman at its center, Alex offers the nonspecific descriptors "artistry" and "best." All three of the residents participate in the recognition of the sign's charged quality. Faye then situates the recognition of Gary Coleman within his professional career by asking whether Alex has watched his television shows. Alex explains that he is not familiar with Gary Coleman, ostensibly meaning something like "as an actor." He then explains that the allure is derived from the actor's current appearance. Alex sums this up when he states, "he's like forty-five and he's a tiny black man." Ryan repeats a line from a popular show in which Gary Coleman served in a major role, in Gary Coleman's "voice." Faye then offers Webster, a TV series in which Emmanuel Lewis plays the lead role. She is, no doubt, drawing a parallel between Gary Coleman and Emmanuel Lewis, as both are small and African American. Alex offers the noncommittal "it's intriguing," and immediately follows by playfully addressing the interviewers and cashing in on a potentially ironic situation. Never in the interview does anyone make explicit that Alex's friend, described and "voiced" as a racially nonnormative white person, has been given the credit for stealing a sign that the residents of Plantation recognize as racially constituted. And never does anyone note that the residents of Plantation, who understand their own sign to be racially underpinned, pick another racially underpinned sign to provide the most celebratory moment in the interview.

Race has long played a part in folklore and anthropological scholarship, often serving to help define groups and communities. In an especially thoughtful consideration, Patrick Mullen (2008) reviews the ways that the work of folklore scholars such as Newbell Niles Puckett, Zora Neale Hurston, John Lomax, Alan Lomax, and Roger Abrahams shows that race is anything but natural and independent of social, cultural, and literary means of representation available in a certain time and place. Mullen explores the unequal power dynamics whereby scholars have reproduced, shaped, and emphasized certain representations of race that present an extremely complex base for later scholars to find new possibilities of representation. Mullen ultimately shows that folklore scholarship is no different from everyday life in the sense that the construction of racial difference rests on the power to represent and to do it selectively:

> As white scholars wrote about African Americans as folk, they not only created images of blackness, they also constructed whiteness, since concepts of the two races were oppositionally determined. Blackness was explicitly described, but whiteness was implicitly imbedded in white descriptions of blacks. (6–7)

Put simply, the representation of the other involves the self, but this is unevenly realized because folklore and its means of representation are born out of and reproduced in situations of inequality.

The discursive racial underpinnings of talk about the Ghetto in Oxford—versus talk about the "real" ghetto—calls for an analysis that is not based on overt racial descriptions. As residents of the Ghetto celebrate life there, especially when nonracial elements of the real ghetto such as the police come to GhettoFest, race seems irrelevant. Residents of named houses in the Ghetto certainly do not see race as relevant. A study of the place of race in rumor hints at the dynamics at work in the celebration of life in Oxford's Ghetto. Gary Fine and Patricia Turner identify different types of rumor, distinctions between which require the consideration of the teller, the rumor itself, and the focal character, all in terms of racial difference. What Fine and Turner call "formula rumors" are those that draw on fundamentally different relationships between protagonist, event, and victim, reflecting a racial basis for their plausibility.[11] They explain, "We find that whites are frightened by black street violence but not by black corporations attempting to poison them. Within the African-American community, white corporations and the white-dominated governmental structure provide the greatest threat" (2001, 23).[12]

The formula rumors comprise a genre radically different from house signs. For example, rumors focus on an event, are short-lived, and reemerge in eerily similar forms. House signs, in contrast, are not primarily descriptive of an event, generally remain for a year or longer, and are connected to the house on which they are displayed. But Fine and Turner's work is helpful in thinking about house signs because the formula rumor presupposes the racialized differences that residents of named houses in Oxford draw on when they reflect on its Ghetto. The very idea of there being a real ghetto in Oxford is understood to be absurd. Life in Oxford's Ghetto can be celebrated because the attributes of the real ghetto, namely its crime and large police presence, largely remain elsewhere, but can offer tension and excitement as students recognize that aspects of the real ghetto come to town at GhettoFest. The racial underpinnings of the notion that a real ghetto's existence in Oxford is absurd become apparent when residents offer their experiences with the "real" ghetto. In the comparatively rare moments when residents do talk about their experiences with the real ghetto, racial difference emerges to provide the image of the real ghetto. The playful celebration based on the notion that a real ghetto's existence in Oxford is absurd is refocused to the real ghetto, and residents of named houses must face the rather uncomfortable racist image that emerges. One might venture to claim that Oxford's Ghetto can only exist as long as the real ghetto contributes nonracial elements; refocusing to the moral geography of the real ghetto shifts attention from Oxford's Ghetto to the particular resident who claims to have had experience in the real ghetto.[13]

There is something about the appearance of "ghetto" in house signs, however, that Fine and Turner's book cannot explain, based as it is on another genre. When considered within house signs' rubric of partying, residents of Oxford's Ghetto can be said to benefit from their residence there. The process through which one group comes to benefit from living in a space defined, to some extent, by another leads away from a consideration of rumor. Work by a handful of linguistic anthropologists, however, points in the direction of the value of language forms and their association with racial groups.

Linguistic anthropologists have become interested in what happens when linguistic forms at the phonological, morphological, and/or syntactic levels cross racial boundaries. When forms cross these boundaries, their pragmatic dimension often changes. Jane Hill (1993), for example, has noted that in the film *Terminator 2*, Arnold Schwarzenegger says, "Hasta la vista, baby" (just before killing someone) without any desire to see the addressee again. She calls such an utterance "Mock Spanish" and points out that it casts the person uttering it in a positive light rather than a person who cannot speak good Spanish.[14] This is possible, she argues, because the form is derived from a language whose speakers' identity is imagined to be a resource for play and even ridicule. She describes the process:

> Mock Spanish borrows Spanish-language words and suffixes, assimilates their pronunciation to English (often in a hyperanglicized or boldly mispronounced form), changes their meaning, usually to make them humorous or pejorative, and uses them to signal that the movement of English-language speech or text thus embellished is colloquial and informal. (2008, 134)

The pragmatic shift involved in Mock Spanish therefore involves the kind of speaker who can benefit from linguistic usage, underpinned by race. Hill argues that Mock Spanish is best used in "white public space" (1998).

Hill notes that although the linguistic dimensions are quite different, the same kind of pragmatic transformation can occur when terms of African American origin are taken up in white discursive interaction. She notes:

> Geneva Smitherman (1998, 206) has pointed out that the ability to maintain one's cool probably originated within African American culture to stay out of trouble and survive in a world of lynch mobs and police brutality. However, in White popular culture "cool" has been flattened into a fashionable aesthetic of the self. (2008, 166)

Linguistically, the crossing manifested in "Hasta la vista, baby" and "cool" is very different since the former exhibits error. But both effect a radical pragmatic transformation in that both can come to benefit a white speaker.

Hill claims that both pragmatic shifts can be likened to the Marxist notion of the capitalist's appropriation of labor. She calls the process in the realm of language "linguistic appropriation." Someone can use some linguistic form for positive effect, but in such a way that indexes inequality between groups. Hill argues that the inequality involves a witty cosmopolitan speaker and a lampooned and mocked racialized other.

> Today, White users of forms appropriated from African American English make a claim on many desirable qualities, especially those assigned to preferred forms of masculinity. These include toughness, urban "street-smarts," and especially "cool," a sort of sexy, edgy unflappability that has a very high value in contemporary American popular culture. (Hill 2008, 166)[15]

Discourse about house signs, those that use "ghetto" on the one hand, and "Plantation" on the other hand, lack linguistic features that indicate racializing play. In the transcriptions presented above, "What you talkin' 'bout, Willis?" is the only utterance that is immediately apparent as exhibiting features of African American vernacular English, and it is quoted from a once-popular television series. Yet signs that use "ghetto" appear on houses whose residents can celebrate their residence there. "Plantation," on the other hand, blocks the potential for celebration because its residents become entangled in accounting for and excusing the racist quality of the sign. Residents of the Ghetto thus enjoy the appropriation of which Hill speaks whereas the residents of Plantation do not. The process of appropriation in the Ghetto does not rely on terms borrowed from a kind of English associated with African Americans, but rather relies on the Ghetto's position in a larger moral geography. Locally, life in Oxford's Ghetto enhances the carefree ambience of the parties held there, and that ambience lies at the heart of the Ghetto's moral geography. The Ghetto is thus able to attain distinction in Oxford's world of house signs more generally because it provides a place where partying can occur to its fullest.

But this local moral geography depends on the existence of the real ghetto and its great distance from the Ghetto. As long as police are the only visitors from the real ghetto, the appropriation of qualities of the real ghetto by residents of the Ghetto and revelers at GhettoFest can commence. The fact that the real ghetto implies racialized difference from the Ghetto, however, becomes apparent at those moments when experience in the real ghetto is invoked. Should one think that race is irrelevant rather than simply absent, its invocation via the real ghetto puts the brakes on celebratory discourse. Indeed, it seems that for the process of appropriation to be successful, overt reference to racial distinctions must be absent. The best fun is had in the Ghetto, comfortably distant from the real ones.

CHAPTER FIVE

Hot Box, Box Office, and Fill'er Up: Reflections on Gender and Sexuality

Never wear patent leather shoes on a date; they reflect. Never wear a red dress; it inflames. Don't eat olives; they're passion pills. Always carry along a telephone book (or a newspaper, or a copy of the *Saturday Evening Post*) in case your date asks you to sit on his lap. A coed must turn the picture of her boyfriend to the wall before undressing at night.

—RICHARD DORSON,
The Folklore of College Students, *American Folklore*

In keeping with the goals of writing this book—particularly the argument for the consideration of language in context—I hope that the passage above prompts a number of questions. All of the statements are rather absolute, and all but the last are commands. We know that the person being commanded is a female college student, and Dorson tells us that the person issuing the commands is the dean of women. The parallel construction of the commands suggests a genre, perhaps a set of rules. We are not told, however, just how these rules came about, what those people to whom they apply (or don't) might have to say about them, and where and in what form they might be found. Did Dorson copy them from some source? Did he compile them from several sources, shaping them into the pleasing form we encounter in his book? Did an actual dean of women hand him the list? To be fair, these concerns themselves must be contextualized. Richard Dorson published his overview of the folklore of the college student in 1959, before concerns about the social location of the textual life of folklore were salient, much less important.

Nevertheless, there are aspects of the "The Folklore of College Students" by Dorson that remain quite relevant to the exploration of house signs, specifically relationships between gender and sexuality depicted on them. Contemporary scholars have become increasingly interested in investigating and demonstrating the immense complexity entailed in the relationship between gender and sexuality. In a review of work on language and gender conducted since Robin Lakoff's seminal publication, *Language and Woman's Place,* in 1975, Penelope Eckert and Sally McConnell-Ginet explain that gender is an especially complex social phenomenon for its reproduction of ideology in service of constructing the natural:

> Gender is the very process of creating a dichotomy by effacing similarity and elaborating on difference, and even where there are biological differences, these differences are exaggerated and extended in the service of constructing gender. (2003, 13)

The quote by Dorson can be used to illustrate Eckert and McConnell-Ginet's claim. Gender is not a symmetrical and equal division between female and male, for example, because the objects that participate in establishing gender difference can be particular to one and not the other. Whereas men might wear patent leather shoes, they do not wear dresses. And these gendered differences far exceed the sexual differences of the clothed bodies in elaborateness and complexity of expression.

Words, as Robin Lakoff points out, can similarly establish gender difference in an uneven way. She notes that descriptors such as "ecru," "lavender," and "mauve" or "adorable," "lovely," and "divine" sound natural only when being used by women (2004, 43–45). Underpinning the gendered status of such words, Lakoff notes, is the idea that only women should be concerned with matters frivolous and unimportant. Lakoff calls such language "women's language" to mean not language used by women but language that emerges from and reestablishes the position of women.[1] Not just objects and words, but ways of moving and speaking can similarly participate unevenly in the construction of gender difference. For example, Dorson says that men ask women to sit on their laps whereas women turn over the pictures of their boyfriends while undressing. Such patterns establish an oppositional dynamic for gendered difference: everything has to fit into two categories. The two sexes are implicated in these gendered scenarios such that the gendered scenarios inform what girls and boys do. Indeed, the social manifestations of difference based in gender exceed the sexual differences entailed in the attributes of bodies. One of the categories is expected to act on the other, which, in turn, is expected to protect itself. In the quote at the beginning of the chapter, only women need a telephone book, a newspaper, or a magazine on a date, and they only need it for protection. Whether a woman's request that her date sit on her lap would be unthinkable or simply innocuous is never raised. Such missing possibilities are indicative of the manner in which gender differences come to seem natural.

In an expanding body of scholarly work, anthropologists have shown that objects, words, ways of moving, and ways of speaking that participate in the construction of gender often have interdependent relationships with those that participate in the construction of sexuality. In their review of such scholarship, Deborah Cameron and Don Kulick explain:

> The three terms—having a certain kind of body (sex), living as a certain kind of social being (gender), and having certain kinds of erotic desires (sexuality)—are not understood or experienced by most people in present-day social reality as distinct and separate. Rather, they are *interconnected.* (2003, 5)

The significance of gender is often established through notions of sexuality, and constructions of sexuality often contribute to the lack of symmetry evident in gender differences. Patent leather shoes can reveal what is usually unseen because women wear dresses. Special caution and modesty characterize a gender category because of the other category's sexual advances or even gaze.

Dorson's examples should not establish a point from which one compares images of gender and sexuality on house signs. Older readers might find unremarkable the ideas that patent leather shoes reflect what should remain hidden and that going on a date is the primary way in which college students initiate a relationship, while younger readers probably find such ideas old-fashioned, if not unfamiliar (and perhaps laughable). One would be wrong, however, to understand the quote taken from Dorson to be indicative of a purer time, somehow more innocent than a world that contains house signs such as Octopussy, Octoballs, and Asspen. A quick tour through research on the folklore of college students suggests that bawdy and lewd behavior has emerged from college life since people began writing about it. If the disembodied rules suggest a world of heterosexual pairs wherein the female should be particularly vigilant not to appear too sexually provocative or available, other accounts from the same period give evidence of incredibly lewd communal licentiousness. In fact, most of the songs, practical jokes, club, fraternity, and sorority initiations and games reported in scholarly work trump anything found on house signs for their salacious qualities.

Oxford's world of house signs presents particular possibilities for reflection and critique by residents. While gendered difference and sexuality become salient in house names by virtue of a great variety of images, personae, and euphemisms, residents tend to simplify such complexity by means of identifying the gender of the residents of the house in question. Some house names allow onlookers to derive the sex of the residents quite easily. Others prove more problematic, and discussion about these is more elaborate. Elaborate discussions about ambiguous cases index the notion that the gender of residents should be easy to determine from the house's name. At the same time, residents pick out sexually charged names as examples. One of the most commonly heard explanations for the derivation of the gender of residents from house names is that males tend to be more salacious than females. This helps to explain why it is that so many residents mention houses with particularly sexual names in which females are imagined to live—Octopussy in particular.

I will consider one interview at length because it was one of the few in which we were able to record women and men talking about house signs together. The interview is with the residents of Hot Box, a group of females, but some of the men who live in Box Office and Fill'er Up join the interview. The women of Hot Box launch subtle critiques of the men's signs, but in the end they claim to have no particular stance. As the women are building their critiques, however, the men interject the names of houses the likes of which the women are in the process of critiquing. The signs happen to involve sexuality and to make overt reference to women's bodies. Such names are uncommon when considered among all house signs that involve gender and/or sexuality because they use euphemisms for women's genitalia at the same time that the houses on which they appear are occupied by men. The women's critiques reveal that men cross gender lines and involve female bodies in their signs while women never involve men's bodies in their signs. The interview with Hot Box depicts the ways in which men might utilize especially sexual house names as well as the ways in which women might undercut their own critiques of such names.

Gender and Sexuality across House Signs

The notion that the social negotiation of sexual activity is a realm of great concern—one might even say anxiety—is as true in the time of house signs as it was when Dorson's overview was published. Gender and sexuality clearly represent two of the most common house sign themes, and many signs involve both themes. The ways in which the themes of gender and sexuality play their parts in the names and designs of signs exhibit the complexity of scholarly work noted above. Table 5.1 shows a number of dimensions of gender and sexuality that residents use to create their house names.

In the first list are those names that refer to some group—person, animal, or object—in a way such that the gender of the referent is explicit. The first name, 4 Non-Blondes, differs from the others because it is a popular rock group that consists of women. One could certainly describe men as "non-blondes," but the rock group's fame makes the possibility of men being the referents for the name unlikely. Another name that invokes the gendered nature of a popular culture persona is The Playm~~ate~~eight Mansion. A "playmate" is a young woman working for Hugh Hefner in the Playboy Mansion. In the other names words like "girls," "belles," "women," and "ladies" do not rely on media and occupational sources, as in the case of 4 Non-Blondes and The Playm~~ate~~eight Mansion, and are used to refer to persons in a way that involves gender.

"Fox" and "chick" are words for animals, but denote gender when used for humans in a metaphorical fashion. "Peeps" are mass-produced marshmallow treats shaped like chicks, and seem to refer to women in the same way that "chicks" does. Another object used for referring to women is "doll." "Hoe" is a shortened version of "whore" that when used for men has to be made more explicit with "man whore." Finally, "beeches" is a manipulation of "bitches" that designates the female within an animal category. The only house sign that uses a word that refers to males is Band of Brothers, based on a movie that depicts a group of GIs in World War II. Thus, whereas all manner of popular cultural and metaphorical references are used to refer to women on house signs, a kin term couched in a popular culture reference is used for men.[2]

Some house signs refer to an animate entity that has no clear gender affiliation. Angels, for example, can be female or male. And some house signs refer to entities some of which are female and some of which are male. For example 3 Chicks and a Cock is complex because "chick" is a word that can

Table 5.1. Gender and Sexuality among House Signs

Female	Ambiguous or Both Gender	Male
* * *		
House name refers to a person, animal, or entity the gender of which is explicit		
4 Non-Blondes	Absolut Angels (A)	Band of Brothers
Collgirls	3 Chicks and a Cock (B)	
Fox Den		
Girls Gone Ghetto		
Girls Gone Wild		
Girls on Top		
Hell's Belles		
Hoe Down		
Little Women		
Peeps		
Poplar with the Ladies		
Spoiled Beeches		
Spring Chicks		
The Chick-Inn		
The Doll House		
The Playm~~ate~~eight Mansion		
Tipsy Chicks		
Uptown Girls		
* * *		
House name contains the name of a body part		
Boxed Inn	ΑΣΣ (A)	6 Pack
Box Office	Asspen (A)	Cocktail
Hooter~~s~~ville	Boutique Hall (A)	Cocktales
Hot Box	Dickens Cider Box (B)	Deez Nutz
Liquor Juggs	Ghetto Booty (A)	Dillywhop
Octopussy		Gutter Balls
Poplar Cherry		Morning Wood
The Boobie Trap		Octoballs
Tuna Sandwich		Pop-N-Wood
		Well Hung Over
* * *		
House name makes gender explicit through popular culture item		
Beech Bunnies		The Heisman
Betty Boops		
Wendy's Backyard		

Table 5.1. *Continued*

Female	Ambiguous or Both Gender	Male
* * *		
House name makes gender explicit through clothing item		
<u>The Panty Shanty</u>		
* * *		
House name makes gender explicit through sexual practice		
<u>Fill'er Up</u>		<u>The Rusty Trombone</u>
<u>Liquor Up Front Poker in the Rear</u>		

Note: House names that are sexual are underlined

FIGURE 5.1. Uptown Girls

FIGURE 5.2. Peeps

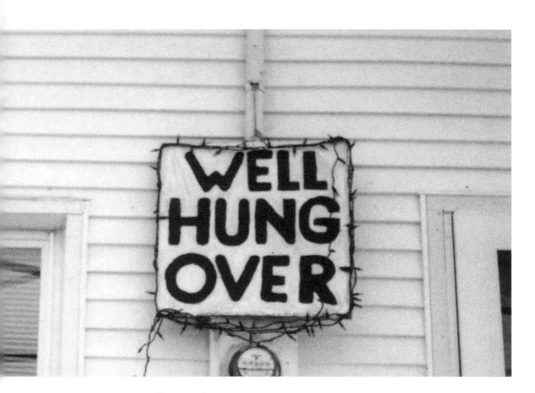

FIGURE 5.3. Well Hung Over

be used for a young woman, but "cock" is not usually used to refer to a man. In keeping with signs listed in the next section of Table 5.1, "cock" invokes gender by way of sexual anatomy. Indeed, all of the names invoke gender by the incorporation of sexual features of anatomy. Thus, "box" and "pussy" are words of common parlance that refer to the vagina. "Tuna," when used to refer to female anatomy, suggests its smell, and like "pussy," "fox," and "bitch," relies on an animal category. "Cherry" is a word that is used to refer to the virginal vagina, and the pun in "Poplar Cherry" involves the popular idiom by which virginity is lost when the "cherry" gets "popped." "Hooters," "jugs," and "boobies" are all words for breasts. Male genitalia are well represented in house names, too. While a "six pack" does not refer to genitalia, it is most commonly used to refer to bodies that are considered male-like because it refers to a well-muscled torso. "Cock" and "dillywhop" are words for the penis, and "wood" is a word for an erect one. To be "hung" is to have a large penis. Both "nuts" and "balls" refer to testicles. "Ass" and "booty" both refer to the buttocks and can also have the more general meaning of sexual activity as in "getting ass" or "getting booty." Buttocks, of course, are common to all people, regardless of sex. Finally, Dickens Cider Box involves words for the penis and the vagina.

The next section lists house names that invoke gender by the popular culture names they use. A "beach bunny" is someone who enjoys hanging out at the beach, displaying one's body. The house sign makes the gender designation of the name explicit because it depicts a bunny that resembles the Playboy emblem. Betty Boop was a female cartoon character, and Wendy is a girl depicted on the eponymous fast-food chain logo. The Heisman is a football trophy and thus won by males.

The remaining sections achieve a gendered image by way of an object or a practice. "Panty" is a word that refers to female underwear. Fill'er Up and Liquor Up Front, Poker in the Rear both position "her" as the recipient of sexual activity, whereas The Rusty Trombone is the name for a sexual practice in which the penis (and anus) is stimulated.

In sum, Table 5.1 shows that gender and sexuality are complexly related when they are considered across house signs. Sometime house signs include words that are often used elsewhere to refer to women or men. Sometime those words include a sexual charge. Sometimes house signs suggest gendered difference through the involvement of genitalia, and sometimes sexual aspects of anatomy do not invoke gender difference. Sometimes a figure, person, or group included on a house sign is either female or male. Finally, clothing and sex acts sometimes rest on gendered difference. These are all possibilities such that there is no easy way to describe the intersection—or lack thereof—of gender and sexuality as they take part in the display of house signs.

Further complicating the relationship between gender and sexuality is the fact that just as some house names invoke gender difference without invoking sexuality, some invoke sexuality without invoking gender difference. Table 5.2 provides a list. The house names that invoke sexuality without gender draw on a number of other domains. Many borrow names from film or television and present them unchanged or manipulate them slightly. *Boogie Nights* is a movie about the adult film industry, and *Risky Business* is a movie about prostitution. Champagne Room, the place where a stripper may give one private attention but may not be touched, is taken from a movie; Genital Hospital is a manipulation of a long-running soap opera's title; *Miami Vice* was a television series; "Simply Irresistible" was the title of a popular song; and "The 'O' Face" is the facial expression one makes on orgasm and is taken from the movie *Office Space*.

Some of the house names present the names of institutions unchanged or manipulate them, whether the institutions are of a commercial, civic, or service nature. Thus Bed Booze & Beyond is a manipulation of the commercial chain Bed Bath & Beyond, Ho-Tel 6 is a graphic manipulation of the name of a hotel chain, Precinct 109 "Spread 'Em" borrows from institutional designations of the police, and Unplanned Parenthood is a manipulation of Planned Parenthood, an organization that offers information about sex and pregnancy. Other signs invoke institutional domains more generically such as The No-Tell Motel and The Petting Zoo.

Other house signs borrow popular phrases. These include Casual Six, which puns on "casual sex"; Come-N-Go, which plays with the ability of "come" to refer to orgasm; Four Play that puns on "foreplay"; Gettin' Lucky, a popular expression for having sex; Live Bait, a phrase for the sexually available; and Pucker Up, an expression for preparations to kiss. Some of the signs invoke alcohol, including Bed Booze & Beyond, Beer Goggles, Champagne Room, and Sex on the Beech, the name of a fruity cocktail. One of my students told me that Pucker Up invokes alcohol because Pucker is the name of a line of fruity liqueurs.

The major difference between the signs that invoke sexuality without invoking gender distinctions and signs that do both is that the signs that only invoke sexuality do not use euphemisms for genitalia. The only examples

FIGURE 5.4. Live Bait

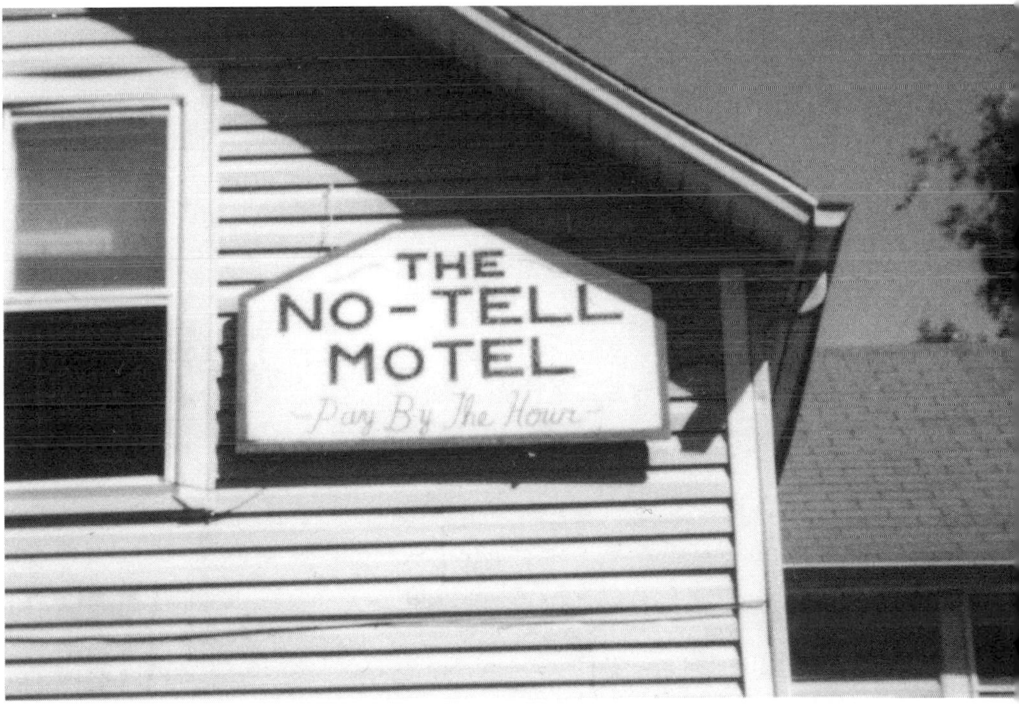

FIGURE 5.5. The No-Tell Motel

Table 5.2. Sexual House Names without Explicit Gender Distinctions

Bed Booze & Beyond	Beer Goggles	Boogie Nights
Boutique Hall	Casual Six	Champagne Room Rules Were Meant to Be Broken
Clothing Optional	Come-N-Go	Four Play
Game On. We Shoot. We Score.	Genital Hospital	Gettin' Lucky
Ho-Tel 6	Kinkytown	Live Bait
Miami Vice	Moist	Pay by the Hour
Pheromones	Precinct 109 "Spread 'Em"	Pucker Up
Risky Business	Sex on the Beech	Simply Irresistible
Six Geese a Layin'	Spring Fever	Strangers with Candy
The Boom Boom Room	The No-Tell Motel	The "O" Face
The Petting Zoo	Top or Bottom?	Unbuckled
Unplanned Parenthood		

that do involve genitalia do so in a way that does not distinguish bodies by sex. Boutique Hall is a pun on the popular phrase "booty call," which refers to a casual sexual encounter. The phrase relies on a euphemism for the butt to stand for sexual activity generally. Genital Hospital is a manipulation of a popular soap opera. Replacing "general" with "genital" does not distinguish bodies by sex. The difference is relevant to the ways in which residents of named houses reflect on house signs that involve gender and sexuality. When residents reflect on signs "worse" than their own, or even on house signs generally, sexual signs that use euphemisms for genitalia emerge as especially notable.

Vulgar Boys and Exceptional(ly Vulgar) Girls

One of the primary ways residents of named houses in Oxford conceptualize issues of gender involved in the display of house signs is through sexuality. Sexually charged signs drew special attention across interviews with residents of named houses, and chapter 3 shows how residents of houses with sexually charged signs make special efforts to obviate responsibility for the display of their signs. However, the images, personae, and themes on which sexual names of houses draw, depicted in Table 5.2, are of limited use in explaining how house residents see gender as relevant to sexual signs. Rather than engage house names' gendered and sexual imagery and themes in their complexity, residents of named houses generally focus on especially charged sexual signs and imagine whether men or women inhabit the houses to which they belong. Across the residents' reflections, only a handful of house names emerge to stand for sexual signs. Residents' reflections on relationships between gender and sexuality ignore much of the complexity between the two that exists across house names.

An interview with the residents of Girls Gone Wild demonstrates that sexual signs, especially those that have to do with euphemisms for genitalia, sexual practices, or both, figure prominently in discussions of signs that might be worse than the residents' own. In chapter 3, residents of Morning Wood mention Strangers with Candy as a sign worse than their own. Strangers with Candy involves no obvious sexual elements via genitalia or a sexual practice. What seems to make the sign particularly objectionable is its predatory nature. However, residents of houses with sexual signs mention other sexual signs that include euphemisms for genitalia and/or sexual practices to claim that those signs trump their own in vulgarity.

The segment of the interview with Girls Gone Wild offered here starts with an explanation of the name's inheritance. Jay and Meg, the student interviewers, ask the residents why they kept the house name when they moved in, something the residents had just mentioned.

JAY: how come you kept the same name
BETHANY: well, since it was already like, Girls Gone Wild, or whatever. we kept it. half the house liked it and half of us wanted to change it
MEG: oh yeah, how come
BETHANY: 'cause we didn't really
VANESSA: we **thought** we could think of something a little bit more creative
CARA: yeah
VANESSA: and funny
BETH: and then we went on spring break, and there were signs and then we just kind of went crazy with the signs, like, saying that was our house name and we all have T-shirts
JAY: are those from the actual show
BETH: uh, yeah

JAY: you guys didn't participate, did you
BETH: no
ALL: #
BETH: not everyone . . . **no, no**
VANESSA: no one in particular
MEG: but if some of you had participated in it, how would you all feel like if one of you . . .
VANESSA: I think we would have been proud of each other . . .
ALL: #
CARA: embarrassed kind of
VANESSA: embarrassed after being on the show
MEG: but you're upholding the name. so that's OK
BETH: not really
VANESSA: we don't exactly, like, **sell the videos**, #, from our front porch, but, the name kind of stuck(3)

The women explain that some of the residents were tempted to coin a new name for the house in order to be more clever and funny, but a trip to spring break brought them into contact with the film crew of the soft-core pornographic video series *Girls Gone Wild*. The residents toy with Jay and Meg, showing them promotional T-shirts from the series, and they are very coy about whether one or more of the residents might have been filmed. Vanessa concludes commentary on the video series by denying that the residents sell the videos from home, a sarcastic image to be sure, and by explaining elusively that "the name kind of stuck."[3]

When Jay asks the residents whether the sign reflects their "identities," the residents answer in a typical way.

JAY: do you think the name has anything to do:: with your identities
ALL: #
CARA: no, no. **no** #
JAY: was it, like a joke, that you put it up there
BETH: not really
ALL: no
CARA: it's just that like, I mean, people know when we say where we live. like by the name so it's just kind of easier 'cause we were thinking of changing it but, then we realized like no one would
JAY: everybody already knows where it is

CARA: yeah

VANESSA: like it was kind of an unspoken like . . . they knew so . . . like the location.

JAY: # what do you think, like, the other people think . . . when they see that sign

BETHANY: well, on nights that we're not doing anything they make fun of us

CARA: oh they . . . people always comment and walk by and say **oo::h Girls Gone Wild**

MEG: who, random strangers

ALL: yeah

CARA: well, yeah, people somewhat, I think, expect us to . . . some people, I don't know. I think they think that we should act in certain ways.

BETHANY: yeah

CARA: 'cause we say oh we live in Girls Gone Wild, but it doesn't mean that to us(2)

JAY: so when you tell somebody that you live in Girls Gone Wild, do you think they are, like, making assumptions

BETHANY: I don't necessarily think that . . .

VANESSA: they'll just say oh, are you crazy

CARA: yeah

VANESSA: you're wild girls, yeah and we're like, **uh-hu::h** we're a::lways crazy. um, I mean in comparison to some of the other names, this is pretty mild, I think

ALL: yeah

When Jay guesses that the residents' responses to his question are due to their understanding of the sign as a joke, they correct him. Indeed, rarely did residents describe their house names as being a joke, but rather as "fun" or "clever." The women introduce a common way of understanding house signs' importance, the recognition of the location of the house by its name. The women explain that one of the reasons they did not change the house name was because people were familiar with the location of Girls Gone Wild. Jay then returns the focus to the ways in which the residents might envision onlookers and what onlookers might make of the residents by way of their sign. Bethany intimates that the sign provides onlookers with an easy means of poking fun at the residents when they are "not doing anything," and Cara imitates what onlookers say with her sarcastic delivery of "Ooh, Girls Gone Wild." After Bethany claims that these are "random strangers," thus establishing that onlookers do make assumptions about the house residents from their sign, Cara admits that the residents do claim to live in the house, but that "it doesn't really mean that to us." She is thus ambiguous about whether the residents make explicit that they do not take the connection between the house name and their behavior seriously when they claim to live in Girls Gone Wild.

The next few utterances are fascinating because Vanessa explains that those people who are told that the residents live in Girls Gone Wild respond with the question, "Oh, are you crazy?" Bethany has already intimated that Jay's offer of making assumptions is not an accurate interpretive characterization for a person discovering that the women inhabit a house named Girls Gone Wild. Vanessa's animation of an imagined interlocutor is most likely sarcastic. "Crazy" approximates wild rather than insane. Then Vanessa animates what such people do say: "You're wild girls." Vanessa thus has the person speaking to the residents using part of the house name to describe the residents. Vanessa thus is able to obviate any more elaborate commentary by nonresidents on the connection between the residents' behavior and their house name. Her response is created with a good degree of sarcasm. Her response, "Uh-huh, we're always crazy," purposely lacks sincerity. In a single stroke, Vanessa affirms that house signs are about partying but that one cannot understand residents or their behavior via their signs. She ends her turn at talk in a way that resembles reflections of residents of other houses with sexual names. She claims that her own house name is mild compared with others.

When Jay presses for examples, the residents are quite willing to offer some. All of the names the residents offer are sexual, and the residents indicate that the sex of the residents of the houses named can be inferred from the name. They make special remarks about names for houses whose residents' sex comes as a surprise.

JAY: yeah, I see what you mean. like what though
BETH: there's Liquor Box, I don't know if that's still a house name.
VANESSA: and Liquor Juggs
ALL: yeah

JAY: Dickens Cider Box is another one over by where I live
BETH: there's Stickamore Inn. I think it's actually girls who live there(2)
VANESSA: oh, there was one, I wouldn't be able to tell my . . .
CARA: Eight Out
BETH: Eight Out
VANESSA: Eight Out, I don't think my parents would let me . . .
JAY: I've never heard of that.
BETHANY: oh, Eight Out's new. they don't have a sign up yet
MEG: Eight Out. **o::h h::o**
BETHANY: eight girls live there
ALL: eight girls
MEG: #, right on
JAY: #
VANESSA: but Girls Gone Wild. my parents were just kind of like, **oh** funny
CARA: yeah
VANESSA: they know it's not real

Beth offers Liquor Box as an example of a house with a name that is less "mild" than that of her own house, and Vanessa adds Liquor Juggs. Both of these names involve euphemisms for genitalia. Jay adds an example, Dickens Cider Box, a name that includes two euphemisms and the suggestion of intercourse. Beth indicates that she understands the imagery when she offers Stickamore Inn, a manipulation of Sycamore Street, on which the house so named is located. She also mentions that the residents are "actually girls." It is true that men reside in all of the houses named thus far in the interview segment, and Beth's caveat intimates that the fact that girls reside in Stickamore Inn is noteworthy.

Vanessa then begins an offer of a house name by foregrounding her imagined inability to tell someone that she lives there. Cara and Beth make evident that the residents might have discussed the house name in question before or at least that the house name is a particularly salient example of a name that is too salacious. They offer the name, Eight Out, before Vanessa can finish her explanation and reveal the name. Eight Out is a pun on cunnilingus and the number of house residents. Vanessa then makes explicit that it was her parents whom she could not tell. Indeed, she reworks her initial claim somewhat.

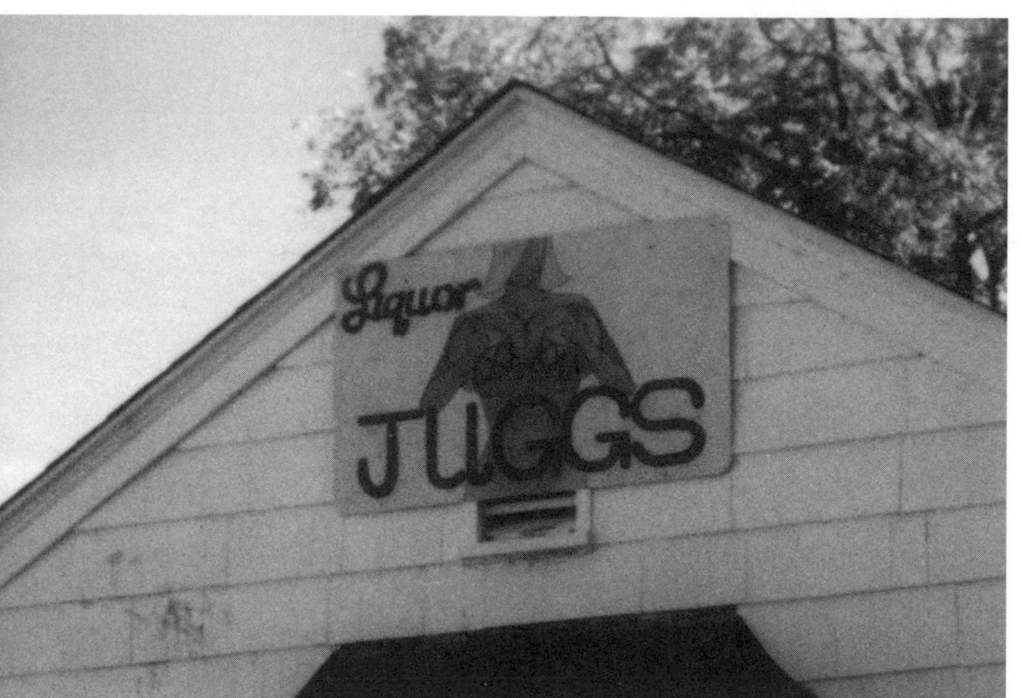

FIGURE 5.6. Liquor Juggs

When Vanessa is finally able to name the people at issue, those people would not let her live in Eight Out. When Jay claims not to have heard of the name, Bethany explains that the residents have not put up a sign yet. Meg, the other student interviewer, repeats the name and then gives evidence that she understands the salacious nature of the pun. Bethany then articulates the connection between the name and the number of residents. She also makes explicit that the residents are girls. This latter fact rests on cunnilingus serving as the basis of the pun. Meg laughs and issues an approving cheer, and Jay laughs, too. Vanessa returns to the issue of parents, but this time to the parents' reaction to Girls Gone Wild, her own sign. In implicit contrast to her parents' imagined reaction to Eight Out, she notes that her parents understand that Girls Gone Wild is funny. And in implicit contrast to the sexual act underpinning Eight Out, Vanessa describes Girls Gone Wild as "not real."

In an interview at The Panty Shanty, residents are less coy about the possibility that their house name can be used to understand their behavior. This is probably due to the rather salient and well orchestrated scenario implied by Girls Gone Wild, based as it is on a pornographic video series. Nevertheless, residents describe the opinions of family members at the same time that they claim not to care about what nonresidents think about their sign.

> DICK: what do you think other people think about your house sign
> KELLI: I don't really care honestly
> ALL: yeah
> KATE: people just kind of laugh when they . . .
> BARB: they think, okay, girls live here
> KATE: yeah, I mean people just sort of laugh and they say, oh, that's cute
> BARB: yeah
> KATE: and my dad thinks it's horrific(2) my grandmother lo::ves it
> BARB: really, oh my grandma . . .
> KATE: she's like you're inviting strange boys in.
> KELLI: my family thinks it's hilarious
> KATE: yeah, my grandma loves it.
> BARB: oh, in fact, whenever my grandma writes me a letter
> KATE: oh yeah
> BARB: she puts The Panty Shanty
> KATE: my grandma always does that, too, and my grandpa yells at her

Kelli claims not to care what others might think of the sign, an assertion with which other residents readily agree. By claiming that "people just kind of laugh" at the sign, Kate joins the larger house sign community of practice in believing that signs should be funny or clever. Barb then offers the imagined interpretation that the house's residents are women, ostensibly based on the fact that the sign includes the name of and depicts women's underwear. Kate renders this connection in the eyes of onlookers as cute and productive of laughter. Family emerges to embody onlookers in the next several utterances. Kate juxtaposes her father's negative reaction to her grandmother's positive one. Barb begins to say something about her own grandmother when Kate interrupts to quote her grandmother's utterance, "You're inviting strange boys in." This comment seems playful rather than admonishing, and Kelli joins in to assert her family's positive feelings. Barb and Kate explain that their grandmothers are so fond of the house name that they use it in correspondence. And just as Kate's father finds the house name "horrific," her grandfather yells at her grandmother for using the name. The fact that a woman approves of the sign in the face of the disapproval of two men seems significant.

Just as in the interview with Girls Gone Wild, the residents of The Panty Shanty begin to offer examples of especially salacious signs after establishing that their own sign is funny. And just as in the interview with Girls Gone Wild, the residents of The Panty Shanty offer house names that refer to genitalia and sexual practices, and they imagine which sex the residents must be based on the house name in question.

BARB: yeah, so many people have horrid house names . . .
KATE: Clitty Clitty Bang Bang.
MARY: that's probably the worst
KATE: [that's horrible
KELLI: [I have never seen it
BARB: wasn't it the worst thing with the picture
KATE: it was the picture. I don't think you saw it(2) we were just taking a walk, two years, I think it was our sophomore year.
DICK: what, what does it have a picture of
KATE: it's like the front of the car and it is a grill shaped like a woman's vagina. it is really, like Kelli and I were walking down the street and just, like e::w, it was obscene. it must have been boys. I mean it's not like I'm really . . . it's just like . . .
BARB: get your bang right here.
KATE: I'm like wha::t
BARB: like **no**
DICK: there's one, I think they're making it on Sycamore. It's called Stickamore Inn
BARB: oh go::d
MARY: it's actually all girls that live there

Barb frames the discussion by describing some house names as being "horrid." Kate offers Clitty Clitty Bang Bang, and Mary describes it as the "worst." When Kelli claims never to have seen it, Kate embarks on a description of the sign and its imagery based on a pun on the name of the car, Chitty Chitty Bang Bang, and on "clit," a shortened form of "clitoris." After she describes the sign as "obscene," Kate asserts that the house residents "must have been boys." Barb and Kate engage in some sarcastic and negative expressions about the sign when Dick, the student interviewer, mentions Stickamore Inn. Mary mentions the fact that the residents are female. She prefaces her statement

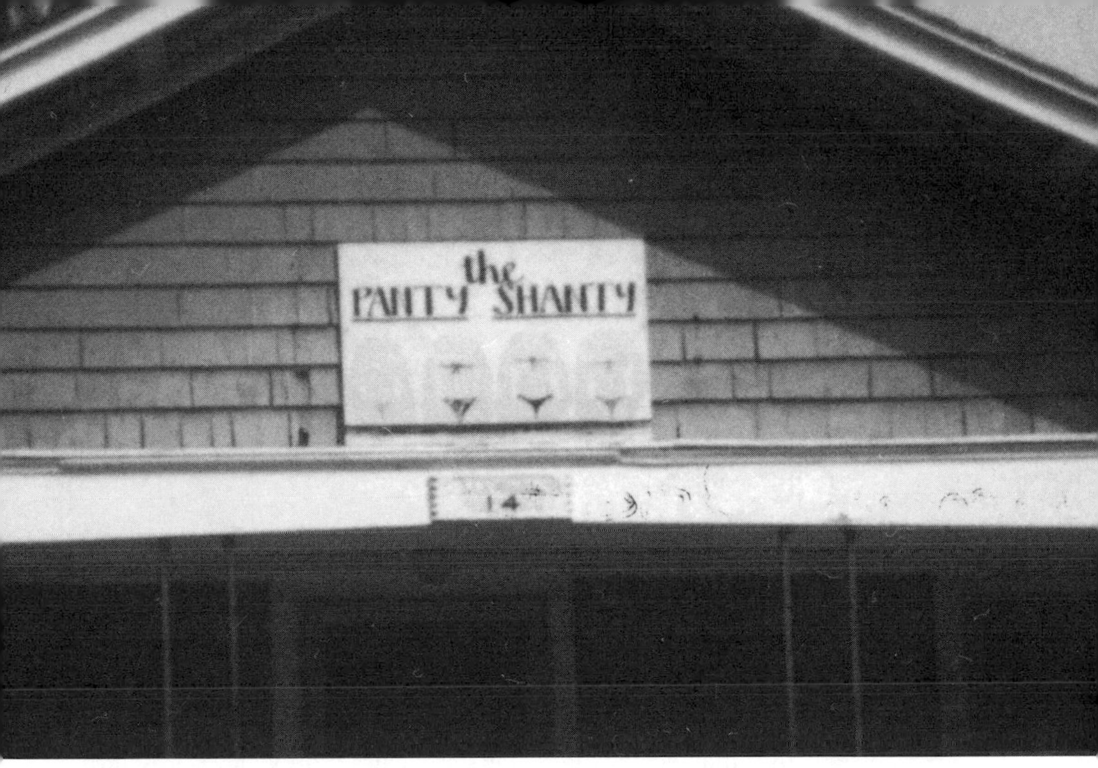

FIGURE 5.7. The Panty Shanty

with "actually," intimating that the sex of the residents comes as a surprise. This claim echoes Beth's of Girls Gone Wild.

The residents of Green House make particularly clear the notion that one can derive the sex of house residents from the name of the house—in the case of particularly sexual signs.[4] Jess, the student interviewer, asks if one can "tell anything about the identity of the people living in the house by the name?" Usually the answer to this question is negative. In most cases, residents understand the question to imply a connection between the house name and their behavior and moral disposition. In the interview with Green House, however, the residents understand the gender of the residents to be a possible referent for identity. This is a possibility never disputed or denied in other interviews because residents' gender was never imagined to be a possible referent for identity. The residents of Green House proceed to list house names, stating the residents to be boys or guys or girls.

> JESS: so do you think you can tell anything about the identity of the people that live in the house by the name
> CASS: you can definitely tell the gender of people that live in a ⌈house
> STACEY: ⌊yeah

CASS: by the name . . . typically, some of them.
JESS: any examples
CASS: Morning Wood is a house of boys
EMILY: Strangers with Candy is a house of **boys**
STACEY: Pissonia
CASS: Gutter Balls
EMILY: Gutter Balls
STACEY: boys, all boys
CASS: with a bowling pin and two balls next to it, yeah
EMILY: Octopussy would be a house of girls
STACEY: eight
CASS: eight, girls obviously

Cass starts with Morning Wood and states that the house is inhabited by boys. While this example allows the derivation of the gender of residents by the sexual imagery of the house name, the next two examples do not. Neither Strangers with Candy nor Pissonia offers any clues. Emily and Stacey intimate that the fact that men reside in the houses accounts for the vulgarity of the names. Cass describes what makes the next sign, Gutter Balls, indicate that its house's residents are male. Octopussy joins Gutter Balls in including the means to connect the sign with the gender of the residents. Thus, when the residents of Green House assert that one can derive the gender of the residents from their house name, no particular criteria emerge to account for all examples. Morning Wood, Gutter Balls, and Octopussy involve genitalia, and Gutter Balls is the only house sign whose imagery is used by the residents of Green House to describe the connection between the house name and the gender of the residents. Strangers with Candy and Pissonia, on the other hand, seem to represent the vulgarity characteristic of male residents generally, outside of any particular way to match house sign and sex of residents.

In an interview with Girls Gone Ghetto, Britt begins by asking Jack, the student interviewer, a question about the relationship between house signs and the gender of the inhabitants. Jack has suggested that signs one would assume to have been created by males can turn out to have been created by females. Britt asks for examples because she can only think of one. She thus intimates that such cases are rare.

BRITT: okay anyways, what were some that you thought would be all guys that actually are girls, like The Dirty Dozen ⌈that's the only one **I** thought would have been guys . . .

JACK: ⌊there's
something that was . . .

AMY: oh did you, Jaundice. I would think Jaundice would be an all-guys' house, it's like this pale yellow house on University

MISSY: **why** would you think Jaundice would be all guys. there's a little girl on the sign(2)

AMY: because like, it's a **disease**

ALL: #

Amy guesses that Jack is thinking of Jaundice. Her description of the house as "pale yellow" suggests the coloring of the illness, but it indicates nothing about the gender of the residents. When Missy points out that there is a "little girl on the sign," Amy pauses to answer. Her assertion that there is a connection between the house name and the fact that its residents are male by virtue of the fact that the house name is a disease draws laughter from all. Amy is also reproducing the notion that the gender of residents can be derived from particularly vulgar house names because males tend to be more vulgar than females. This follows Britt's assertion that only very rarely do such house names turn out to coined by female residents.

In sum, when reflecting on house signs, residents of named houses try to make sense of enormously complex possibilities for the involvement of gender and sexuality. The topic often arises because residents identify other signs as worse than their own. Whether the topic arises in a comparative mode or in a discussion of house signs more generally, there are two ideas that residents of named houses try to make compatible. One is that there is a connection between the genitalia and/or sexual act depicted on the sign, on the one hand, and the sex of the house's residents, on the other hand. The other is that boys are responsible for especially vulgar signs. The second notion is necessary to explain the gender of residents of such houses as Strangers with Candy, Pissonia, and Clitty Clitty Bang Bang. Women who are salacious in their house signs are deemed exceptions. The three signs listed here include either no overt indication of sexual difference or an indication of the "wrong" sex, and thus they are assumed to be male creations. When the ideas do not coincide, and residents of houses with vulgar names are not male, people comment on the fact explicitly and intimate that this comes as a surprise. Reflective talk about house signs excludes the vast majority of signs that involve gender and/or sexuality and reproduce the idea that men are more salacious than women.

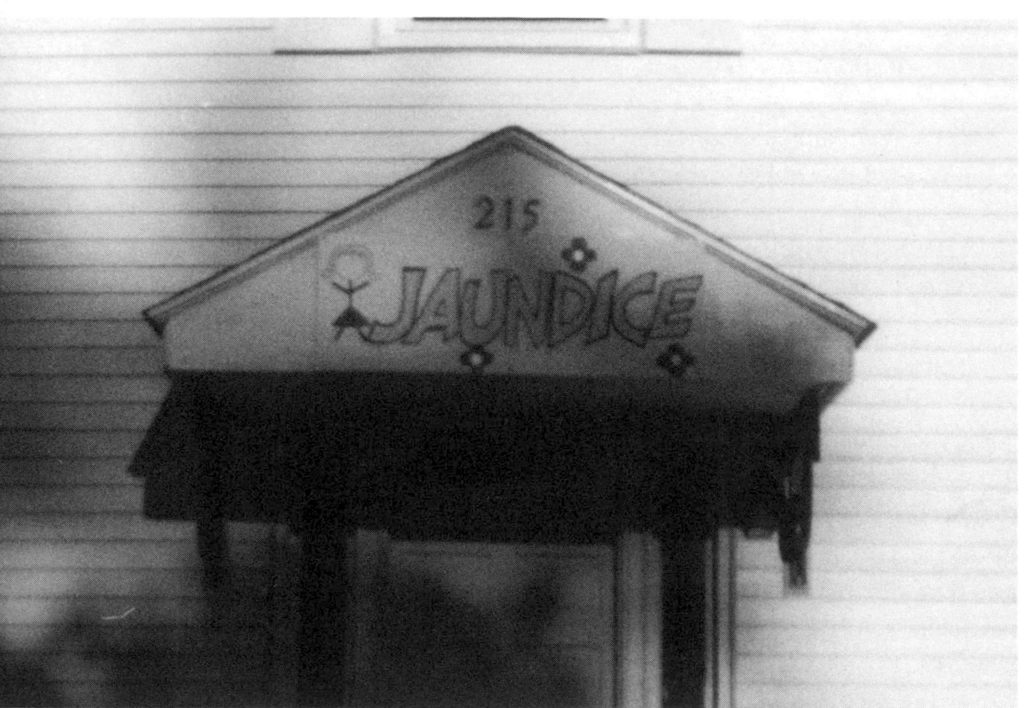

FIGURE 5.8. Jaundice

Hot Box with Box Office and Fill'er Up

Our interview with the residents of Hot Box provided us with a rare opportunity to consider the ways in which women and men might reflect on house signs in the presence of one another. During our interview with Jackie, Lily, and Meg, Wade and Willy of Box Office and Simon and Patrick of Fill'er Up paid a visit and joined our discussion. This was highly unusual, since the people conducting the interviews always made an initial visit to ascertain interest, shared paperwork approved by the institutional review board for the protection of human subjects, and made an appointment for an interview in order to include as many house residents as possible. Once we started interviewing, we quickly surmised that most residents must be telling their friends about their engagement between first contact and the interview because interviews were interrupted very rarely. The participation by the men provides the chance to explore what happens when a mixed-sex group reflects together on house signs. Most generally, we will see that gender and sex emerge as an important feature structuring the interaction of the people involved in the interview, not just the messages on house signs or residents' notions about how others—variously defined—might be affected or not affected by their sign.

Before the arrival of the men, Lily, Jackie, and Meg of Hot Box give evidence that they are especially aware of the ways in which others might construe their house name. Thus they exhibit reflections on their sign in a manner very much like the residents whose signs feature sexual elements. Initially, at least, Jackie points to possibilities of interpreting Hot Box that are not sexual. Lily quickly adds other possibilities that are more likely sexual. When asked what their sign means, Jackie points to two domains and Lily adds two more:

> JACKIE: our house is small and it's hot, is one . . . vague . . . meaning
> LILY: um, smoking, and, um, girls, Hot Box

The attributes offered by Jackie have to do with the house itself. Ostensibly, Jackie's "small" corresponds to the second word in the house's name, "box," and her "hot" repeats the first word of the house's name. Lily reframes the understanding of Hot Box to include its residents. Her "smoking" invokes a practice in which the house residents engage and most likely corresponds to the first word of the house's name, and her "girls" most likely corresponds to "Box," understood as a word for female genitalia. Laughter works in tandem with the move from interpretations having to do with the house to ones having to do with the residents. Jackie seems to laugh as an acknowledgment that there is something in the house's name that she is leaving out, just as Lily's laughter seems to register the hilarity of the name's involvement of girls. Lily also creates an intertextual link with other house names, of course, by indexing notions of partying encountered across our interviews with residents of named houses.

This intertextual link would take awhile to emerge, for me at least, because I initially understood "smoking" to refer to the activity in which everyone except one of the student interviewers was engaging at the time: smoking cigarettes. This struck me as rather benign, since smoking cigarettes never counted in our interviews as the consumption of a substance that might contribute to partying. Later, Jackie made the inclusion of smoking as a possible construal of Hot Box quite relevant to the partying indicated by house signs. Jenny begins a line of discussion by using a word that is ambiguous in that it can refer to one who consumes cigarettes and/or to one who consumes marijuana: “smoker.” It quickly becomes apparent that the residents understand Hot Box to include both and that such inclusion enhances the charged quality of the sign.

> JENNY: okay so, do everybody who lives here are they all smokers
> MEG: what kind
> ALL: #
> JENNY: um, well like cig, you guys are all smoking cigarettes, but I, I mean, obviously like the Hot Box doesn't have to do with really cigarettes usually
> JACKIE: we all smoke cigs, we smoke weed
> GIRLS: yeah

Jenny was indeed the one person not smoking cigarettes at the time, but her question plays on the dual possibilities of “smoker.” This only becomes apparent in the various replies to her question. Meg playfully acknowledges that “smoker” might mean something other than what was presently happening with her reply, “What kind?” The residents and the interviewers, myself included, laugh at Meg's explicit acknowledgment that “smoker” might mean something else. Jenny's response that the house name must not be limited to the residents' cigarette smoking habit makes apparent that Jenny had been aware of the possibility that “smoker” might include marijuana from the start. With her mention of “weed,” Jackie names the substance the consumption of which constitutes the other meaning of “smoker.” Jenny's suspicion that smoking cigarettes is not illicit enough to create an intertextual link with “partying,” realized across house signs, proves to be warranted.

After Jackie makes explicit that Hot Box includes smoking marijuana and not just cigarettes, that possibility of the house's meaning disappears for all but one moment of the rest of the interview. Fifteen minutes later, Willy, a resident of another house who has paid a visit to Hot Box and joined the conversation since the last excerpt, explains why he thinks the name is a good one:

> WILLY: because, as you can, you can't really see right now but like, whenever I walk in this house when it's, getting close to twelve o'clock, you can't even see this wall from all the smoke that's in here so I think it ⌈works well #
> JACKIE: ⌊cigarettes, too

LILY: too
ALL: #

Jackie's utterance, "cigarettes, too," implies that the smoke about which Willy spoke emanates from a source other than cigarettes and that the smoke we were currently creating accounted for only some of the smoke described by Willy. Everyone laughs when Lily laughingly calls attention to the word "too." Allusions to marijuana in our interview with Hot Box are thus playful, productive of laughter, and even produced by a visitor.

Much more productive of discussion, however, is the notion that Hot Box in particular and house signs more generally can refer to aspects of human anatomy and/or sexual activity. Perhaps one factor in the interview with Hot Box that contributed to the focus on the inclusion of genitalia and sex in house signs was that Wade and Willy, both residents of Box Office, and Simon and Patrick of Fill'er Up paid a visit to Hot Box five minutes after the interview had started. The residents of Hot Box had not told them about the interview. Thus we were all surprised by their arrival, and the four visitors had no idea what we were doing.

At the door, Jackie said to them, "Wait. guys. Willy, we're in an interview," to which he responded, "Oh really?" and Wade, "For what? What are you, what are you gonna interview, what are you guys gonna interview for?" Wade assumed that Jackie and her housemates were interviewing someone, and she explained otherwise and invited the four in, telling them to remain quiet. Jenny, Ali, Chris, and I explained that the interview was part of the class I was teaching and that the four could join the interview if they were willing to read and sign the consent forms approved by the institutional review board. Patrick was the only one who refused to sign the form, claiming that he would like to listen but not participate. He blurted out things twice during the interview, once to tease Willy, and once to talk about his house sign. Both times, the interview team offered to let him read the forms and sign them so that he would know that his participation in the project would be anonymous and the recording of his voice subject to his review, but he declined.

Between Jackie's assertion, "we all smoke cigs, we all smoke weed," and the arrival of the four guys, the residents of Hot Box explained that they changed the name of the house on moving in. The shift from the previous name and occupants to the present ones involved gender, but this cannot, per se, be derived from the name change. Lily begins the excerpt about the name change by talking about the previous residents and their house name.

LILY: so, like we, pretty much like stole it from those boys and so they were like, we just didn't wanna, have any . . .
JACKIE: 'cause they had been that like seven years so it was kind of like their name so, we didn't want . . .
LILY: we thought that they would probably want us to change it but it turned out like, they were mad that we changed it
JENNY: did they call you or . . .
MEG: they tried to steal our sign
JACKIE: our sign got stolen once, like when it wasn't even hung up after we painted the first one, and then . . . homecoming, we thought it was gonna get stolen again, but, it didn't
JENNY: did you eventually get it back
LILY: no, we made another one
JENNY: oh really, do you know, you know who stole it though
MEG: yeah
LILY: well . . .
JACKIE: there's a bunch that live across the street that . . .
LILY: and like people walk by and like they're just like "it's **Boxed I::nn**" like, you know, and we're just like "haha," so like . . .
JENNY: so you guys get harassed
MEG: I think it's mostly like the senior, well, the people that were supposed to live here live across the street, so like . . .
JACKIE: but really our landlord wouldn't have rented to boys again, so she was looking for girls, so we didn't really steal it like from them but, saved our landlord more than like, ⌈tried to steal it from them
MEG: ⌊but of course, they're not gonna blame her they probably would just put the blame on us it's easier that way

Lily starts the excerpt by making explicit that the previous residents were male. She uses the verb "stole," but one is left wondering just what was stolen. Jackie invokes the idea that the long-term usage of a house name creates the ownership of a tradition across various sets of occupants when she explains that what was stolen was "their name." She also demonstrates that such pedigree can be imagined to apply to the current residents of the house when she states, "they had been that for seven years," when she knows that the residents had occupied the house for two years at most. Lily, Jenny, and Meg then explain that they were mistaken in their belief that the previous owners wanted them to change their name. To give evidence, they explain that their new sign was stolen. The significance of long-term maintenance of a name is thus ambivalent in the residents' talk. The residents of Hot Box express recognition that the maintenance of a house name enhances its salience and fame, but also explain that they believed that the previous residents did not want this fame transferred to them.

By understanding the tensions brought on by house succession solely in terms of the fact that the name had changed, the residents of Hot Box fail to reflect on the fact that the name change might be related to the change in the sex of the residents. Their mention of homecoming is probably oriented to alumni visits to campus and associated fears about the desire of former residents of the house to steal the changed sign. Near the middle of the excerpt, Lily finally gives the previous name, Boxed Inn, while explaining that various passersby have reacted negatively to the name change. Meg states two different points about the people who have been mentioning the former name. One gets the impression that at least some of the people living across the street might have occupied Boxed Inn during their junior year. One cannot be sure because the residents of Hot Box are not explicit about the issue. What seems to be more focal is the fact that calling out a former house name is a way to index the fact that current house residents have changed the name. By mimicking "Inn" in Boxed Inn, Lily is mimicking an onlooker's emphasis on the element missing in Hot Box.

Jackie again mentions the fact that the previous residents were male, intimating that the sex of the residents was relevant to the transition from former residents to present ones. Jackie explains that the decision to switch the sex of renters was not the current residents' but rather the landlord's. Jackie explains that she and the current residents thus "saved our landlord" rather than "tried to steal" the house from the former residents. Meg explains that the former residents do not identify who is really culpable in their taunts because it is easier "to put the blame on us."

An unsettled question emerges out of the ruminations of the residents of Hot Box. They explain that the landlady was indeed interested in renting to women after several years of renting to men. They explain that the former house residents of their house (of Boxed Inn), some of whom, at least, now live across the street, are angry that the residents of Hot Box changed the name.

What they do not address is whether the change in gender had anything to do with their choice of name. While this point might seem rather trivial, the relationship between the sexual element in a house sign and the sex of its house's residents will come to pattern the interaction between Jackie, Lily, and Meg, on the one hand, and Wade, Willy, and Simon, on the other.

After three of the four visitors agree to participate, Wade explains to me that the name of his house is Box Office. Jackie notes the similarities in the names when she states, "We're Hot Box and Box Office, oh god, that's bad news." Everyone erupts into laughter. At this point, Jackie is focusing on the shared use of "box." The relationship between the speech play of a house sign and the sex of the same house's residents has not yet emerged as significant. This will change shortly.

The men next ask how long the interview will take. Jenny redirects the interview to the focus just before the men arrived, a discussion about "clever" or "offensive" signs. Jenny mentions The Rusty Trombone, ostensibly an example of an offensive sign.

> JENNY: so, have, can you think of any other signs, like we didn't really, you said, you were trying to think of signs that, that like you think are clever, or like, or any that you think are offensive, like have you heard of The Rusty Trombone
> LILY: the one I hate is . . .
> MEG: Fill'er Up
> LILY: Juggs . . .
> JACKIE: Liquor Juggs
> LILY: Liquor Juggs . . . it's sort of funny but, I don't know
> JENNY: why do you hate it
> LILY: I, just . . .
> MEG: I don't know, I just think it's sort of dumb, like . . . I guess
> LILY: I'm trying to think, there's so many that I really . . .
> WADE: what about the Liquor Box from last year, do you like that one
> JACKIE: I like Subject to Blackout
> MEG: until they [changed it
> LILY: [I liked that too

While Jenny asks the residents whether they find house signs offensive, Lily uses the verb "hate." Meg interjects "Fill'er Up," and though one cannot be sure, this might make sense of the fact that Patrick of said house was unwilling to participate in the interview. Simon lives in Fill'er Up, too, so one cannot be sure whether Meg's mention of the name indicates much at all about her opinion of her visitors. What becomes significant, though never explicitly described, is that the residents of Hot Box express intense dislike for houses occupied by men whose house names represent women as passive sexual objects or utilize euphemisms for female genitalia.[5] The grammatical parallel between the imperatives Fill'er Up [fill her up] and Liquor Juggs [lick her jugs] is striking.

The residents of Hot Box are not explicit about these relationships, however, and relegate themselves to the criticisms commonly launched in the house sign community of practice generally. Thus Lily claims ambivalently, "It's sort of funny," and Meg describes the same sign as "sort of dumb." Neither of these descriptors affords Lily and Meg the disposition that "hate" allows. Wade then offers another sign that indexes his recognition of the parallelism of Fill'er Up and Liquor Juggs: Liquor Box. Wade seems to be taunting the women somewhat with his suggestion. He uses the verb "like" with a sexual sign that fits with signs the women earlier claimed to hate. Rather than expressing dislike, however, Jackie offers positive feedback about Subject to Blackout, thereby drawing the focus away from examples involving females as sexual objects erected by men. In so doing, Jackie does not acknowledge Wade's participation in the production of examples.

Wade tries again, immediately after the last excerpt. In the first line, he indexes recognition that the women have reframed the set of house signs with their offer of Subject to Blackout.

> WADE: we're talking about offensive ones though right
> JENNY: oh no you guys can talk about anything like anything that you think is clever, or offensive, and like why you think they're clever kind of
> WADE: what about um, Dickens Cider Box
> LILY: where's that
> WADE: you've never seen that one, Dickens Cider B, well obviously if you haven't . . .
> JACKIE: I think Dirty South is a cool sign and . . .
> LILY: Dirty South has a nice sign
> JACKIE: yeah, they have a nice sign, it's like 3-D, and fun

Once again, Wade offers the name of a sign that focuses on female genitalia, this time being penetrated by a penis. And once again, the residents of

Hot Box do not recognize his offer by offering yet others. Lily first implicitly claims not to be familiar with Wade's example. When Wade expresses gentle dismay, Jackie offers the name of a house that has nothing to do with the representation of genitalia, at least those that are sex-specific. Unlike in the case of sexual signs that prompted ambivalent responses, Dirty South prompts "cool," "nice," "3-D," and "fun." The residents have no trouble using the evaluative discourse of house signs for Dirty South.

At this point, one might make the argument that the women who reside in Hot Box have a dislike for houses that involve genitalia in their punning. In addition, they seem not to want to engage Wade as he produces more names that fit with those the women have already offered as ones that they "hate." Only the latter argument turns out to be true. The residents of Hot Box quickly return to signs that involve genitalia, and this time their evaluation is positive. Their offer of a house name that involves genitalia does not seem to have been prompted by Jenny. Indeed, Jenny begins the next excerpt by addressing the residents' discussion of the comparatively nonsexual Dirty South.

> JENNY: oh, I see, that's kind of cool, so do you think that like, the actual like sign itself and like what it, like the, I don't know artwork or whatever on it has a lot to do with like how you, like think about the . . .
> LILY: like Morning Wood, that's a pretty nice sign
> JENNY: why do you think that's pretty good
> MEG: you know
> JACKIE: the face, the boner . . .
> LILY: because it's . . .
> JENNY: well yeah the face like I never even like noticed the face until like they pointed it out like . . .

When Jenny tries to characterize the descriptors for Dirty South used by the residents of Hot Box, Lily offers a sign that involves genitalia, this time men's. Jackie makes the sexual nature of Morning Wood explicit when she explains that "the face, the boner" make the sign "nice." "Boner" is an expression for an erection. The women thus are not squeamish at all when offering a sign that involves male genitalia. They claim to express approval of the sign, calling it "nice." Just whom Jenny is talking about when she refers to "they" is unclear, but she does not mention the sexual aspect of the sign in her concluding line. She intimates that the sexual aspect of Morning Wood is rather obvious.

Jenny next presses the residents of Hot Box for additional examples that they find funny. Meg begins to answer but then evaluates examples offered by Jackie and Ali.

JENNY: what do you think is funny, which ones?
MEG: like . . .
JACKIE: Sex on the Beech
MEG: that's kinda funny
ALI: Spoiled Beeches
MEG: yeah, I like that one
LILY: that's, isn't that where Veronica lives
MEG: she lives at Simply Irresistible
WADE: I don't care what a sign says or pertains to just it's, if it makes me think like, for it, like think about it for a second and then all of a sudden I get it like if it's really clever like that's the kind of signs I like

Earlier, the residents of Hot Box expressed hatred for signs involving women in a sexualized way. In this latest excerpt, however, they express approval of Sex on the Beech and Spoiled Beeches. The first name puns on the name of the street on which the house is located and the name of a popular cocktail. The second name is less complex and puns, like the first, on the name of the street and on the possibility of "bitch" standing in for "beech" to render the sign Spoiled Bitches. The second sign's invocation of "bitch" might be read into the first sign, Sex on the Beech, to render a particularly heinous and offensive pun, though no one present seems to notice this.

Notice the ways in which the residents of Hot Box manage to draw on the names of house signs toward the production of very specific indexical activity while remaining true to the very vague and general reflexive evaluations available in the house sign community of practice. On the one hand, they interject Sex on the Beech and Spoiled Beeches, names that involve sexuality and women. On the other hand, the names are offered as examples of funny signs, and the residents stick to that level of generality when discussing them. While one might argue that the residents are interjecting these two names because they share a pun on the street name, their appearance in the larger series of excerpts dealing with gender and sexuality lends the interjections continuity. Wade does not contribute but rather reflects quite generally on what makes a sign clever. He effectively removes the issue of sex from the discussion. This shift in Wade's behavior coupled with the Hot Box residents' offer of the two names suggests that the gendered and sexual nature of the house signs being discussed and the gender of the people involved might have something to do with one another.

Indeed, the interview with Hot Box, when considered alongside others, provided a rare opportunity to consider what happens when women and men reflect on house signs in the presence of one another. The fact that Meg, Jackie, Lily, Willy, Wade, and Simon focus their discussion of house signs with names involving sex is not surprising given that they reside in Hot Box, Box Office, and Fill'er Up. The first two share the use of a euphemism for the vagina, "box," and the last uses a common command at the gas pump to refer to heterosexual intercourse and male orgasm. But the stances the women and men take vis-à-vis one another is fascinating and complicates the ways in which one might interpret residents' dispositions to gender and sexuality from house names themselves.

For example, one might see the women's christening of themselves as Hot Box and maintaining the sexualized pun of their house predecessors, Boxed Inn, to be in conflict with their offer of Fill'er Up and Liquor Juggs as signs that they hate. When one considers that the residents of Fill'er Up and Liquor Juggs (and Boxed Inn) are all male, however, the disposition of the residents of Hot Box to house signs emerges as quite consistent, even if unstated. The women consistently express disapproval of signs that invoke women as sexual when the houses to which they belong are inhabited by men. When the women of Hot Box reflect on signs that invoke women as sexual, but are displayed on houses occupied by women, they are quite positive in their evaluation. The women thus create a disposition to issues of gender and sexuality that approves of residents erecting sexually charged signs when the gender invoked in the sign matches the gender of the house's residents.

When house residents violate this general rule, the women of Hot Box step out of the typical means of evaluation of house signs as "clever" and "funny" or "dumb" and "gay," and use the verb "to hate." Such an extreme emotional descriptor is rare in reflections on signs, and when students do express an individual stance toward a particular name (as opposed to the offer of a descriptor of the sign, e.g., "dumb"), they most often use the verb "to like." The women never make their stance to the issue of gender in sexual signs explicit, but rather demonstrate their stance toward the issue with the offer of particular names and generalized approval or disapproval.

The notion that the residents of Hot Box approve of sexual signs when the gender of house residents match the gender invoked in the name is reinforced

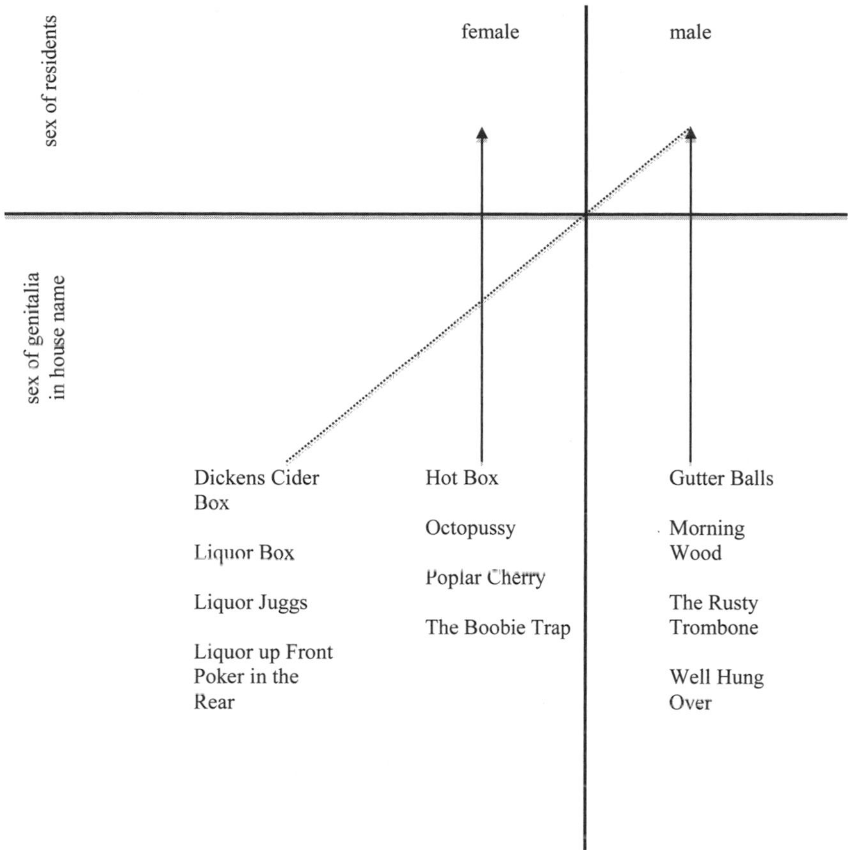

FIGURE 5.9. Relationships between Sexual House Signs and Sex of Residents

in an excerpt taken from a later point in the interview. This time, the residents reflect on Boxed Inn, the name of the house in which Wade and Willy live. Jenny begins the excerpt by addressing Simon, who has been relatively quiet.

JENNY: what house do you . . . where do you live
LILY: Fill'er Up
SIMON: our sign just got stolen
JENNY: are you sure you don't want to talk about it
SIMON: I'm pretty sure
JENNY: okay, excellent
LILY: Simon, will you get me a beer [Simon leaves for the kitchen]
JENNY: so, house names that you guys talked about

WILLY: oh, um . . . well, we live in the house that was formerly known as Blue Moon, it's right down here on the corner, and it's the gas leak house, okay, yeah, we're fine, in case you were worried, um, but uh, we were gonna call it something, we were gonna try and play off of that, and we were gonna do something like uh, like Natural High, or um, we were gonna do um, uh we were just gonna call it straight up Gas Leak, just to kind of like, get back at our landlords a little bit, you know, but uh, we figured that if we made a sign that said Gas Leak on it they would find a reason to make us take it down so, we didn't do that one, um, there's, #, Crackin, 'scuse me, uh, one of my roommates has a, was thinking about, we have this huge um, like, uh, squirrel that they stole from a putt-putt course in Pleasantville, and it's, you can, we could bolt it to the, to the roof of our house, and we were gonna do that and maybe, call it the Nut House but, we didn't really like the Nut House ⌈that much

JACKIE: ⌊I like that one, ⌈by the way, a lot

LILY: ⌊I like that too, I like that way better than Box Office

MEG: so do I

LILY: how come I never thought of that idea

WILLY: well that's, it just came out like last week

LILY: I like that one

Lily answers for Simon, who then explains that his house sign has been stolen. Jenny seems to understand that he is genuinely upset about the theft. Lily then asks Simon to get her a beer, and he exits the room to return in the middle of Willy's explanation. Willy recounts the other house names the residents of Box Office considered. The name was Blue Moon when they moved in. The first two possibilities they considered referred to a gas leak in the house. Willy seems to recognize that Natural High seems to engage in the clever quality a house name is supposed to possess when he uses the verb "to play" and that Gas Leak does not when he describes it as "straight up." The latter's rather literal description of the condition, Willy explains, would be too threatening.

The next possibility that Willy mentions ostensibly remains incomplete. He laughs at the thought of the name and then offers an apology. Willy apologizes in recognition that he has not provided an explanation whereby one might understand the (incomplete) name he has offered, a name that turns out to be unrelated to the gas leak. After a few failed starts, he explains that his roommate (and roommate's friends, presumably) stole a large squirrel statue and that the name Nut House might go well with it. That Willy's incomplete offer of "Crackin'" relates to Nut House is clear, but Willy never reveals what the rest of the first name was. Jackie offers, in contrast to the lack of enthusiasm reported by Willy, that she is fond of the name. She emphasizes her feeling with "a lot." Lily asserts a similar feeling and contrasts her positive feeling about the unrealized Nut House with her feeling for Willy's current house name, Box Office. Meg signals unanimity with "so do I." Lily goes so far as to regret never having thought of the name herself. In the face of the enthusiasm of the residents of Hot Box, Willy explains that the residents of Box Office only thought of Nut House the week before the interview.

Jenny then asks two questions, both of which focus on the giant squirrel rather than the sexual connection between Nut House and male genitalia.

JENNY: so do you have the squirrel
WILLY: yeah we have the squirrel, it's pretty big
MEG: it's like life-sized almost, it's like as big as me it's huge
JENNY: and you can bolt it to the top of your house
WILLY: 'cause it was bolted to the, eighteenth hole of the putt-putt
course so it's got the holes already
ALI: why do you ladies like . . . what was it, the Nut House. why did
you like that one
MEG: uh, ⌈well, the sign would be . . . yeah, the sign would be pretty cool
JACKIE: ⌊I think that'd be funny if they had the squirrel on their,
the squirrel's funny, and they have, ⌈I just think it would be
funny, yeah
LILY: ⌊the sign, the squirrel,
⌈boys' anatomy, all the things
JENNY: ⌊so would the squirrel own the sign
WILLY: something like, we didn't really think of the logistics of it
yet, you know, it's, it's still uh, it's still in, ⌈in the works
LILY: ⌊that's a way better
name than Box Office

Meg reveals that the women have indeed known about the squirrel prior to the interview. This makes sense of the fact that Lily earlier expressed regret for not having thought of Nut House as a possible name.

Ali shifts the discussion to Meg, Jackie, and Lily's approval of Nut House and away from the logistics of the squirrel's display on the house. Meg and Jackie stay within the means of reflection on house signs realized across interviews when Meg explains that the sign would be "cool" and Jackie uses the word "funny" three times in one utterance. Lily is the first to make an explicit connection between the various parts of the potential sign toward the invocation of sex. By "sign," she probably is referring to the potential name, Nut House. Jenny returns to the issue of the squirrel by using the colloquial expression, "to own," meaning something like a combination of "to be in control of" and "to be worthy of." Willy doesn't seem to understand her question and focuses on the problem of mounting the squirrel to the house. Lily concludes by reiterating that Nut House is a better name than Box Office.

All of the residents of Hot Box express approval of Nut House, and Lily explains that "boy's anatomy" is one of the things that makes the name such a good one. Furthermore, Lily compares Nut House quite favorably with Willy and Wade's current house name, Box Office. When one considers that "box" is a euphemism for the vagina, and "nut" is a euphemism for the testicle, the stance of Jackie, Meg, and Lily is rendered consistent with that taken earlier in the interview. Willy and Wade live in a house whose name invokes female genitalia. They would do better to pick a name that invokes their own genitalia. Nut House would do the job whereas Box Office fails.

The women and men interject names that achieve their sexual charge through distinctions in sex. Consistently, the women express approval for names that invoke female genitalia or females through punning on beech/bitch when the houses are occupied by women. They express approval for names that invoke male genitalia when the houses are inhabited by men. They express annoyance at house names that invoke female genitalia when the occupants are men. When considered against the backdrop of house signs and the residents of the houses to which the signs belong, this stance constitutes a revealing critique. Though the women of Hot Box never make the fact explicit, women do not invoke men sexually when naming their houses. Indeed, the only exception we knew about was Pop-N-Wood. Meg, Jackie, and Lily implicitly recognize that men—including their present company—have transgressed a dictum that gains their approval: stick to your own genitalia when coining your house's name. Women do indeed engage in erecting sexually charged house signs, but they rarely sexualize men while doing so.

While the residents of Hot Box critique signs when the residents of the house use genitalia of the opposite sex in the name, they do not do so explicitly in a manner that would have them take a stance. The women's expressions of disapproval of house names that use euphemisms for genitalia of the opposite sex do implicate the names of the two men present at the interview, but never do the women of Hot Box criticize the men. Indeed, a few minutes after the women express like or dislike for particular signs, they make explicit that a moral stance on the men's house signs would indicate that the onlooker in question has taken signs too seriously. Jenny, one of the student interviewers, begins the line of discussion by asking the collective whether there are pictures on house signs (as opposed to verbal elements) that they might find offensive.

JENNY: so, what pictures on the signs did you think are offensive kind of, if there are any
WILLY: well I mean . . .
JACKIE: certain kinds ⌈of box . . .
SIMON: ⌊my house . . . people ⌈bitch about my house
JENNY: ⌊what's your house, again
SIMON: there's just a, there was a picture of uh, a girl . . .
JENNY: Liquor Juggs
JACKIE: Fill'er Up
LILY: there's one, what is the one that's Liquor Juggs though isn't that right on . . .
JACKIE: yeah Liquor Juggs is on, over right over there
LILY: yeah Liquor Juggs is like, isn't it isn't it like two big breasts and like . . .
JACKIE: but it's like two beers too or something like . . . it's like pour, I think she's like taking two beers and like pouring it on her chest maybe, ⌈it's something like that
CHAISE: ⌊have you guys complained directly or . . .
SIMON: we, like, we've just had a few girls come by, not come by but girls that have like been over that have been like, oh we don't like your sign

Willy begins to answer the question but Jackie defines a group of signs by their use of "box." Her answer is fascinating because it invokes her own sign as well as Willy's sign. Ostensibly, what makes hers benign and his offensive is the earlier rationale that signs put up by women should involve female genitalia and that signs put up by men should involve male genitalia. If one understands Jackie to implicate Willy with her comment, Simon's offer of "my house" might be seen as an attempt to take the focus away from Willy. Simon claims rather vaguely that people complain about his house when Jenny asks for him to remind her of its name. He begins to describe its pictorial elements when Jenny guesses its name, but is incorrect. Jackie provides the correct answer, but Jenny's guess becomes the focus of description. First, the residents of Hot Box discuss its location rather vaguely, and then its involvement of beer and a woman's chest. I mistake their descriptions for the expression of disapproval and offense with which Jenny began. Simon, downplaying the consequence of the expression of dislike, with "just" and "few," explains that girls have said, "Oh, we don't like your sign."

The visitors' expression of dislike reported by Simon differs from the expressions of dislike offered earlier in the interview by the residents of Hot Box. Ostensibly, both Simon's visitors and the women of Hot Box present at the interview do not like signs put up by men who use euphemisms for female genitalia on them. But when Simon reports the words of his female visitors, he uses a possessive pronoun, "your," to represent the sign. This involves the owner of the sign in the expression of dislike. There is no hesitation in saying whose sign is the target of dislike, something not true of the criticism launched by the residents of Hot Box earlier. Indeed, Simon's animation of the female visitors with "oh we don't like your sign" sets into relief the indirection that characterizes the statements of the residents of Hot Box as they repeatedly offer disparaging comments about house signs, including those of the two men present, but never refer to the men by way of their signs (or vice versa). It also sets into relief the men's maintenance of the women's indirection as the men do not respond to the women's mention of their signs.

Willy then introduces another sign that uses female genitalia, Liquor Box.

WILLY: people probably hated the Li, the Liquor Box sign I though was even, was real creative 'cause they . . .

SIMON: what's the Liquor Box sign

WILLY: 'cause they made it into a mouth that was wide open, and then, the teeth, the way they made the teeth it spelled out Liquor Box, inside of it, so that, that was pretty clever

LILY: I just think it's all fun and games and you just have to live with it like I just, ⌈don't think there's any need to get offended

SIMON: ⌊our Liquor Box idea was just a girl with her legs spread with a big box of [indecipherable] liquor, in between her legs #

JENNY: but what's your sign have on it now
SIMON: just a, big . . . titted woman
ALL: #
SIMON: with, with, with an empty beer mug in the house called Fill'er Up, and that's it
LILY: see like I mean like you're gonna walk past that and be like at least I would and like, laugh to myself like I wouldn't be like "oh **god**" like, "who are those **people** in there, rrr" and like get . . .
JENNY: do you think anybody does that
LILY: I'm sure people do
JACKIE: I'm sure there are people like that

Willy invokes the omnipresent notion that the determination of a house sign's cleverness should be the most important task confronting a person engaged in reading a house sign. Thus those who "probably hated" the Liquor Box sign were missing its creativity. Willy never does explain why anyone might have hated the sign, however. Rather than expressing dislike for the sign, as the residents of Hot Box did when they were in control of offering examples of house names, Lily offers a general comment applicable to all house signs. She explains the entire phenomenon of the creation and display of house signs as "fun and games" and decries the kind of stance toward house signs that would enable one to "get offended."

Just to whom Simon is referring with his use of "our" is uncertain, especially given that Simon has just expressed a lack of familiarity with Liquor Box. It could very well be that he is trying to trump Willy's description of the sign by moving the focus from the mouth to between the legs. Jenny brings the discussion back to Simon's sign by asking him what was on it. He answers vulgarly, using "tit" instead of "breast" and "chest," words the women of Hot Box had used earlier. The vulgar answer draws a laugh from all. He completes the description less vulgarly and does not explain the connection between the woman and the empty beer mug on the sign.

In a way, Lily's response provides a parallel with Simon's earlier animation of the visiting girls who say, "Oh, we don't like your sign," and Willy's intimation that such people cannot appreciate the clever elements of Liquor Box. Lily explains that she would "laugh to myself" on seeing a sign like Fill'er Up. She performs the stance that should not meet the sign, one by which someone would say "Oh god, like, who are those people in there, rrr." Imbedded within the critical statement offered by Lily is the imagination of what residents are like via their house sign. This, too, is shared by Simon's earlier animation of the opinion of the girls visiting his house. Lily's animation of criticism differs from Simon's, however, because Lily is relaying a hypothetical stance and not one she has overheard. Jackie reinforces Lily's imagined stance when she says, "I'm sure there are people like that."

In the extended transcript of the interview with the residents of Hot Box and their guests, the residents consistently express approval of house names that indicate the sex of the residents, making no distinction in vulgarity, and express disapproval for house names that indicate the sex different from that of the residents. In doing so, the women show—but never state explicitly—that men involve female genitalia or position women as sexual objects in their signs whereas women relegate involvement of female genitalia in their house signs. The men present at the interview hint at why this might be so when they repeatedly interject names of houses inhabited by men that involve female genitalia or female sexual objectification. Salacious signs, thought to be produced by men, emerge as the most notable at the same time that Willy and Simon interject the names of houses inhabited by men that depict female sexuality. Those signs seem to pack the most (pragmatic) punch and the idea that men put up particularly vulgar signs lends support.

In the meantime, the vulgar signs erected by women are rendered exceptional. The female residents of houses with vulgar names who give evidence that they know that male-generated signs depicting female sexuality are especially notable and transgressive fall short of launching a critique for fear of being seen as taking house signs too seriously. Thus, "boys" get to enjoy the infamy of producing a very particular possibility in an extremely complex array of gendered and sexual motifs, and others, even those who are aware of what the "boys" are doing, fail to thwart their efforts.

CONCLUSION

Remarks on Cultural Production and Ethnography

This book has focused largely on some of the ways in which college students at Miami University who display house signs in Oxford reflected on the phenomenon during interviews conducted by my students and me. Emergent from these reflections are general lessons about the production of language and culture, as well as the importance of ethnography in its exploration. We learned quickly, for example, that interpretation happens while people respond to ongoing activity, and their responses can reveal a great deal about the history of their disposition to that activity. House signs have emerged recently in the United States. Yet their relevance to collegiate fun brings to bear the deeper historical context of the wider institution. Indeed, house signs reveal that college students today are very much like their forebears in that having fun remains central to what is perceived to be a complete undergraduate experience. Signs also show that the means and modes of having fun have shifted drastically since a time when fewer students embodied the opposition between college men and outsiders. Historical shifts in the lives of college students come to the fore because when house signs are understood in relationship to earlier ways of having fun, they are peculiar.

House signs do not represent all college students' ideas about fun, however, because they rest on the resources of a specific social class and enrollment at a four-year institution where few students commute daily. House signs pick out a certain kind of student attending a certain kind of institution.

One might qualify signs' representation of fun by pointing out that students' ways of entertaining themselves have changed along with increasingly complicated institutional distinctions in which they are involved.

An ethnographic approach enables us to find different positions from which house signs emerge as meaningful. Some people, for example, look for values in house signs against the backdrop that there is little moral organization in students' lives. My class, in contrast, started with the assumption that the messages displayed on house signs could reveal their significance, and we proceeded eagerly to sort the messages using various categories. As we talked with residents, we realized that neither values nor categories emerged as paramount. Rather, we learned that residents, some of whom had designed their signs, and others who kept using the ones displayed when they moved in, see convenience, cleverness, and a generalized indication of partying. Students living in named houses often had no idea why previous residents had given particular names to the rental houses.

Even at this stage of ethnographic exploration, such insights show that ethnography constitutes a metacultural representation of culture that offers something new. No one, for example, was positioned to see in house signs all three possibilities of their interpretation: that they express college students' values, express categories important in the lives of college students, and embody the habits of interpretation common to named house residents themselves. By presenting all of these as possibilities, this study widens the frame of interpretation for those readers ensconced in one of the positions—or readers who began knowing little or nothing about house signs—such that multiple possibilities of cultural production are realized for the same phenomenon. Description—what is often assumed to be the mere recounting of what is there in space and time—can be creative depending on the listener or reader's disposition to habits of description and events described. Because ethnography always ventures to bring together multiple dispositions, one can make the claim that ethnography is an inherently creative endeavor.

Pointing out the ways in which ethnography can bring multiple interpretive positions forward simultaneously is not my only goal, however. If one were to consider this study to be a metacultural response to the cultural phenomenon of house signs, one might call it a critical one in addition to an exploratory one. By considering residents' reflections on house signs during interviews, for example, I was able to piece together what residents understood signs to accomplish. Most often, residents understood house signs to accomplish little, but I have been able to make the case that the benign quality claimed for house signs is itself something that residents' signs meet unevenly. Residents who see their house signs as tied to their Christian faith stand in relationship to ways of interpreting house signs very differently than most residents of named houses. Indeed, when most residents of named houses see a house sign that is supposed to be an indication of residents' Christian faith, they see only convenience, wit, or evidence of partying. The claim that this book provides a critical approach to house signs rests, in part, on the fact that the goals are realized unevenly, and that such unevenness emerges outside of awareness of those who display house signs. Identifying what makes the perpetuation of interpretive unevenness possible helps to explain why people participate enthusiastically in endeavors when the goals of their participation are thwarted.

Not only do house signs make it possible for some to participate in their display without realizing their goals, but they also make it possible for people who do not (and most probably never will) participate in their display to be involved. The inner city and its residents are salient to the display of house signs even though residents of named houses claim that such places and people are not present locally. Oxford's Ghetto embodies the qualities said to make house signs important and enjoyable. They include a lack of care, freedom to do what one wants, and a massive party. At the same time, when a resident of a named house describes a real ghetto and its inhabitants, the focal characters are defined by race. My discussion of Oxford's Ghetto and its importance to house signs is a critical one because it shows what is necessary for the perpetuation of the involvement of the Ghetto in house signs: an ambivalence about race whereby places locally absent must remain unmentioned. As long as such places and their inhabitants are absent and unmentioned, their qualities can be invoked. This book's discussion of the Ghetto and house signs is critical because it demonstrates the involvement of racist stereotypes in a situation in which no obvious linguistic, sartorial, or other marker emerges.

This study also provides a critical approach to house signs in that it shows that even when there is evidence of some recognition of inequality in what house signs presuppose and reproduce, house residents are reticent to make such recognition explicit. Some women who display sexually charged signs give evidence that they realize that some men do something with house signs that women almost never do: some men name their houses such that they involve female genitalia. This case differs from the display of house signs as indications of residents' Christian faith or the use of "Ghetto" in house signs because the residents of houses with sexual signs described in chapter 5 present the possibility of the existence of a critical approach within the house signs community of practice. The women of Hot Box indicate that they understand that men do something with signs that almost no women do and that they would prefer that those men did not. By situating these women within the larger habits of interpretation among residents of named houses, the study provides an explanation of why the critical potential of the reflections on house signs of the residents of Hot Box is not realized. House signs thwart the agency of those who see their Christian faith in them, those whose imagined attributes are selectively appropriated, and, finally, those who themselves have seen the unequal uses of house signs.

NOTES

INTRODUCTION

1. In another publication, Williams explains, "We are concerned with meanings and values as they are actively lived and felt, and the relations between these and formal or systematic beliefs are in practice variable" (1977, 132). Keywords lie at the intersection of life and definition.

2. For a discussion of the same theoretical terrain in folklore, see Noyes (2003). For a seminal discussion in folklore, see Bauman (1972).

3. By engaging residents of named houses in interviews, we were opening up the possibility of metacultural apprehensions of house signs, in the rubric of the next chapter, other than our own.

4. For a seminal critical discussion on interviewing as a technique in research, see Briggs (1986).

5. For a lively debate on how speech is rendered with respellings and to what representational effects, see Preston (1982), then Fine (1983), and then Preston (1983).

6. When considered among colleges and universities across the United States, these percentages are not atypical. Sharon Gmelch notes that such percentages vary widely from institution to institution, but average nationally 5 percent for African Americans (1998, 95).

1. BED BOOZE & BEYOND

1. Although the description of its historical development as a category exceeds the capacities of this book, childhood is also a social position that has been shown to be in flux.

2. For a review of the literature on youth culture, see Bucholtz (2002). There are instructive contrasts between Miami University students who can afford to pay rent off-campus and the members of the most studied and theorized groups of youths, British postwar youth cultures. Often studied under the rubric of subcultures, such groups include Teddy Boys, Mods, Rockers, skinheads, punks, and football hooligans. The study of these subcultures has changed over time in its approach to these groups and their ori-

gins. See Bennett and Kahn-Harris (2004) and Muggleton and Weinzierl (2003). Dick Hebdige's 1979 classic *Subculture, the Meaning of Style* is a good example in arguing that the subculture's appropriation and recombination of elements from mainstream culture represents a form of resistance. No such claims are made for American students enrolled at colleges or universities, although scholars do see resistance in their activities, for example, in arguments that account for collegiate fun as a form of mild rebellion against adult figures due to psychological insecurity.

3. The house name Short Bus predates the movie of the same title.

4. See Baker (1983), Bronner (1995), Mullen and Place (1978), and Tucker (2005, 2007) for particularly comprehensive reviews.

5. Holland and Eisenhart (1990) argue that women decades later continued to be extremely concerned with measuring the status of their female peers by the status of the men with whom they should be paired.

6. The type of display that Nathan calls the "official imagery of dorm life" included bulletin boards for which resident assistants were largely responsible. She notes that approximately one-fifth of the bulletin board displays focused on academic matters such as "dealing with test anxiety" or "ten steps to academic success." Just over one-fifth of the displays dealt with health, ranging from sexual assault and sexually transmitted diseases, drugs and alcohol, and body image problems. Some boards offered comic relief with their service-oriented messages, such as "Fifty Things Admissions Never Told You about College," "Crazy Things to Do for under $10," and "Fifty Fun Things to Do at Wal-Mart." Just under one-fifth of the bulletin board displays warned students of dangers (suspension/expulsion, AIDS, jail, STDs, pregnancy, sickness, even death) (2005, 21–22).

7. Here, house signs contrast with one of the more nefarious possibilities of photographic reproduction, whether posted on the Internet or not (see McDowell 2008). Some of my own students at all of the campuses where I have taught, Miami University, Southern Connecticut State University, and Hamilton College, have told me that they keep albums of photographs depicting similar practices of "shaming," and that the practice predates the emergence of the Internet. Nevertheless, house signs do not provide a platform for the practice.

8. My project parallels that of Ortner (2006) in that she considers the social construction of Gen X and its dependence on the media for its emergence. I show the relevance of faith, race, and gender to a seemingly boundless pastiche of imagery recycled from the media, whereas Ortner shows that the fears of decline embedded in the idea of Gen X presuppose racial exclusions.

9. Lizabeth Cohen (2003, 306) confirms that the perception of incompatibility that Frank describes was salient even as the transition to market segmentation occurred.

10. A popular understanding of the youth counterculture of the 1960s is that its ethos was incompatible with the simultaneous growth of marketing in advertising. Through a review of advertising for cars and men's clothes in the 1960s and 1970s, Frank argues rather that youthful rebellion became a stock feature of advertising such that "youth became a consuming position to which all could aspire" (1998, 25).

11. Helena Wulff (1995, 15) argues that studies of youth culture have usually not made any substantive contribution to the development of the concept of culture, but she sees Willis (1977) as an exception.

12. Stallybrass and White (1986, 53–56) have questioned the utopian universalism of Bakhtin's argument, pointing out that Jews, for example, suffered in the carnival imagery of Rabelais's day. Sutton-Smith (1997) makes the more encompassing argument that ideas about play are susceptible to changing moral, ethical, or functional constructions of human action and its evaluation. Dentith (1995, 14) notes that Bakhtin's utopianism could have been fueled by social upheavals in Russia in the early twentieth century.

2. WITTY HOUSE NAME

1. By "meaning" I mean "denotational value," what makes possible the reference to the same phenomenon across events (Agha 2007).

2. Other ethnographic accounts of names and naming include Alia (2007) and Roth (2008).

3. For particularly clear explanations of the sign's different relationships with objects as Firsts (icons), Seconds (indexes), and Thirds (symbols), see Mertz (1985), Parmentier (1994), and Singer (1984).

4. Sometimes such messages make the temporal dimension explicit by situating a state of affairs by the use of dates and times.

5. An indexical possibility of the first sign, the one that displayed its message digitally, might be that the power is on. This possibility does not exist in the case of the second, unless the second sign was illuminated by some nonsolar or nonlunar source. One might, however, point out that the first sign has a solar panel attached to it.

6. See, for example, Hodge and Kress (1988), Kress and van Leeuwen (1996, 2001), Scollon and Scollon (2003), van Leeuwen (2004), and van Leeuwen and Jewitt (2001).

7. See Ahearn (2001b), Barton and Hamilton (1998), Blommaert (2008), Collins and Blot (2003), Cook-Gumperz (2006), Gregory and Williams (2000), and Street (1984) for accounts of literacy that resonate with my approach. These authors conceptualize visual language as it emerges in particular contexts such that all manner of temporally and spatially inflected aspects of knowledge open possibilities for and impose constraints on people.

8. Indeed, one might argue that the use of such names indexes those civic entities.

9. Penelope Eckert and Sally McConnell-Ginet define a community of practice as "an aggregate of people who come together around mutual engagement in an endeavor" (1992, 464). Community of practice is a conceptual device that replaces a focus on a linguistic form and the identification of its users and contexts of use with a focus on an interpretive habit within and across contexts. See Holland et al (1998), Lave (1993), Lave and Wenger (1991), and Wenger (1998). Bourdieu (1977, 1990) was inspirational to scholars who developed the notion "community of practice," especially in their conceptualization of the notion's relational qualities. See Ortner (1984) for a widely cited overview of the influence in anthropology of Bourdieu's ideas, as well as a call for further application.

10. For an excellent account of the development of the notion of community of practice and a critique of the tendency of many who have used it to stress interpretive alignment and coordination, see Barton and Tusting (2005).

11. For a contrasting case in which college students do care about the opinions of onlookers regarding their playful creations, see McDowell (1985).

3. INN PURSUIT . . . OF CHRIST

1. My vignette about driving offered in the previous chapter illustrates this point.

2. Julia Kristeva (1980) introduced the somewhat parallel notion of "intertextuality," which has been applied to practices of folklore by Bauman (2004) and Kapchan (1996).

4. GHETTO FABULOUS AND PLANTATION

1. The College Prowler books present facts about enrollment profiles in terms of sex ratio, test scores, and financial aid; broad overviews of student life within categories ranging from "local atmosphere" to "finding a job or internship"; and anonymous quotes from students.

2. Many people, whether living in the Ghetto or not, could tell us the street names forming its boundaries.

3. Many faculty and a handful of students qualified this last claim by noting that rents might be cheaper in the trailer park on the northwestern outskirts of Oxford, well beyond the boundaries of the Mile Square and adjacent student apartments and suburban neighborhoods.

4. Note that Jack has begun to use "down here" to refer to the Ghetto. The interview is taking place in the Ghetto, whereas Jack lives more than ten blocks away. Within twenty minutes that have elapsed so far, he has begun to orient himself in alignment with the residents of the house where the interview is being conducted.

5. Jess uses "North Campus" when she reports talking to colleagues and coworkers. It is in recognition of their lifelong residence in Oxford that she switches to "the Ghetto." The area, according to students, is dominated by them, but new and surprising to freshmen and old hat to residents of the town who are not students.

6. I use pseudonyms because the townspeople are not elected officials, commonly represented in the minutes of the city council.

7. At this point, one might describe the residents as being engaged in what Kristen Myers (2005) has called "racetalk" for their heavily stereotyped exegesis of the phrase "ghetto fabulous" without the explicit mention of racial distinctions.

8. ECM is also a large record label, but it produces mostly jazz.

9. When the student interviewers asked the house residents whether they would like to have parts of the tape erased, they replied that they would not. When Jack mentioned Amy's request to erase her words, she said that she was not being serious.

10. We would have liked to have interviewed the residents of Gary Coleman Fan Club, but the sign was gone by the time of our research.

11. Fine and Turner (2001, 21–22) identify two other types of rumor. "Mirror rumors" are those that circulate identically in black and white communities, the only difference being the race of the focal character. Another kind is the "Topsy/Eva rumor," after a popular doll in the nineteenth century that is Little Eva, "white, well-dressed, blond, and blue-eyed," and when turned upside-down is Topsy, "black, poorly dressed, kinky-haired, and dark-eyed" (22). Like mirror rumors, Topsy/Eva rumors focus on a similar focal event, but represent it differently when spread through white and black groups.

12. Patricia Turner (1994, 2002) has written more extensively about rumors that circulate specifically in the African American communities and the folklore that represents those communities from afar.

13. For an example of how complex a moral geography can become without the possibility of distancing the real from the fake, see Modan (2007). For an example of how national boundaries can play complex roles in the creation of moral geographies, see Mendoza-Denton (2008).

14. In the 1993 article, Hill actually uses "Junk Spanish," but I use "Mock Spanish" to reflect her use of the term in her more recent work.

15. See also Bucholtz (1999), Chun (2001), and Cutler (1999, 2003).

5. HOT BOX, BOX OFFICE, AND FILL'ER UP

1. Lakoff points out, for example, that men might very well use such language but that the usage would be recognized as indicating something significant about what he was saying. His speech might be seen as emergent, for example, from the stance of a gay man or an academic.

2. Thus "sisters" is not used for women, and "bulls" and "stallions" are not used for men.

3. A spring break trip also provided the explanation for the origin of Che, described in chapter 2, but the resonance of popular media in the case of Girls Gone Wild enables the house residents to escape characterizations of the house name as an inside joke.

4. In the terms of Michael Silverstein's 1993 work on semiotic mediation, the residents of Green House engage in particularly overt metapragmatic discourse in that they claim that one can derive a contextual feature of house signs (the sex of house residents) by way of describing the semiotic sign (the house name).

5. The Rusty Trombone, the example that Jenny offers as an offensive sign, in contrast to Fill'er Up and Liquor Juggs, represents men as sexualized. It does not challenge the larger point being made through the offer of house names by the residents of Hot Box, however. The Rusty Trombone might focus attention on men as the object of sex, but men live in the house.

REFERENCES

Abrahams, Roger D. 1993. Phantoms of Romantic Nationalism in Folkloristics. *Journal of American Folklore* 106 (419): 3–37.

Agha, Asif. 1998. Stereotypes and Registers of Honorific Language. *Language in Society* 27 (2): 151–93.

———. 2007. *Language and Social Relations*. Cambridge: Cambridge University Press.

Ahearn, Laura. 2001a. Agency. In *Key Terms in Language and Culture*, ed. Alessandro Duranti, 7–10. Malden, Mass.: Blackwell.

———. 2001b. *Invitations to Love: Literacy, Love Letters, and Social Change in Nepal*. Ann Arbor: University of Michigan Press.

———. 2001c. Language and Agency. *Annual Review of Anthropology* 30: 109–137.

Alia, Valerie. 2007. *Names and Nunavut: Culture and Identity in Arctic Canada*. New York: Berghahn Books.

Altbach, Philip G. 1993. Students: Interests, Culture, and Activism. In *Higher Learning in America, 1980–2000*. Baltimore: Johns Hopkins University Press.

Amit-Talai, Vered, and Helena Wulff, eds. 1995. *Youth Cultures: A Cross-Cultural Perspective*. London: Routledge.

Apte, Mahadev. 1985. *Humor and Laughter: An Anthropological Approach*. Ithaca: Cornell University Press.

Babcock, Barbara. 1984. The Story in the Story: Metanarration in Folk Narrative. Supplementary essay in *Verbal Art as Performance* by Richard Bauman. Long Grove, Ill.: Waveland Press.

Bacchilega, Cristina. 2007. *Legendary Hawai'i and the Politics of Places: Tradition, Translation, and Tourism*. Philadelphia: University of Pennsylvania Press.

Bailey, Beth L. 1988. *From Front Porch to Back Seat: Courtship in Twentieth-Century America*. Baltimore: Johns Hopkins University Press.

———. 1999. *Sex in the Heartland*. Cambridge: Harvard University Press.

Baker, Ronald L. 1983. The Folklore of Students. In *Handbook of American Folklore*, ed. Richard Dorson, 106–114. Bloomington: Indiana University Press.

Bakhtin, Mikhail. 1981. Discourse in the Novel. In *The Dialogic Imagination—Four Essays*, ed. Michael Holquist, trans. Caryl Emerson and Michael Holquist, 259–422. Austin: University of Texas Press.

———. 1984. *Rabelais and His World.* Trans. Hélène Iswolsky. Bloomington: Indiana University Press.

———. 1986. The Problem of Speech Genres. In *Speech Genres and Other Late Essays,* ed. Caryl Emerson and Michael Holquist, trans. Vern McGee, 60–102. Austin: University of Texas Press.

Barlow, Alexandra. 2006. Police Clarify Off-Campus Party Rights. *Miami Student,* http://media.www.miamistudent.net/media/storage/paper776/news/2006/09/12/Community/Police.Clarify.OffCampus.Party.Rights-2266578.shtml.

Barton, David, and Mary Hamilton. 1998. *Local Literacies: Reading and Writing in One Community.* London: Routledge.

Barton, David, and Karin Tusting. 2005. Introduction. In *Beyond Communities of Practice: Language, Power, and Social Context,* ed. David Barton and Karin Tusting, 1–13. Cambridge: Cambridge University Press.

Basso, Keith. 1996. *Wisdom Sits in Places: Landscape and Language among the Western Apache.* Albuquerque: University of New Mexico Press.

Bauman, Richard. 1972. Differential Identity and the Social Base of Folklore. In *Toward New Perspectives in Folklore,* ed. Américo Paredes and Richard Bauman, 31–40. Austin: University of Texas Press.

———. 1982. Conceptions of Folklore in the Development of Literary Semiotics. *Semiotica* 39 (1/2): 1–20.

———. 1984. *Verbal Art as Performance.* Long Grove, Ill.: Waveland Press.

———. 1986. *Story, Performance, Event: Contextual Studies of Oral Narrative.* Cambridge: Cambridge University Press.

———. 1993. The Nationalization and Internationalization of Folklore: The Case of Schoolcraft's "Gitshee Gauzinee." *Western Folklore* 52 (2–4): 247–69.

———. 1995. Representing Native American Oral Narrative: The Textual Practices of Henry Rowe Schoolcraft. *Pragmatics* 5 (2): 167–83.

———. 2004. *A World of Others' Words: Cross-Cultural Perspectives on Intertextuality.* Malden, Mass.: Blackwell.

———. 2008. The Philology of the Vernacular. *Journal of Folklore Research* 45 (1): 29–36.

Bauman, Richard, and Charles L. Briggs. 2003. *Voices of Modernity: Language Ideologies and the Politics of Inequality.* Cambridge: Cambridge University Press.

Ben-Amos, Dan. 1972. Toward a Definition of Folklore in Context. In *Toward New Perspectives in Folklore,* ed. Américo Paredes and Richard Bauman, 3–15. Austin: University of Texas Press.

———. 1974. Folklore in African Society. *Folklore Reprint Series* 2 (1): 1–32.

Bendix, Regina. 1992. National Sentiment in the Enactment of Discourse of Swiss Patriotic Ritual. *American Ethnologist* 19 (4): 768–90.

———. 1997. *In Search of Authenticity: The Formation of Folklore Studies.* Madison: University of Wisconsin Press.

Bennett, Andy, and Keith Kahn-Harris, eds. 2004. *After Subculture: Critical Studies in Contemporary Youth Culture.* New York: Palgrave Macmillan.

Berger, Harris M., and Giovanna P. Del Negro. 2004. *Identity and Everyday Life: Essays in the Study of Folklore, Music, and Popular Culture.* Middletown, Conn.: Wesleyan University Press.

Blommaert, Jan. 2005. *Discourse: A Critical Introduction.* Cambridge: Cambridge University Press.

———. 2008. *Grassroots Literacy: Writing, Identity, and Voice in Central Africa.* London: Routledge.

Blount, Jim. 2000. *The 1900s: 100 Years in the History of Butler County, Ohio.* Hamilton, Ohio: Past Present Press.

Blum, Susan D. 2009. *My Word! Plagiarism and College Culture.* Ithaca: Cornell University Press.

Bogatyrev, Petr. [1936] 1976. Costume as Sign (The Functional and Structural Concept of Costume in Ethnography). Trans. Yvonne Lockwood. In *Semiotics of Art: Prague School Contributions,* ed. Ladislav Matejka and Irwin Titunik, 13–19. Cambridge: MIT Press.

Bogle, Kathleen. 2008. *Hooking Up: Sex, Dating, and Relationships on Campus.* New York: New York University Press.

Bourdieu, Pierre. 1977. *Outline of a Theory of Practice.* Trans. Richard Nice. Cambridge: Cambridge University Press.

———. 1990. *The Logic of Practice.* Trans. Richard Nice. Stanford: Stanford University Press.

Boyer, Ernest L. 1993. Campus Climate in the 1980s and 1990s: Decades of Apathy and Renewal. In *Higher Learning in America, 1980–2000,* ed. Arthur Levine, 322–32. Baltimore: Johns Hopkins University Press.

Briggs, Charles L. 1986. *Learning How to Ask: A Sociolinguistic Appraisal of the Role of the Interview in Social Science Research.* Cambridge: Cambridge University Press.

———. 1993. Metadiscursive Practices and Scholarly Authority in Folkloristics. *Journal of American Folklore* 106 (422): 387–434.

Briggs, Charles L., and Richard Bauman. 1992. Genre, Intertextuality, and Social Power. *Journal of Linguistic Anthropology* 2 (2): 131–72.

———. 1999. "The Foundation of All Future Researches": Franz Boas, George Hunt, and the Textual Construction of Modernity. *American Quarterly* 51 (3): 479–528.

Briggs, Charles L., and Clara Mantini-Briggs. 2003. *Stories in the Time of Cholera: Racial Profiling during a Medical Nightmare.* Berkeley: University of California Press.

Bronner, Simon. 1986. *Grasping Things: Folk Material Culture and Mass Society in America.* Lexington: University Press of Kentucky.

———. 1995. *Piled Higher and Deeper: The Folklore of Student Life.* Little Rock: August House.

Bucholtz, Mary. 1999. You da Man: Narrating the Racial Other in the Production of White Masculinity. *Journal of Sociolinguistics* 3 (4): 443–60.

———. 2000a. Globalization: Language and Youth Culture. *American Speech* 75 (3): 280–83.

———. 2000b. The Politics of Transcription. *Journal of Pragmatics* 32 (10): 1439–65.

———. 2002. Youth and Cultural Practice. *Annual Review of Anthropology* 31: 525–52.

Cameron, Deborah, and Don Kulick. 2003. *Language and Sexuality.* Cambridge: Cambridge University Press.

Campus Squeeze. n.d. "The Sixteen Best College Themed Movies." http://www.campussqueeze.com/post/16-Best-College-Movies.aspx.

Chun, Elaine. 2001. The Construction of White, Black, and Korean American Identities through African American Vernacular English. *Journal of Linguistic Anthropology* 11 (1): 52–64.

City of Oxford. 2003. City Council & Mayor—Agenda: Tuesday, April 15, 2003. http://www.cityofoxford.org/Agendas.asp?Display=Minutes&AMID=696.

Coe, Cati. 1999. The Education of the Folk: Peasant Schools and Folklore Scholarship. *Journal of American Folklore* 113 (447): 20–43.

Cohen, Arthur. 1998. *The Shaping of American Higher Education: Emergence and Growth of the Contemporary System.* San Francisco: Jossey-Bass.

Cohen, Lizabeth. 2003. *A Consumer's Republic: The Politics of Mass Consumption in Postwar America.* New York: Vintage Books.

Cohen, Stanley. [1972] 2002. *Folk Devils and Moral Panics: The Creation of the Mods and the Rockers.* 3d ed. London: Routledge.

CollegeTips.com. n.d. College Party Themes and Ideas. http://www.collegetips.com/college-parties/party-themes.php.

Collins, James, and Richard K. Blot. 2003. *Literacy and Literacies: Texts, Power, and Identity.* Cambridge: Cambridge University Press.

Cook-Gumperz, Jenny, ed. 2006. *The Social Construction of Literacy.* 2d ed. Cambridge: Cambridge University Press.

Cresswell, Tim. 1996. *In Place/Out of Place: Geography, Ideology, and Transgression.* Minneapolis: University of Minnesota Press.

Cutler, Cecilia. 1999. Yorkville Crossing: White Teens, Hip Hop, and African American English. *Journal of Sociolinguistics* 3 (4): 428–42.

———. 2003. "Keepin' It Real": White Hip-Hoppers' Discourses of Language, Race, and Authenticity. *Journal of Linguistic Anthropology* 13 (2): 211–33.

Delaney, Carol. 2004. *Investigating Culture: An Experimental Introduction to Anthropology.* Malden, Mass.: Blackwell.

Dentith, Simon. 1995. *Bakhtinian Thought: An Introductory Reader.* London: Routledge.

DeSantis, Alan D. 2007. *Inside Greek U.: Fraternities, Sororities, and the Pursuit of Pleasure, Power, and Prestige.* Lexington: University Press of Kentucky.

Dorson, Richard. 1959. The Folklore of College Students. In *American Folklore,* 254–67. Chicago: University of Chicago Press.

Dundes, Alan. 1966. Metafolklore and Oral Literary Criticism. *Monist* 50: 505–516.

———. 1971. On the Psychology of Legend. *American Folk Legend: A Symposium,* ed. Wayland Hand, 26–29. Berkeley: Publications of the UCLA Center for the Study of Comparative Folklore and Mythology.

Duranti, Alessandro. 2001. Intentionality. In *Key Terms in Language and Culture*, ed. Alessandro Duranti, 129–31. Malden, Mass.: Blackwell.

———. 2004. Agency in Language. In *A Companion to Linguistic Anthropology*, ed. Alessandro Duranti, 451–73. Malden, Mass.: Blackwell.

Eble, Connie. 1996. *Slang & Sociability: In-Group Language among College Students.* Chapel Hill: University of North Carolina Press.

Eckert, Penelope, and Sally McConnell-Ginet. 1992. Think Practically and Look Locally: Language and Gender as Community-based Practice. *Annual Review of Anthropology* 21: 461–90.

———. 2003. *Language and Gender.* Cambridge: Cambridge University Press.

Eco, Umberto. 1989. *The Open Work.* Trans. Anna Cancogni. Cambridge, Mass.: Harvard University Press.

eHow.com. n.d. How to Have Fun in College without Drinking. http://www.ehow.com/how_5355220_fun-college-drinking.html.

Ellison, Curtis W., ed. 2009. *Miami University, 1809–2009: Bicentennial Perspectives.* Athens: Ohio University Press.

Errington, J. Joseph. 1985. On the Nature of the Sociolinguistic Sign: Describing the Javanese Speech Levels. In *Semiotic Mediation: Sociocultural and Psychological Perspectives*, ed. Elizabeth Mertz and Richard Parmentier, 287–310. Orlando: Academic Press.

Fabian, Johannes. 1998. *Moments of Freedom: Anthropology and Popular Culture.* Charlottesville: University of Virginia Press.

Fass, Paula S. 2008. Childhood and Youth as an American/Global Experience in the Context of the Past. In *Figuring the Future: Globalization and the Temporalities of Children and Youth*, ed. Jennifer Cole and Deborah Durham, 25–47. Santa Fe: School for Advanced Research Press.

Fine, Elizabeth. 1983. In Defense of Literary Dialect: A Response to Dennis R. Preston. *Journal of American Folklore* 96 (381): 323–30.

———. 1984. *The Folklore Text: From Performance to Print.* Bloomington: Indiana University Press.

Fine, Gary Alan, and Patricia Turner. 2001. *Whispers on the Color Line: Rumor and Race in America.* Berkeley: University of California Press.

Frank, Thomas. 1998. *The Conquest of Cool: Business Culture, Counterculture, and the Rise of Hip Consumerism.* Chicago: University of Chicago Press.

Freud, Sigmund. 1905. Jokes and Their Relation to the Unconscious. In *The Standard Edition of the Complete Works of Sigmund Freud*, ed. James Strachey and Anna Freud. London: Hogarth.

Gal, Susan, and Judith Irvine. 1995. The Boundaries of Language and Disciplines: How Ideologies Construct Differences. *Social Research* 62 (4): 967–1001.

Gal, Susan, and Kathryn Woolard. 2001. Constructing Languages and Publics: Authority and Representation. In *Languages and Publics: The Making of Authority*, ed. Susan Gal and Kathryn Woolard, 1–12. Manchester, UK: St. Jerome.

Garrett, Tiffany, and Erin Shultz. 2005. *Miami University of Ohio: Off the Record.* Pittsburgh: College Prowler.

Gell, Alfred. 1998. *Art and Agency: An Anthropological Theory.* Oxford: Oxford University Press.

Gmelch, Sharon Bohn. 1998. *Gender on Campus: Issues for College Women.* New Brunswick: Rutgers University Press.

Gregory, Eve, and Ann Williams. 2000. *City Literacies: Learning to Read Across Generations and Cultures.* London: Routledge.

Gregory, Kaila. 2004. Police Prepare for GhettoFest: 35 Officers Will Be Patrolling on April 24. *Miami Student:* http://media.www.miamistudent.net/media/storage/paper776/news/2004/04/23/community/Police.Prepare.For.Ghettofest-939654.shtml.

Grigsby, Mary. 2009. *College Life through the Eyes of Students.* Albany: State University of New York Press.

Gumprecht, Blake. 2008. *The American College Town.* Amherst: University of Massachusetts Press.

Handler, Richard, and Joyce Linnekin. 1984. Tradition: Genuine or Spurious. *Journal of American Folklore* 97 (385): 273–90.

Hanks, William. 1993. Metalanguage and Pragmatics of Deixis. In *Reflexive Language: Reported Speech and Metapragmatics,* ed. John Lucy, 127–57. Cambridge: Cambridge University Press.

Harding, Susan Friend. 2000. *The Book of Jerry Falwell: Fundamentalist Language and Politics.* Princeton, N.J.: Princeton University Press.

Hartigan, John. 2005. *Odd Tribes: Toward a Cultural Analysis of White People.* Durham: Duke University Press.

Hebdige, Dick. 1979. *Subculture, the Meaning of Style.* London: Methuen.

Herzfeld, Michael. 1982. *Ours Once More: Folklore, Ideology, and the Making of Modern Greece.* Austin: University of Texas Press.

Hill, Jane H. 1993. Hasta La Vista, Baby: Anglo Spanish in the American Southwest. *Critique of Anthropology* 13 (2): 145–76.

———. 1995. The Voices of Don Gabriel: Responsibility and Self in a Modern Mexicano Narrative. In *The Dialogic Emergence of Culture,* ed. Dennis Tedlock and Bruce Mannheim, 97–147. Urbana: University of Illinois Press.

———. 1998. Language, Race, and White Public Space. *American Anthropologist* 100 (3): 680–89.

———. 2008. *The Everyday Language of White Racism.* Malden, Mass.: Wiley-Blackwell.

Hill, Jane H., and Judith Irvine. 1992. Introduction. In *Responsibility and Evidence in Oral Discourse,* ed. Jane H. Hill and Judith T. Irvine, 1–23. Cambridge: Cambridge University Press.

Hodge, Robert, and Gunther Kress. 1988. *Social Semiotics.* Oxford: Polity.

Holland, Dorothy, and Margaret Eisenhart. 1990. *Educated in Romance: Women, Achievement, and College Culture.* Chicago: University of Chicago Press.

Holland, Dorothy, William Lachicotte Jr., Debra Skinner, and Carole Cain. 1998. *Identity and Agency in Cultural Worlds.* Cambridge, Mass.: Harvard University Press.

Horowitz, Helen. 1987. *Campus Life: Undergraduate Cultures from the End of the Eighteenth Century to the Present.* Chicago: University of Chicago Press.

Hymes, Dell. 1981. *"In Vain I Tried to Tell You": Essays in Native American Ethnopoetics.* Philadelphia: University of Pennsylvania Press.

Irvine, Judith. 1996. Language and Community: Introduction. *Journal of Linguistic Anthropology* 6 (2): 123–25.

Irvine, Judith, and Susan Gal. 2000. Language Ideology and Linguistic Differentiation. In *Regimes of Language: Ideologies, Polities, and Identities,* ed. Paul Kroskrity, 35–84. Santa Fe: School of American Research Press.

Jaffe, Alexandra. 2000. Introduction: Non-Standard Orthography and Non-Standard Speech. *Journal of Sociolinguistics* 4 (4): 497–513.

———. 2007. Variability in Transcription and the Complexities of Representation, Authority, and Voice. *Discourse Studies* 9 (6): 831–36.

Jakobson, Roman. [1933–34] 1976. What Is Poetry? Trans. M. Heim. In *Semiotics of Art: Prague School Contributions,* ed. Ladislav Matejka and Irwin Titunik, 164–75. Cambridge: MIT Press.

Kapchan, Deborah. 1996. *Gender on the Market: Moroccan Women and the Revoicing of Tradition.* Philadelphia: University of Pennsylvania Press.

Kapchan, Deborah, and Pauline Turner Strong. 1999. Theorizing the Hybrid. *Journal of American Folklore* 112 (445): 239–53.

Keane, Webb. 1997a. From Fetishism to Sincerity: On Agency, the Speaking Subject, and Their Historicity in the Context of Religious Conversion. *Comparative Studies in Society and History* 39 (4): 674–93.

———. 1997b. *Signs of Recognition: Powers and Hazards of Representation in an Indonesian Society.* Berkeley: University of California Press.

Kirshenblatt-Gimblett, Barbara. 1998. *Destination Culture: Tourism, Museums, and Heritage.* Berkeley: University of California Press.

Kirshenblatt-Gimblett, Barbara, and Joel Sherzer. 1976. Introduction. In *Speech Play: Research and Resources for the Study of Linguistic Creativity,* ed. Barbara Kirshenblatt-Gimblett, 1–16. Philadelphia: University of Pennsylvania Press.

Kress, Gunther, and Theo van Leeuwen. 1996. *Reading Images: The Grammar of Visual Design.* London: Routledge.

———. 2001. *Multimodal Discourse: The Modes and Media of Contemporary Communication.* London: Arnold.

Kripke, Saul A. 1972. *Naming and Necessity.* Cambridge, Mass.: Harvard University Press.

Kristeva, Julia. 1980. *Desire in Language: A Semiotic Approach to Literature and Art,* ed. Leon S. Roudiez, trans. Thomas Gora, Alice Jardine, and Leon S. Roudiez. New York: Columbia University Press.

LaDousa, Chaise. 2007. "Witty House Name": Visual Expression, Interpretive Practice, and Uneven Agency in a Midwestern College Town. *Journal of American Folklore* 120 (478): 445–81.

Lakoff, Robin. 2004. *Language and Woman's Place: Text and Commentaries,* ed. Mary Bucholtz. Oxford: Oxford University Press.

Lave, Jean. 1993. The Practice of Learning. In *Understanding Practice: Perspectives on Activity and Context,* ed. Seth Chaikin and Jean Lave, 3–34. Cambridge: Cambridge University Press.

Lave, Jean, and Etienne Wenger. 1991. *Situated Learning: Legitimate Peripheral Participation.* Cambridge: Cambridge University Press.

Lesko, Nancy. 2001. *Act Your Age! A Cultural Construction of Adolescence.* New York: Routledge and Falmer.

Levine, Arthur, and Jeanette Cureton. 1998. *When Hope and Fear Collide: A Portrait of Today's College Student.* San Francisco: Jossey-Bass.

McDowell, John Holmes. 1985. Halloween Costuming among Young Adults in Bloomington, Indiana: A Local Exotic. *Indiana Folklore and Oral History* 14: 1–19.

———. 1992. Speech Play. In *Folklore, Cultural Performances, and Popular Entertainments: A Communication-Centered Handbook,* ed. Richard Bauman, 139–44. New York: Oxford University Press.

———. 2008. "Folklore of Student Life: Rituals." http://www.indiana.edu/~f351jmcd/rituals.html.

Mendoza-Denton, Norma. 2008. *Homegirls: Language and Cultural Practice among Latina Youth Gangs.* Malden, Mass.: Blackwell.

Mertz, Elizabeth. 1983. A Cape Breton System of Personal Names. *Semiotica* 44 (1–2): 55–74.

———. 1985. Beyond Symbolic Anthropology: Introducing Semiotic Mediation. In *Semiotic Mediation,* ed. Elizabeth Mertz and Richard J. Parmentier, 1–19. Orlando: Academic Press.

Modan, Gabriella. 2007. *Turf Wars: Discourse, Diversity, and the Politics of Place.* Malden, Mass.: Blackwell.

Moffatt, Michael. 1989. *Coming of Age in New Jersey: College and American Culture.* New Brunswick: Rutgers University Press.

Moll, Richard. 1985. *The Public Ivys: America's Flagship Undergraduate Colleges.* New York: Penguin.

Muggleton, David, and Rupert Weinzierl, eds. 2003. *The Post-Subcultures Reader.* Oxford: Berg.

Mullen, Patrick. 2008. *The Man Who Adores the Negro: Race and American Folklore.* Urbana: University of Illinois Press.

Mullen, Patrick, and Linna Funk Place. 1978. *Collecting Folklore and Folklife in Ohio.* Washington, D.C.: Ethnic Heritage Studies Program, Department of Health, Education and Welfare.

Munro, Pamela. 1989. *Slang U: The Official Dictionary of College Slang.* New York: Harmony Books.

Myers, Kristen. 2005. *Racetalk: Racism Hiding in Plain Sight.* Lanham, Md.: Rowman and Littlefield.

Nathan, Rebekah. 2005. *My Freshman Year: What a Professor Learned by Becoming a Student.* Ithaca: Cornell University Press.

Noyes, Dorothy. 2003. Group. In *Eight Words for the Study of Expressive Culture,* ed. Burt Feintuch, 7–41. Urbana: University of Illinois Press.

Nuwer, Hank. 1999. *Wrongs of Passage: Fraternities, Sororities, Hazing, and Binge Drinking.* Bloomington: Indiana University Press.

Nuwer, Hank, ed. 2004. *The Hazing Reader.* Bloomington: Indiana University Press.

Ochs, Elinor. 1979. Transcription as Theory. In *Developmental Pragmatics,* ed. Elinor Ochs and Bambi Schieffelin, 43–71. New York: Academic Press.

Ohio Department of Public Safety. 2006. Investigative Unit Activity Report Between 4/7/2003 and 4/23/2003. http://www.publicsafety.ohio.gov/news/2003/04070413.pdf.

Olson, Reginald. 2000. *Please Sign In: A Study of Oxford House Signs Pointing to Students' Values.* Self-published.

Oring, Elliot. 1996. Humor. In *American Folklore: An Encyclopedia,* ed. Jan Harold Brunvand, 374–76. Garland Reference Library of the Humanities (vol. 1551). New York: Routledge.

Ortner, Sherry. 1984. Theory in Anthropology since the Sixties. *Comparative Studies in Society and History* 26 (1): 126–66.

———. 2003. *New Jersey Dreaming: Capital, Culture, and the Class of '58.* Durham: Duke University Press.

———. 2006. *Anthropology and Social Theory: Culture, Power, and the Acting Subject.* Durham: Duke University Press.

Paniagua, Melissa. 2002. Hey Baby, What's Your Sign? *Miami Student Amusement,* January 24, 4.

Parmentier, Richard J. 1994. *Signs in Society: Studies in Semiotic Anthropology.* Bloomington: Indiana University Press.

Peirce, Charles Sanders. [1894] 1998. What Is a Sign? In *The Essential Peirce: Selected Philosophical Writings,* vol. 2 *(1893–1913),* ed. Nathan Houser, Jonathan Eller, Albert Lewis, André De Tienne, Cathy Clark, and D. Bront Davis, 4–10. Bloomington: Indiana University Press.

Pettitt, Ruth, ed. 2007. *Growing Up in Oxford, Ohio: African-American Stories.* Coral Springs, Fla.: Llumina Press.

Pred, Allen. 1990. *Lost Words and Lost Worlds: Modernity and the Language of Everyday Life in Late Nineteenth-Century Stockholm.* Cambridge: Cambridge University Press.

Preston, Dennis R. 1982. 'Ritin' Fowklower Daun 'Rong: Folklorists' Failures in Phonology. *Journal of American Folklore* 95 (377): 304–26.

———. 1983. Mowr Bayud Spellin': A Reply to Fine. *Journal of American Folklore* 96 (381): 330–39.

———. 1985. The Li'l Abner Syndrome: Written Representations of Speech. *American Speech* 60 (4): 328–36.

———. 2000. Mowr and Mowr Bayud Spellin': Confessions of a Sociolinguist. *Journal of Sociolinguistics* 4 (4): 614–21.

PubClub.com. n.d. PubClub.com's Top 10 College Party Schools: "Win or Lose, We Booze!" http://www.pubclub.com/collegefootball/index.htm.

Putnam, Hilary. 1975. *Mind, Language, and Reality: Philosophical Papers.* Vol. 2. Cambridge: Cambridge University Press.

Robbins, Alexandra. 2004. *Pledged: The Secret Life of Sororities.* New York: Hyperion.

Roller, Brett A., and Anna Michael. 2003. GhettoFest Faces Uncertainty. *Miami Student,* http://media.www.miamistudent.net/media/storage/paper776/news/2003/04/11/FrontPage/Ghettofest.Faces.Uncertainty-938369.shtml.

Roth, Christopher. 2008. *Becoming Tsimshian: The Social Life of Names.* Seattle: University of Washington Press.

Rymes, Betsy. 1996. Naming as Social Practice: The Case of Little Creeper from Diamond Street. *Language in Society* 25 (2): 237–60.

———. 2001a. *Conversational Borderlands: Language and Identity in an Alternative Urban High School.* New York: Teachers College Press.

———. 2001b. Names. In *Key Terms in Language and Culture,* ed. Alessandro Duranti, 158–61. Malden, Mass.: Blackwell.

Sanday, Peggy. 2007. *Fraternity Gang Rape: Sex, Brotherhood, and Privilege on Campus.* 2d ed. New York: New York University Press.

Scollon, Ron, and Suzie Wong Scollon. 2003. *Discourses in Place: Language in the Material World.* London: Routledge.

Seaman, Barrett. 2005. *Binge: Campus Life in an Age of Disconnection and Excess.* Hoboken, N.J.: John Wiley.

Sherzer, Joel. 1978. "Oh! That's a Pun and I Didn't Mean It." *Semiotica* 22 (3–4): 335–50.

———. 2002. *Speech Play and Verbal Art.* Austin: University of Texas Press.

Shuman, Amy. 1993. Dismantling Local Culture. *Western Folklore* 52 (2–4): 345–64.

———. 2005. *Other People's Stories: Entitlement Claims and the Critique of Empathy.* Urbana: University of Illinois Press.

Shuman, Amy, and Charles Briggs. 1993. Introduction. *Western Folklore* 52 (2–4): 109–134.

Silverstein, Michael. 1993. Metapragmatic Discourse and Metapragmatic Function. In *Reflexive Language: Reported Speech and Metapragmatics,* ed. John Lucy, 33–58. Cambridge: Cambridge University Press.

Singer, Milton. 1984. *Man's Glassy Essence: Explorations in Semiotic Anthropology.* Bloomington: Indiana University Press.

Smitherman, Geneva. 1998. Word from the Hood: The Lexicon of African American Vernacular English. In *African American English: Structure, History, and Use,* ed. Salikoko S. Mufwene, John R. Rickford, Guy Bailey, and John Baugh, 203–225. London: Routledge.

Sperber, Murray. 2000. *Beer and Circus: How Big-Time College Sports Is Crippling Undergraduate Education.* New York: Henry Holt.

Stallybrass, Peter, and Allon White. 1986. *The Politics and Poetics of Transgression.* Ithaca: Cornell University Press.

Stevenson, Michael R. 2007. Diversity Update—Student Edition. http://www.miami.muohio.edu/documents_and_policies/diversity_facts/pdfs/Diversity_Update_2006_Student.pdf.

Stewart, George R. [1945] 2008. *Names on the Land: A Historical Account of Place-Naming in the United States.* New York: New York Review Books.

Stewart, Susan. 1991. Notes on Distressed Genres. *Journal of American Folklore* 104 (411): 5–31.

Street, Brian V. 1984. *Literacy in Theory and Practice.* Cambridge: Cambridge University Press.

Suslak, Daniel F. 2009. The Sociolinguistic Problem of Generations. *Language and Communication* 29: 199–209.

Sutton-Smith, Brian. 1997. *The Ambiguity of Play.* Cambridge: Harvard University Press.

Syrett, Nicholas L. 2009. *The Company He Keeps: A History of White College Fraternities.* Chapel Hill: University of North Carolina Press.

Thelin, John R. 2004. *A History of American Higher Education.* Baltimore: Johns Hopkins University Press.

Titon, Jeff Todd. 2003. Text. In *Eight Words for the Study of Expressive Culture,* ed. Burt Feintuch, 69–98. Urbana: University of Illinois Press.

Toelken, Barre. 1986. The Folklore of Academe. In *The Study of American Folklore: An Introduction,* 3rd ed., ed. Jan Harold Brunvand, 502–528. New York: W. W. Norton.

———. 1996. Academe, Folklore of. In *American Folklore: An Encyclopedia,* ed. Jan Harold Brunvand, 3–4. Garland Reference Library of the Humanities (vol. 1551). New York: Routledge.

Tucker, Elizabeth. 2005. *Campus Legends.* Westport, Conn.: Greenwood Press.

———. 2007. *Haunted Halls: Ghostlore of American College Campuses.* Jackson: University Press of Mississippi.

Turner, Patricia. 1994. *I Heard It through the Grapevine: Rumor in African American Culture.* Berkeley: University of California Press.

———. 2002. *Ceramic Uncles and Celluloid Mammies: Black Images and Their Influence on Culture.* Charlottesville: University of Virginia Press.

Turner, Victor. 1969. *The Ritual Process: Structure and Anti-Structure.* Ithaca: Cornell University Press.

Urban, Greg. 2001. *Metaculture: How Culture Moves through the World.* Public Worlds, vol. 8. Minneapolis: University of Minnesota Press.

Urciuoli, Bonnie. 1995. Language and Borders. *Annual Review of Anthropology* 24: 525–46.

van Leeuwen, Theo. 2004. *Introducing Social Semiotics.* London: Routledge.

van Leeuwen, Theo, and Carey Jewitt, eds. 2001. *Handbook of Visual Analysis.* London: Sage.

Vesey, Laurence R. 1965. *The Emergence of the American University.* Chicago: University of Chicago Press.

Vološinov, V. N. 1930. Slovo i jego social'naja funkcija [The Word and Its Social Function]. *Literaturnaja učeba* [Training in Literature] 5: 45–46.

Wechsler, Harold S. 1977. *The Qualified Student: A History of Selective College Admission in America.* New York: John Wiley.

Wenger, Etienne. 1998. *Communities of Practice: Learning, Meaning, and Identity.* Cambridge: Cambridge University Press.

Williams, Raymond. 1977. *Marxism and Literature.* Oxford: Oxford University Press.

———. 1983. *Keywords: A Vocabulary of Culture and Society.* Rev. ed. Oxford: Oxford University Press.

Willis, Paul. 1977. *Learning to Labor: How Working-Class Kids Get Working-Class Jobs.* New York: Columbia University Press.

Wirtz, Kristina. 2007. *Ritual, Discourse, and Community in Cuban Santería: Speaking a Sacred World.* Gainesville: University Press of Florida.

Wolfe, Tom. 2004. *I Am Charlotte Simmons.* New York: Farrar, Straus and Giroux.

Wulff, Helena. 1995. Introducing Youth Culture in Its Own Right: The State of the Art and New Possibilities. In *Youth Cultures: A Cross-Cultural Perspective,* ed. Vered Amit-Talai and Helena Wulff, 1–18. London: Routledge.

INDEX

Italicized page numbers refer to illustrations.

Chaise LaDousa
is Associate Professor of Anthropology at Hamilton College in Clinton, N.Y.